World Class
Manufacturing

World Class Manufacturing

The Lessons of Simplicity Applied

Richard J. Schonberger

THE FREE PRESS
A Division of Macmillan, Inc.
NEW YORK

Collier Macmillan Publishers
LONDON

The Free Press
A Division of Macmillan, Inc.
866 Third Avenue, New York, N. Y. 10022

Collier Macmillan Canada, Inc.

Printed in the United States of America

printing number

2 3 4 5 6 7 8 9 10

Library of Congress Cataloging-in-Publication Data

Schonberger, Richard.
  World class manufacturing.

  Bibliography: p.
  Includes index.
  1. Industrial management. 2. Production management.
3. Manufacturing processes. I. Title.
HD31.S3385 1986   658   85–24719
ISBN 978-1-416-59254-9

Contents

Contents

Preface

Stock market crashes, political assassinations, declarations of war, and oil shocks are the sorts of events that trigger social or economic upheavals. Dawning awareness, on the other hand, tends to usher in modest change instead of upheaval.

What I am bent on describing is a dawning awareness that came on with a rush and triggered an upheaval. The upheaval is occurring in the industrial sector, and the title of this book, *World Class Manufacturing,* is what the upheaval is about.

Blaming Ourselves

Public awareness of industrial decline was marked by numerous reports in the popular and business press in the late 1970s and early 1980s. Those accounts mainly concerned losses of markets, plant closings, and people thrown out of work. The blame for the decline was not carefully fixed.

Today the many companies that have made a resolution to become world-class manufacturers are blaming themselves. Their managers, their engineers, their technicians, their staff experts, and their supervisors went about their jobs under mistaken notions of how a manufacturing enterprise ought to operate.

The labor unions must shoulder some of the blame for worsening competitive positions, but today's industrial leaders are far less apt to use labor as the scapegoat. The enlightened view is: If there were labor problems, what did management do wrong? And how can management improve itself to create good relationships with labor? The answer is not to be nice, not to trust each other, but to find grounds for mutual gain. I believe that those grounds are now known and are quite different from what the universities have been teaching. We take up the people issue in several chapters, especially Chapters 2, 3, and 6.

Changes in attitude extend to another common target for blame: suppliers of component parts and materials. If suppliers have not met our needs, the customer is beginning to ask, what did we do wrong? And how can we foster good relations with our suppliers? Those questions, too, have firm answers. Harley-Davidson has adopted the excellent slogan *partners in profit.* Harley is one of many Western manufacturers that see folly in the once popular game of supplier musical chairs. Under world-class manufacturing (WCM), adversarial relationships between customer and supplier are out, and a whole new set of buying and contracting practices is in.

Government regulators were also handy targets. Our industrial leaders still lobby aggressively for less interference, but today (with a few exceptions) the lobbying is more constructive and less accusatory.

Thanking the Japanese

The manufacturing upheaval is worldwide, and it comes in response to Japan's post–World War II industrial recovery and ascendency. The first wave of accounts on the Japanese "miracle" raised our consciousness, created healthy forebodings, and lowered our complacency. We took the trouble to visit Japan to see and study. We saw that Japanese manufacturers are not given to quarreling with their unions, their suppliers, and their regulators. The four seemed like parties to a partnership.

How could the cooperation be explained? Some observers came up with answers that were plainly tautological: Japanese workers were treated well because Japanese bosses treated them well. Suppliers were loyal to their customers out of a sense of loyalty.

More probing study—mostly by savvy visitors from our biggest manufacturers—found vastly better quality and much tighter controls on waste. Surprisingly those were achieved with far fewer inspectors and controllers. Were we going to settle for tautology again—excellent quality because of emphasis on quality, little waste because of emphasis on waste elimination?

The observant visitors found the real reasons. I refer to people like Ed Hay, then of Fram Corp.; John Rydzik of GE; Jack Warne of Omark Industries; Lloyd Stone, Len Ricard, and Fred McCallum of GM; and William Harahan of Ford. They saw manufacturing concepts and techniques being practiced in Japan that sometimes were 180 degrees out of phase with our own. They told everyone who would listen. A few people from the academic institutions found out, too, and began to write articles and books, and a few of us went out on the lecture circuit. (Besides me, those few include Robert Hall of Indiana University, and Robert Hayes, the late William Abernathy, Earl Sasser, and Steven Wheelwright, all of Harvard. We must also include W. Edwards Deming, Joseph Juran, and Armand Feigenbaum. Having been influential in Japan's quality movement years before, those three gentlemen's wisdom finally became valued in the rest of the world as well.)

The message learned and then told was that Japanese success is not culture-based. Its basis is a quite different set of concepts, principles, policies, and techniques for managing and operating a manufacturing enterprise. All of it is easy to understand, not hard to accept (once known), eminently teachable and learnable, and not so difficult to apply.

Transformation

We know it is not hard to apply, because there are so many Western success stories in such a short time: defect rates cut tenfold and more; manufacturing lead times cut twentyfold in a number of cases; triple the sales volume in half the plant space; stockrooms emptied and converted to manufacturing; storage racks, automated stock handling systems, and conveyors dismantled; fork trucks eliminated; complicated and costly computer systems replaced by manual charts and blackboards, with data entered and interpreted by operators; existing machines upgraded to process capability and moved into cells that make and feed parts forward just in time for the next machine to use them; reduced numbers of inspectors, suppliers, part numbers; whole layers of management eliminated.

The greatest success stories are in the young electronics industry, which has fewer bad habits to break: Hewlett-Packard, Intel, Apple,

Tektronix, Motorola, and others. Accomplishments are more modest in large old-line companies and industries, but zeal for change is widespread and touches most industries that manufacture something.

The zeal extends downward, too. As the top companies act out their aspirations to become world-class, they pull suppliers with them. Large suppliers—for example, Intel supplying 8088 memory chips for IBM personal computers—can take the initiative themselves to become world-class suppliers. Small suppliers need help, and they are getting it from some of their large customers.

The central task of purchasing departments in this decade is *supplier development*. The task is half done when both the supplier and the component part have been "certified" so that the customer no longer has a need to inspect or count materials or fret about late deliveries from the supplier. The task is complete when the supplier has taken up the crusade for simplification, waste removal, and a fast-paced campaign for rooting out causes of error. There now are small supplier companies in North America that have been transformed in that way.

Rejuvenation

What is most gratifying to some of us is to see a rejuvenation going on among large numbers of people whose work lives had fallen into a rut. Dennis Butt, who launched just-in-time production when he was plant manager at Kawasaki in Nebraska, once told me that the "old warhorses" weren't adaptable, and I thought he surely was right. Now I know that to be false (and probably Dennis, in his current position in the thick of WCM at Outboard Marine, sees it too). The twenty-, thirty-, and forty-year veteran manufacturing managers are in many cases leading the upheaval (Dennis is one of them). Why? It's just like competitive golf, tennis, bowling, or even fishing. A steady succession of wins yields enormous personal pleasure and satisfaction. After years of losing in manufacturing, it's great to win, and to know exactly what to do to keep on winning. The hard work involved seems more like hard play.

The manufacturing upheaval is just beginning to have rejuvenation effects on the majority: the operators and assemblers on the factory floor. Participatory leadership, industrial democracy, quality circles, quality-of-work-life programs—all of these have offered hope for a better work life. Those programs, however, are peripheral to the upheaval. World-class manufacturing involves the operators in activities

:hat once were owned by the supervisors, technicians, trainers, engineers, inspectors, handlers, controllers, and managers. WCM makes operators owners of the processes and the first line of attack on the wide array of problems that spring up on any shop floor.

WCM requires that no one have a job that consists only of chunking out parts all day. There are already a few American manufacturing plants where the category "direct labor" is no longer used, where the accounting system treats all operators as indirects. On the whole, however, the tradition of treating operators like machines that can take verbal orders is still strong. The manufacturing upheaval may be called a revolution when the last wall, the wall around the operators, is fully breached.

Does this book present theory, concepts, or implementation? The answer is all three. Throughout the book, I present a WCM concept and include actual examples of how various companies put it to work. I also offer commonsense reasons behind the concepts and the ways of implementing them as well. The fancy word for the reasons that guide our actions is theory.

World Class
Manufacturing

Chapter 1

Faster, Higher, Stronger

In the 1950s through the 1970s, running manufacturing companies became gentlemen's work. Decisions and policies were made by people twice and thrice removed from the manufacturing arena. Authority was in the hands of staff people who sifted data from other staff people. Venturing out into the plant was, well, venturing. It was prudent to stick around offices and conference rooms and make sure your backside was covered. Excitement in industry was confined to high-tech R&D. Manufacturing was stagnant.

How quickly things change. While the changes have scarcely touched small companies, the well-known manufacturers are caught up in revival, renewal, recovery, and renaissance. A popular term among those caught up is *world-class manufacturing* or a term like it. World-class manufacturing may sound like Madison Avenue hyperbole, but it is not. The term nicely captures the breadth and the essence of fundamental changes taking place in larger industrial enterprises. A full range of elements of production are affected: management of quality, job classifications, labor relations, training, staff support, sourcing, supplier and customer relations, product design, plant organization, scheduling, inventory management, transport, handling, equipment selection, equipment maintenance, the product line, the accounting system, the role of the computer, automation, and others.

The Goal and the Path

World-class manufacturing (WCM) has an overriding goal and an underlying mind set for achieving it. The overriding goal may be summarized by a slogan suggested to me by a manager at the Steelcraft division of American Standard, where I was presenting a seminar. During the afternoon break, the fellow told me that he had digested all that had been said, and he concluded that the whole thing was like the motto of the Olympic Games: *citius, altius, fortius.* From the Latin the English translation is "faster, higher, stronger." The WCM equivalent is *continual and rapid improvement.*

A few years ago we didn't even know the factors of manufacturing that ought to improve. There was little agreement on what excellence in manufacturing is, because we thought in terms of tradeoffs. Plant managers or their corporate overseers picked one set of high-priority targets one year (for example, defect rates and warranty costs) and another, seemingly conflicting, set to work on the next (perhaps overhead costs and customer service rates). The high priorities were where problems seemed most severe. Lacking manufacturing principles, we tackled the problem with trade-off analysis.

Today there is wide agreement among the WCM "revisionists" that continual improvement in quality, cost, lead time, and customer service is possible, realistic, and necessary. There is now good reason to believe that those goals may be pursued in concert, that they are not in opposition. One more primary goal, improved flexibility, is also a part of the package. While some of our leading manufacturers have trouble avoiding pitfalls that lead to inflexibility (pitfalls that *are* avoidable), the goal itself is not an issue. With agreement on the goals, the management challenge is reduced to speeding up the pace of improvement.

The improvement journey follows a surprisingly well-defined path. The journey requires clearing away obstacles so that production can be simplified. A fast-growing body of writings (including my own 1982 book, *Japanese Manufacturing Techniques: Nine Hidden Lessons in Simplicity*)[1] offers lists of obstacles to remove and ways to simplify: fewer suppliers, reduced part counts, focused factories (focused on a narrow line of products or technologies), scheduling to a rate instead of scheduling by lots, fewer racks, more frequent deliveries, smaller plants, shorter distances, less reporting, fewer inspectors, less buffer stock, fewer job classifications.

Beyond the Basics

In the pre-WCM era we thought that production could be managed "by the numbers." The numbers would show what to make, what to buy, whom to blame. If, for example, the latest cost report shows a negative cost variance in welding, the onus is on the welding supervisor to cut costs. But *how?* There are no data on the causes of the cost overage. The supervisor may crack the whip to get more output for the same labor cost. Alternatively, ask industrial engineering or quality engineering to "do a study."

The numbers failed to show causes. Mostly they did not even show symptoms of *real* problems.

Numbers *do* serve the world-class manufacturer—when they show how good the product and service are, how much improvement is occurring, what problems to attack next, and what the likely causes are. WCM mandates simplification and direct action: Do it, judge it, measure it, diagnose it, fix it, manage it on the factory floor. Don't wait to find out about it by reading a report later.

Some of that may sound like "back to basics." Basics they are, but going back we are not. It is true that some of the emergent WCM techniques were in use in an earlier era—and then forgotten. In the main, however, the good old days in manufacturing never were all that good. Quality concepts were primitive by today's standards. While some plants had an ethic of continual improvement (applied very selectively), the norm was to transform simplicity into complexity, which sowed the seeds of decline.

Turning Point

There is reseeding going on, and there seems to be a single year that could be called the turning point: the year 1980. In that year a few North American companies (and perhaps some in Europe) began overhauling their manufacturing apparatus. Those first WCM thrusts followed two parallel paths. One was the quality path, and the other was the just-in-time (JIT) production path.

One of the first to try just-in-time in North America was General Electric, which started up two JIT projects in 1980. Kawasaki in Nebraska and Toyota truck in Long Beach, California, began shifting from standard to JIT production in the same year.

3

The first North American companies to take the quality path, also in 1980 (give or take a few months) were Nashua Corp. in New Hampshire, Tennant Co. in Minneapolis, and IBM. (A bit earlier Matsushita in Franklin Park, Illinois; Sanyo in Forrest City, Arkansas; and Sony in San Diego *began* their U. S. operations with a quality focus. These may be thought of as imports from Japan rather than as turning points in existing North American companies.) Nashua got its start by bringing in W. Edwards Deming, the American who, along with Joseph Juran, was instrumental in getting Japan's quality movement going in the 1950s. Tennant and IBM hired Philip Crosby, who was known to a few people as the author of a fine little 1979 book, *Quality Is Free.* [2] Tennant provided early support for Crosby to form a quality college in Florida.

Those stirrings in a few companies in 1980 may someday be chronicled as the third major event in the history of manufacturing management. The first two: (1) coordinating the factory through use of standard methods and times, Frederick W. Taylor, Frank Gilbreth, *et al., circa* 1900; and (2) showing that motivation comes in no small measure from recognition, the Hawthorne Studies at Western Electric, *circa* 1930.

The 5–10–20s

World-class manufacturing could not become the third major event if it were to peter out. The signs that it will not, that WCM is much more than a fad, are persuasive. The list of companies that have already made order-of-magnitude improvements in quality and manufacturing lead time is getting long. For example, I have compiled (and continue to update) a list of the "5-10-20s," which refers to companies, factories, or parts of factories where fivefold, tenfold, or twentyfold reductions in manufacturing lead time have been achieved. The list, with explanatory comments in some cases, is provided as an appendix at the end of this book. Stories about some of the 5-10-20 plants will be told in later chapters.

My 5-10-20 list does not do justice to WCM developments outside of North America, nor is it at all complete for North America. I have conducted seminars and provided consultancy at manufacturing plants in a number of European and Pacific Basin (besides Japan) countries and have found the WCM fever to be globe-spanning.

With so short a history, WCM has not had a chance to mature

in all of its natural habitats. What surprises many is the progressive unearthing of more and more natural habitats. I refer not to different continents and countries but to different industries and types of production. That is, what makes a world-class manufacturer in one industry also seems to work in many other industries. Let us see why that should not be surprising.

Streamlined Flow

Consider how a restaurant fills a customer's order: The cook puts meat from the grill onto the platter, goes to the range to scoop some vegetables, opens the oven to get a baked potato, heads for the salad bar to extract a salad, and so forth. It goes fast, because a kitchen is small and the cook puts only one serving of each food item on the platter.

Stop-and-Go

A machine shop, a sheet metal shop, a printed-circuit-board shop—any shop or factory that makes to order—is just the same. As long as the shop or factory is small, production is usually quite fast. But who wants to stay small? We have plants—for final goods and component parts alike—with thousands of employees and hundreds of thousands of square feet of space. Now the work goes through the plant at a snail's pace. Plant management has its hands full trying to prevent gridlock.

If a restaurant kitchen grew the way our factories do, the platter would go to the grill area for a piece of meat and then move by slow conveyor to the vegetable area. The meat would get cold—and might even fall to the floor once or twice on the way. At the vegetable area, the massive cookers might be tied up making vegetables other than the kind ordered for the platter, which means waiting until the next batch is cooked.

Growth is not the problem. The problem is the more-of-the-same approach to growth. A restaurant is a little *job shop,* to use the manufacturing term. It will not work if it becomes a big job shop—where a job (platter) has to traverse vast distances from one shop to another, waiting for one thing or another at most of the shops. Growth must be accompanied by a transformation to preserve speed, to avoid stop-and-go production.

Over the years we came to believe that stop-and-go production was the fate of the job shop. We also believed that job shops were the fate of industry, because customers are fickle; they want the variety that job shops can provide. Job shop people looked enviously at the flow shops, where work just flows down a production line or through pipes continuously (as patrons flow down a cafeteria line).

That view is out of style, because we have learned how to streamline our job shops, to make them behave more like flow shops. Some go so far as to simplify products and regularize schedules, and thereby transform themselves into flow shops. Many others—those that stick with customers who demand variety—will not become flow shops, but they can come close. The chameleon cannot ever be a leaf, but it can look like one. So it is in manufacturing.

Imperfect Flows

What tools and techniques make job shop transformations possible? At the top of the list are the set known as just-in-time production techniques. They were perfected by Toyota in Japan in the 1960s and 1970s. Toyota's techniques caused work to move through parts fabrication processes fast and get to final assembly just in time for use.

JIT was shaped in the flow shop mold. Continuous-flow industries—the "pure" flow shops—have been around for a hundred or two hundred years. Examples are bottling, tableting, and canning; extruding and weaving; milling and refining. Some of the processes are tightly coupled. The work leaves one process and flows, perhaps through a pipe, to arrive just in time for the next. In that sense, JIT was around long before the people at Toyota thought of it.

In reality the flows are usually not all that continuous. The grain mills, the food processors, the medicine makers, the cloth producers, and the rest are stop-and-go producers, too. They go for a time on one size, style, model, or chemical formulation, then shut down for a complete changeover in order to run another. Shutdowns for change-over are one concern. The massive quantities that build between changes—the raw and semiprocessed material, and especially the fin-ished goods pushed out well in advance of customer needs—are a greater concern. All are forms of costly waste.

There are dominant WCM precepts for treating the ailment. One is a JIT principle: The smaller the lot size, the better. World-class manufacturers of cars, tractors, and motorcycles have some lot sizes down to one unit by becoming adept at changeovers between models. This permits making some of every model every day, almost like continuous-flow processing. With that capability, they outdo the flow processors they started out trying to copy.

A second precept is the total quality control (TQC) principle: Do it right the first time. In the flow industries this means setting up for a new run so that the first yard of cloth, linear foot of sheet steel, length of hose, can, bottle, or tablet is good.

A third set of precepts is called "total" preventive maintenance (TPM). Maintain the equipment so often and so thoroughly that it hardly ever breaks down, jams, or misperforms during a production run. There is nothing like an equipment failure to turn a continuous processor into its opposite number.

Mass Production—Just in Time

While the JIT *concept* (if not the application) is natural in the flow industries, it took Henry Ford and his lieutenants to get JIT worked out in discrete goods manufacturing. Ford has been called the father of mass production. His Highland Park and, later, River Rouge plants mass-produced the parts just in time for assembly, and his assembly lines pulled work forward to next assembly stations just in time, too.

By 1914 the Highland Park facility was unloading a hundred freight cars of materials each day, and the materials flowed through fabrication, subassembly, and final assembly back onto freight cars. The product was the Model T, and the production cycle was twenty-one days. At River Rouge, about 1921, the cycle was only four days, and that included processing ore into steel in the steel mill that Ford built at River Rouge.[3]

That roughly equals the best Japanese JIT auto manufacturing plants today. But it was much easier for Henry Ford, because his plants followed his now famous dictum, "They can have it any color they want, so long as it's black."

Isn't it easy to look like a continuous-flow producer, with very short manufacturing lead times, when every unit is the same as every other? Ford's Tin Lizzies almost could have flowed through a huge pipeline with intersecting pipes bringing in the components at just the right locations and times.

The Model-T factories were what is known as *dedicated* plants and production lines. Where capacity is cheap (cheap equipment or labor) or volume is high, dedicated JIT lines make sense. Most producers of television sets, radios, videotape recorders, and personal computers today have enough volume to follow the easy dedicated-line path to JIT. Most automobile manufacturing is of lower volume and cannot achieve JIT so easily. Nissan in Oppama, Japan, sets up a dedicated line only if sales volume is 10,000 cars a month or more. Since most models they make fall below that number, other approaches are necessary. Some of the other approaches are examined next.

Making Just What Is Sold—Every Day

Whether making things that pour (the flow industries) or things that are counted in whole units (discrete goods), a WCM precept is to produce some of every type every day and in the quantities sold that day. Making more than can be sold is costly and wasteful, and the cost and waste are magnified manyfold as the resulting lumpiness in the demand pattern ripples back through all prior stages of manufacture, including outside suppliers.

Makers of highly seasonal goods sometimes have sound reason for building at least some stock days or weeks before use or sale. Most of industry's chronic mismatches between demand rate and production rate are not caused by seasonality, however. Those mismatches are fixable. Companies in the flow industries need to figure out how to change over flow lines so fast that there is no reason for a long production run of one type. Since the flow industries have been investing for years in inflexible equipment that resists quick changeover, it is not an easy fix.

In the assembly industries it tends to be an easy fix. Assembly— of personal computers, washing machines, boats, trucks, furniture, and hundreds of thousands of other products—is still largely manual. Humans are adaptable and can change from one model to another with ease—and efficiency, too. Assembly is efficient, however, only if the work place is orderly, with every part and tool exactly placed. If the assembler has to search, the efficiency is gone.

In *Japanese Manufacturing Techniques* I told about working for the fastest bricklayer in North Dakota and about how he yelled at me if I didn't place bricks so that he could reach and find them without looking. That concept—exact placement of all the parts to eliminate search—has enabled the world's motorcycle manufacturers

8

and some tractor producers to change models after each unit. That is called *mixed-model production*, and the lot size is one.

Ten years ago, all motorcycle and tractor manufacturers produced in large lots: maybe five hundred of model A; then shut down for a day or two to change over for a run of five hundred of model B; and so on.

Marketing hates this. Marketing might come to manufacturing and say, "Which model are you running this week?" Manufacturing says, "model A."

"Oh, that's too bad. We, ah, overestimated demand for A. In fact, we have a whole warehouse full. When are you going to make E?" Manufacturing looks it up in the master schedule: "Week 9."

"That's bad, too. We *underestimated* demand for E. We're out and losing sales. Can you possibly move it forward in the schedule?" Manufacturing replies, "No way. Our suppliers will not begin delivering raw materials until week 8."

Manufacturing then blames marketing for doing a bad job of forecasting. The fault is not marketing's. Manufacturing gets the blame, because the production schedule pushed the planning horizon out to week 9, and it is impossible to guess (forecast) right that far out.

Now, at Harley-Davidson, Honda, Kawasaki, Yamaha, John Deere tractor, and the others, some of every model is made every day. Marketing therefore has some to sell every day. If marketing comes to manufacturing and says, "Can you increase model E by 10 percent and decrease A by 10 percent next week?" manufacturing says, "Yes, we can." The assemblers are quick-change artists. The makers of the components parts could still be an obstacle, but they can learn quick-change artistry, too.

> *If a world-class manufacturing effort fails to make it easier for marketing to sell the product, then something is wrong.*

High-Variety JIT Production

Some plants or parts of plants seem doomed to have long manufacturing lead times. Western manufacturers of machine tools and thousands of kinds of industrial components, from motors to pumps to hydraulics, take weeks, often months, to produce something. The problem is that those manufacturers are high-variety, low-volume job shops. Ten thousand different part numbers is normal, fifty thousand is not uncommon, and no one knows which ones are going to be needed in the next customer order. There may be four thousand work orders open in the plant at any given time, with a hundred completed and a hundred new ones added every day. How can such a production environment be anything but chaotic?

We know the answer. It is to divide the ten thousand part numbers into families—production families, not marketing families. A production family is a group of parts that follow about the same flow path. Say, for example, that five hundred of those ten thousand parts go from blanking to grinding to drilling to welding to painting. You empty out a square area on the floor and move the following into it in a U-shaped loop: one blanking press, one grinder, one drill press, one welding station, and one paint dip tank. If there is a lot of drilling to be done, move two drill presses into the loop.

The result is a cell, a mini-production line, almost a pipeline that similar parts flow through. The machines are so close together that there is no need for a container, storage rack, or fork-lift truck. An operator, chute, or simple transfer device can move one piece at a time from station to station. Different part types are made in the cell, but all types go through the same machines (a few part numbers may skip one or more of the stations). Also, the parts in the family have similar setup times, cycle times, tool and fixture requirements, and needs for inspection. While the cells do not make the same part over and over again, they make the same *family* of parts over and over again, hence the term "family repetitive" production in Figure 1–1. The figure also shows the three other modes of production, discussed above, that are valid for the world-class manufacturer.

Next, find another family and move the needed machines and work stations into cell 2. Then create cell 3, and so on. Engineers sometimes call this approach *group technology,* although many prefer to use the more descriptive term *cellular manufacturing.*

The approach is much more than industrial engineering and plant layout, however. Cells create responsibility centers where none existed before. A single supervisor or cell leader is in charge of matters that used to be fragmented among several shop managers. The leader and the work group may be charged with making improvements in quality, cost, delays, flexibility, worker skills, lead time, inventory performance, scrap, equipment "up time," and a host of other factors that distinguish the world-class manufacturer.

Large numbers of Western manufacturers are following this path in their quest to become world-class. The machine-tool, aerospace, and shipbuilding industries are especially active in reorganizing their

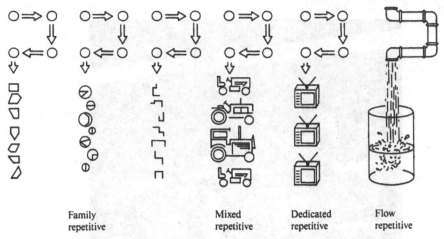

		Mixed	Dedicated	Flow
Family				
repetitive		repetitive	repetitive	repetitive

Figure 1-1. Repetitive Manufacturing

plants into cells. That is natural in view of the mind-boggling numbers of parts that go into large machines, ships, aircraft, rockets, and tanks.

General Electric has transformed its dishwasher plant in Louisville, Kentucky, into a WCM showcase, and moving machines into cells was a basic step. Punch presses that had been in punch-press shops were dispersed to form cells or spurs off other cells or production lines. Figure 1-2 is a photo of one of the moved presses. A sign tacked to it proudly proclaims "point-of-use manufacturing." Other presses and other machines around the plant have the same kinds of signs. GE's success in transforming the dishwasher plant has served as a model for the rest of GE's Appliance Park in Louisville. Refrigerator, range, and washer plants are being converted the same way.

Universals of Manufacturing

The metal fabrication industries have no prior claim on cellular manufacturing. It is emerging as a *prescription for much of the world of work,* on a par with "Do it right the first time." Most of our plants' facilities and people are organized with giant barriers to problem-solving, and the same goes for most of our offices. No one is in charge. Distances between processes are too long for decent coordination. Flow times are too long for us to reconstruct chains of causes and effects when things go wrong—and they go wrong so often.

The immensity of the task would be daunting if we were unsure

Figure 1–2. Point-of-Use Manufacturing

of what paths to take. We *know* what paths to take, because there are many role models. Western manufacturers that have executed the WCM formula have been getting the same spectacular results that Japanese manufacturers did a bit earlier: product defects down from several percentage points to just a few per million pieces, and lead times cut by orders of magnitude. Knowing what it takes to get such results turns on the adrenalin pumps. The competitor whose pump does not get primed is the loser.

That is not to say that the company or plant involved in the WCM quest is completely surefooted. How, for example, can progress be measured? How do the movers get reinforcement so that they stay inspired? The answer is to choose the right goals of improvement and to organize the enterprise for continual progress against those goals. A host of WCM subgoals can be contained within two overriding goals. One is reduction of deviation, and the other is reduction of variability.

Deviation Reduction

Deviation reduction takes many forms, two of which rank above and subsume the rest: (1) Reduce deviation from zero defects. (2) Reduce deviation from zero manufacturing lead time.

Zero defects (ZD) got its start in the United States in the early 1960s. ZD has been elevated to the top—a key component of CEO-level strategic planning—in many Fortune 500 companies. Philip Crosby provided much of the inspiration; W. Edwards Deming, Joseph Juran, and Armand Feigenbaum provided tools and concepts for fitting ZD into companywide total quality control. Visible measures of success are the driving force.

There are many believers in the ZD goal—and never mind if it can never quite be achieved. The number of believers in zero lead time as a superordinate target is still small but is growing fast.

One by one, top companies are coming to the conclusion that reducing lead time is a simple and powerful measure of how well you are doing. The manufacturing people at both Motorola and Westinghouse have chosen lead time reduction as a dominant measure; various divisions of Hewlett-Packard and General Electric have too.

Lead time is a sure and truthful measure, because a plant can reduce it only by solving problems that cause delays. Those cover the gamut: order-entry delays and errors, wrong blueprints or specifications, long setup times and large lots, high defect counts, machines that break down, operators who are not well trained, supervisors who do not coordinate schedules, suppliers that are not dependable, long waits for inspectors or repair people, long transport distances, multiple handling steps, and stock record inaccuracies. Lead times drop when those problems are solved. Lead times drop fast when they are solved fast.

Lead time to get ready must not be overlooked. Short lead time to produce the designs and the specifications are vital to the world-class manufacturer. In halting its declining fortunes in the copier industry, Xerox has vastly improved its ability to get a new product to market. Fewer than 350 R&D people spent just two and a half years developing Xerox's top-of-the-line 9900 copier, as compared with over five years and four times more people for such products in the past.

Time to convert from a first-generation product to its successor is an equally critical concern. That is, we want to become more *flexible* to make product line changes, which translates into *cutting the conversion lead time.*

Lead time is easy to measure: Just stamp the hour and date on a product (or service) in its raw stage, stamp it again when it is finished, and subtract. Take a number of samples and average them. (The Village Inn Pancake House chain does this, using time-stamping machines, in processing food orders.)

It is good policy to put up large lead time charts, one for each important product or family. Plot results on the chart at least once a month. List the improvements—problems solved—on charts nearby, and heap praise on those coming up with each solution.

For practical purposes deviation is usually an average: Perhaps on the average, the lead time target of ten minutes and the quality target of 10 grams have been met on the nose. But what of variability around the averages? Universal goal number 1, deviation reduction, has a companion.

Variability Reduction

The second universal goal is variability reduction. Variability of what? Why, of everything. Variability is a universal enemy. That view once was held by just a few prominent people in the quality community, but it is spreading.

If a ticket taker can sell a ticket in "exactly" thirty seconds nine out of ten times, but then the machine jams and it takes three hundred seconds to sell the ticket to tenth customer, consider the effects. Not only has the tenth customer been poorly served, but at a rate of one customer every thirty seconds, ten new customers will have arrived, only to get in line and wait while the jammed machine gets fixed.

Varying only once in a while from the thirty-second standard requires wasteful solutions: Extra space for customers to line up; staff to manage the queue and sooth the customers; perhaps an extra, mostly redundant, ticket seller to keep the line from getting too long. Costly responses of that sort are called for regardless of the source of the variability. The machine that jams sometimes, the tool that must be searched for sometimes, the assembler who does the task the wrong way sometimes, the part that arrives late sometimes, the blueprint that is wrong sometimes, the part that is off the mark sometimes—all of these and many more require costly sets of "solutions." They are not true solutions, because they provide ways to live with the problems.

In Western industry variability of lead time has been extreme, to say the least. Normal practice in scheduling an order is to use an average lead time figure (stored in the routing file), and then expedite the orders that become late relative to the average. We have taken pride in being able to compress lead time for a hot job from many weeks to a few days; that is an action taken to avoid a late delivery to a customer. In other words, we have put our energies into making on-time deliveries through heroic actions on a case-by-case basis.

With regard to component materials, there is another, more subtle cost of variability. Say that a shaft is supposed to fit into a hole. Engineers state the allowances for shaft and hole diameters. The shop that forms the shaft produces 100 percent within tolerance, and so does the shop that drills the holes. Yet when a shaft at the upper limit of its tolerance (maximum diameter) is paired with a hole at the lower limit of its tolerance (minimum diameter), the shaft won't go into the hole. The opposite case results in a shaft so loose in the hole that it, too, is unacceptable.

This effect is called "tolerance stackup." Western automakers have been made painfully aware of it because of notoriously ill-fitting car doors, fenders, dashboards, and trim. Ford Motor Co. has been aggressive in combating the problem through variation reduction. Ford's manuals on the subject have been widely distributed, and they have helped companies in other industries to get on the variation-reduction bandwagon.

There are many forms of variability, and its cousin, deviation, that ought to be measured frequently. Paper the walls with charts showing the measured results. If such course of action is vigorous, it will take not years but only months to begin looking world-class—head and shoulders above the laggard and endangered competition.

Challenge and Response

This chapter reads, I suppose, like a pep talk, Olympic motto and all. If there were no substance to the message, it would fall on deaf ears, because we've all heard many pep talks—followed by business as usual. There *is* substance to the talk about world-class manufacturing. If Gallup or Harris were to take a poll and ask people to name the twenty best manufacturers (not marketers, not financial empires) in the world, how many would be American, Canadian, French, English, German, Italian, Swedish? Chances are good that many or most would be Japanese. There is substance to the Japanese formula for success in manufacturing.

It took Japanese industry three decades to make its remarkable climb. It used a collection of Western basics, plus common sense, high literacy, and lack of space and natural resources to spur them on. Now the rest of the world is stirred out of its complacency. In some cases manyfold improvements have come after just a year or two of real effort. The Appendix at the end of this book lists some enterprises that have improved in that manner.

WCM clearly is not reserved for the Japanese. In fact, I believe the Western temperament is better suited for rapid and continuous improvement than the Japanese temperament. We in the West have badly misused a chief asset, namely inquisitive minds and innovative spirits. Our greatest challenge is to undo the harm, to change a work culture and unleash natural tendencies.

So far, the 5-10-20s listed in the appendix have had most of their success by changing things, procedures, and concepts—not so much the work culture itself. The things, procedures, and concepts are the easy part and are presented in Chapters 4 through 12. The greatest of all challenges, changing the work culture, comes next in Chapters 2 and 3.

Chapter 2

Line Operators and Operating Data

A factory is like Moby Dick, and the managers are like Captain Ahab. They sink a few harpoons and hang on for dear life. The only way Moby Dick could be steered would be to surround it with a thousand boats and have a thousand harpooners penetrate the whale's hide. Likewise, the only way a factory can be steered is for the factory people to sink a thousand probes. There are enough people there. The trick is to get them to sink the probes.

Indulgency

We keep telling ourselves that it all boils down to people. A book by Rensis Likert in 1961 provided more than three hundred studies on the power of "democratic-participative" leadership.[1] Massive training of supervisors followed, and today it is hard to find managers who haven't heard that they are supposed to elicit the participation of their subordinates.

We know this. We believe in it. But we have not known how. Sometimes it takes an outsider to see what is wrong. Robert Reich, a political scientist, writes briefly on the "profession of management" in his book, *The New American Frontier*. Reich explains the subtle ways that human-social management was being exercised:

Specialists in organization development swarmed over the workplace, conducting encounter groups and "sensitivity-training" sessions. Industrial psychologists provided group counseling and programs of "job enrichment." Some companies instituted collaborative teams and "quality circles" within which workers could offer ideas for improving productivity—so long as they refrained from challenging the structure of authority in the enterprise. Management consultants espoused "Theory Y" or, better still, "Theory Z." But these factory-tested techniques for making workers feel better simply constructed a façade of workplace collaboration. The distinction between thinkers and doers remained intact. Ever more sophisticated strategies for improving the "quality of working life" shied away from actually altering the organization of production.[2]

I favor job enrichment, collaborative teams, quality circles, Theory Y, Theory Z, and quality-of-work-life concepts. They help clean out the clogged arteries through which the lifeblood—information—is supposed to flow. Those programs are never failures.

On the other hand, they are rarely rousing successes either. For a manufacturer to become world-class, mere participation and communication is not nearly enough. Too often the participation is limited to matters like the company benefits package, the recreational program, and the air conditioning. There must be massive *involvement* in the minute-to-minute problems that operators face on the shop floor. Alteration of the "organization of production," as Reich put it, is the issue.

How to do it has become crystal clear. The jobs of everyone in the factory must be changed. Most of the line jobs were direct labor (operator or assembler), nothing more nor less. The new line jobs are direct labor plus a variety of indirect duties—like preventive maintenance—plus some activities that have *always been done by managers and staff specialists*. I refer to *data recording, data analysis,* and *problem-solving*.

Pencils and Chalk

Data recording comes first. The tools are cheap and simple: pencils and chalk. Give those simple tools for recording data to each operator. Then make it a natural part of the operator's job to record disturbances and measurements on charts and blackboards. The person who records data is inclined to analyze, and the analyzer is inclined to think of solutions. Success depends on recording the right kind of data at the right time.

Yellow Lights

One approach is for operators to record a piece of data each time there is a work slowdown or stoppage. The vital piece of data to be captured is the *cause* of the slowdown or stoppage. I'll use an actual case to show how it should work. The plant is Hewlett-Packard's Greeley, Colorado, facility, which is the site of one of the early JIT successes in the United States.

Figure 2–1 is a layout drawing of H-P, Greeley's, first just-in-time

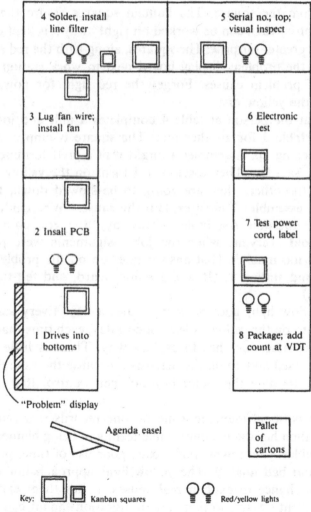

Figure 2–1. Flexible Disc Drive Line

pilot project. (The drawing shows the layout as it was in early 1983, before the JIT line was extended backward to include the full manufacturing cycle.) The product is a flexible disc drive called the Sparrow. It was assembled, tested, and packed in the eight-station U-shaped production cell shown in the figure. This is progressive assembly, one unit at a time, and the product is featureless, except that some are single-disc and some are dual-disc models.

On each work table yellow tape marks off a "kanban square" the size of one unit. An assembler at one table puts a completed unit on the square in easy reach of the next assembler at the next table. No more units may be completed until the next assembler removes the one from the square. The kanban squares assure that waste—more inventory than can be worked on right away—is kept out. There is another, greater purpose: The squares, along with the red and yellow lights and the problem display board next to work station 1, permit capture of problem causes. Forget the red light for now while we see about the yellow one.

Say that the person at table 4 completes a unit and looks to the square on table 3 for another one. The square is empty. Assembler 3 is not keeping up. Assembler 4 might wait a predetermined number of seconds, say, ten. Then assembler 4 turns on the yellow light. The light tells the others they are going to be slowed down, too. More important, assembler 3 must explain the cause. "Why can't you keep up?" is the question. Assembler 3 may say, "I've got too much work to do. I told everyone when the job assignments were passed out that I had too much." That answer goes up on the problem display board behind station 1. (It was a white board, and felt-tip markers were used.)

The yellow light goes on many times a day. Every assembler is likely to turn on the yellow at least once a day; each time that happens, the previous assembler has to explain why. There is little reason to get embarrassed and go on the defensive, because the assemblers have the chance to state the factor beyond their control that causes the slowdown.

In conventional manufacturing no one records real causes. Each assembler then has the uncomfortable feeling of being blamed for most of the troubles: shutdowns, high costs, poor use of time, poor housekeeping, and bad quality. The yellow-light approach not only gives people the chance to explain real causes; it has them explain right when the event occurs, so there are no questions about bad memories and guessing.

Data Analysis

Something has to be done with the data on the display board. At H-P, Greeley, they held a twenty-minute meeting every day after they had met the day's production schedule. The agenda for the meeting was on the easel shown at the bottom of Figure 2–1. One or more problems from the day's problem display board should be agenda items. The team of assemblers, and anyone else they might invite, discuss the problems and brainstorm to try to come up with solutions.

Figure 2–2 is an example of a problem display board at the end of the day. The chart actually would not be arranged with problems in descending frequency or order of importance, a form called a Pareto chart, but it would be easy to rearrange the data into the Pareto form.

Notice that most of the responses came from assembler 3, and "too much work" is the most serious problem. The group discusses the problem and resolves it by taking some small tasks away from assembler 3 and giving them to assemblers 2 and 4; so as not to overload 2 and 4, more small tasks are shuffled to assemblers 1 and 5; the juggling of tasks continues until the production line is fully rebalanced.

It is quite all right for industrial engineers to plan the initial job assignments based on time standards, but we should think of that as *rough* line balancing. Industrial engineers balance to the mythical standard person, but half the population are faster than that, and half are slower. Thus, after the line runs for a while, the assemblers and the supervisor should fine-tune by balancing the work to the capabilities of each assembler. The yellow lights provide good data for the rebalancing. (At Kawasaki in Nebraska they use the phrase "balancing the line by watching the lights.")

PROBLEMS	
3. Too much work	‖‖‖‖‖ ‖‖‖‖‖ ‖‖‖‖‖ ‖‖‖‖‖ ‖
8. Out of boxes	‖‖‖‖‖ ‖
3. Bad bolt	‖‖‖‖
1. Out of drives	‖‖‖‖
6. Tester light out	‖‖

Figure 2–2. Problem Display Board

Once the line is rebalanced, it starts up again, and yellow lights go on again throughout the day. It would not be unusual for assembler 3 still to be the bottleneck—the one with the most responses on the problem display board. Perhaps assembler 3 has cited the bad bolt problem fifteen times in a day, as compared with only four bad bolt tallies before the line was rebalanced. Part of the earlier "too much work" might now be traced more accurately to the bolt trouble.

If someone is skeptical about the causes being posted, assembler 3 may be asked to explain: "Well, you see, I install the fan with four bolts from my bolt tray. I put four bolts into four holes, and then I screw them down. But I get some bolts with mangled threads. I try to screw them down and they won't go. You can see why I am slowed up sometimes."

At its next meeting the group knows what to do. Someone calls the purchasing department and invites the buyer of the bolt to one of the group's meetings. The buyer probably will rush right down to that very meeting. The group leader will say, "Look at our problem chart. That cheap little bolt turns out to be the worst problem we've had lately. Can you take care of it?"

Of course, the answer is yes. The buyer calls the supplier of the bolts and other hardware, tells about the problem—an actual defect frequency can even be cited—and says, "Can you please sort out the bad ones before shipping to us? Or better yet, improve your process so it doesn't make bad bolts. If your people have never done a process capability study or put in statistical process control before, we have quality engineers who will come to your plant to show you how."

The bolt problem gets solved, never to occur again.

Red Lights

Figure 2-1 shows red lights as well as yellow lights. The red light goes on when the problem is so severe the whole production line must shut down. If the production line is conveyor-paced, the assembler who hits the red light switch causes the conveyor to stop as well. Then managers and engineers come on the run.

Although stopping the whole line is costly, the world-class manufacturer gives assemblers the authority—and the button—to do so. The idea is to give assemblers time to do the job right and to stop and fix any problem that stands in the way of doing it right. Our fixation used to be to keep those lines running. We closed our eyes to the parts that were missing or installed wrong, or we tore the product down and repaired the damage on rework lines later at enormous additional cost.

At Kawasaki in Nebraska, the goal is for red light—line shutdown—time to average thirty minutes a day. If it is less than that, assemblers must be pressing too hard and making too many mistakes, which increases end-of-line rework. Furthermore, each red light (or yellow light) event is precious, because it signals a problem, gives an opportunity to record a cause, and leads to a permanent solution. (A GM spokesman commented on adjustments assemblers had to make at the GM-Toyota joint venture in Fremont, California: One of the most difficult things to accept was that the plant did not have an area for rejected parts.)

Most of the North American auto industry and major appliance industry are making the switch to operator control of production lines. There are many variations, including shunting a unit off the main conveyor track and back on only after it is right. At General Electric's dishwasher plant in Kentucky people on the assembly line have four different colored handles to pull. One, the green, means okay and sends the unit forward. The other three signal three degrees of severity of problems. The worst, the red handle, brings everybody to a halt.

There is one type of red light that has been around in Western factories for years. It is up high for all to see, and it goes on when a machine or conveyor jams or malfunctions. Sometimes an operator turns on the light, and sometimes the equipment is rigged so the light goes on automatically. Its Western purpose is to summon fast help from maintenance to get production going again.

It is a shame to use the red lights only for that purpose. I recall consulting visits to four factories where there were red light systems. One had the lights hooked to tire-building equipment, another to printed-circuit-board testers, another to can-filling machines, and the fourth to injection-molding machines. In each case the red light summoned the maintenance person pronto, but I could find no evidence that the *causes* of the repair trip were tallied on a chart.

On the other hand, at a textile plant where I consulted, hundreds of looms were equipped with lights, and in this case every time a light goes on, the cause is entered on a small card. Normally it is better to record on a large blackboard. In this case so many looms were tended by so few trouble-shooters that a large blackboard for each machine is probably not necessary. As long as the trouble-shooters on the floor have first chance at analyzing the data on the cards—

before they go to the maintenance engineers—the cards are all right.

World-class manufacturing requires world-class equipment, which means machines that do not break down. That means recording every cause in detail, sorting the causes, and organizing project teams to solve permanently the problems that recur.

Schedule Versus Actual

Another way to capture problem data is to do so at regular intervals, usually hourly. Hourly data may be recorded on a display board like the one shown in Figure 2–3.

The daily production rate, as the figure shows, is seven hundred units, which reduces to one hundred per hour for seven hours. One hundred good units were produced in each of the first three hours. In the fourth hour there was trouble; only eighty-four good units were made. When hourly production is short, the reason must be explained. The assembler or machine operator says the problem was a whole tray of bad bolts, which is recorded on the chart. There are no further bad hours that day. Part of the eighth hour is used for catchup: Sixteen units are made so that the day's rate is achieved.

Process-Control Data

In the above methods a "bad event," like a stoppage, is what triggers data collection. The goal, of course, is to expose and later eliminate the bad events. Since there are many possible kinds of bad events,

Hour	Schedule	Actual	Problem
1	100	100	
2	100	100	
3	100	100	
4	100	84	Bad bolts
5	100	100	(whole tray)
6	100	100	
7	100	100	
8	0	16	
Total	700	700	

Figure 2–3. Recording Problems at Regular Intervals

this may be thought of as a shotgun approach to data collection. The shotgun approach needs to be supplemented by a rifle approach.

The best of the rifle approaches is known as statistical process control (SPC). SPC takes aim at one or a few critical factors in a process. The most common type of critical factor relates to product quality: diameter, capacitance, hardness, sharpness, data-entry errors, misspelled words, missing parts or data, and others. SPC may also be used to check on timeliness of deliveries, usage of material or other resources, or almost any measurable factor. Data from SPC tells when to stop the process, whereas the preceding methods use a stoppage or other bad event as a signal to record data.

In the hands of staff specialists from quality assurance, SPC is just another run-of-the-mill technique. When used as it is supposed to be used—as a basic operator's tool akin to a screwdriver or wrench—SPC is elevated to a top position on the list of WCM tools.

Without going into details, here is the idea: At regular intervals, the operator measures a small sample of the output of the process. The operator plots the average of the readings on a chart. If the average falls between preset upper and lower control limits, do nothing. If the plotted point is outside the limits, take action.

If the action is nothing more than stopping the process and calling the boss, the powers of SPC have been unleashed: The importance is in the cycle of *doing and checking, doing and checking.* Craftsmen, artists, and scientists follow the do-and-check cycle. We shall not be able to attain high rates of improvement in manufacturing unless assemblers and operators of machines get involved—or reinvolved (as they were in the age of the craftsman)—the same way. In retrospect, it is tragic that so much control was taken away from shop floor people that the cycle was broken.

SPC is not of much use in a job shop, because job order quantities are usually too small to draw samples from. There are other ways to keep processes under control:

- Keep tools clean and sharp, gauges calibrated, equipment in top condition, blueprints and specifications correct, tools and material put in their proper places, and procedures up to date and on display. Mess, confusion, and sloppiness have been the nature of job shops; they can't be tolerated if the job shop is to be world-class.
- Don't build partial units and don't allow rework to build up. These measures help minimize clutter, confusion, and lost or

"robbed" units, and prevent damage to stock in a "hold" condition.
- For process control of small lots, use run diagrams and precontrol charts.

Some of these examples are discussed below and in later chapters.

Care of Gauges, Tools, and Machines

Job shops tend to hire skilled machinists, tool-and-die makers, and other journeymen. The skilled tradesman often can read blueprints and should know how to gauge the output and adjust the tool. Since Western industry employs many skilled tradesmen, we may feel that process control in the skill areas should be in good hands.

In some cases it is. More often, neglect has set in. Gauges are often crude, poorly calibrated, rarely recalibrated, harshly thrown into tool kits, not kept clean, and misplaced. Hand tools and machine tools are in equally bad shape. Adjustment levers and cranks are broken off, shafts are bent, and work surfaces are dinged by a thousand hammer blows. In fact, a joke in industry has it that the most commonly used tool is the BSW—Bohemian speed wrench—which is a hammer. (Actually, the ethnicity of the slur varies. I could have used Russian, Irish, WASP, or any other, but I can get away with Bohemian most easily, because my ancestry on my father's side is mostly Bohemian.)

A strong thread in the JIT, TQC, and WCM tapestry is good housekeeping. Keep it clean, sharp, lubricated, calibrated, in an exact, nearby location, and ready to use. Figure 2–4 is a photo taken at Tennant Co., which ranks high among American companies in activity to become world-class. The photo shows one of the tool cases in the area where Tennant's 240 line of industrial sweeper is assembled. The assembly tools are as neatly arranged as a child's chemistry or microscope set when the wrapping is first torn off.

I do not have a good North American example of especially fine care of gauges. A Japanese example sticks in my mind, however. My first trip to Japan included a visit to a refrigerator plant in the Matsushita family of companies. The factory was a WCM showcase and was laid out in such a way as to impress the touring visitor. As eye-catching as anything on the tour were glass cases that contained gauges. They were located in work centers along the tour path. The glass was clean, the cases were under lock and key, and the gauges were

Figure 2–4. Tool Organization at Tennant Co.

displayed like jewels in a jewelry store. An operator or supervisor was holder of the key and in charge of keeping everything just right.

Strong Management of Skilled People

Our largest manufacturers are finally becoming aware that bad housekeeping has bad consequences. For those resolved to improve, the question is, how? The answer lies in supervision. The battalion commander who does white glove inspections and bounces quarters off tightly made barracks beds is not a bad model. A factory, however, is far more complex than a barracks. The factory supervisors need tools and techniques to put some system into their efforts to get the little things done right. Two examples of such supervisory tools follow; the first is from Japan.

Weekly Checkup

My second trip to Japan included a visit to a very small factory that at first glance looked to be anything but world-class (see photos from that factory in Figure 2–5). The company, Nihon Chukuko (Japan Hollow Steel Company), at that time had only fifty production employees. Chukuko had become contractually linked to Isuzu Motors; more than 90 percent of Chukuko's production of metal parts went into Isuzu trucks.

Chukuko was just one of Japan's multitude of small, below-average enterprises before the Isuzu contract. Isuzu molded Chukuko into a top-notch supplier, and one of the obvious keys is the way Isuzu shaped up Chukuko in the area of housekeeping.

The plant and equipment are old, gray, and ugly. Little in the plant, however, goes unmanaged. The plant's walls, partitions, columns, and posts hold handwritten displays. Machinists, welders, painters, and other shop people prepare the displays as a normal part of their jobs. The displays tell how to make the part, how to care for the machine or tool, how to use the gauge, how to plot the quality (on simple charts, since customer order quantities are too small for SPC), and how to keep things where they belong.

Chukuko's employees are not among Japan's elite, not the ones with lifetime job security, not the ones with the highest entry-level qualifications and pay. How, then, does Chukuko get them to toe the line, to exhibit the high discipline it takes to follow the instructions on the wall displays?

Their supervisor, the plant manager (the plant is too small to have intermediate levels of management) sees to it. The plant manager employs more than mere personal contact and observation. He is required to use Isuzu's simple system of evaluating the housekeeping and related factors once a week. Six main factors are evaluated:

1. Putting things in order; arrangement of work site
2. Management of stock on hand
3. Equipment and tools
4. Inspection
5. Self-control and management of production processes to guarantee quality
6. Prepare manuals and notices on the wall

Each Friday the plant manager makes the rounds. He rates every employee on the six factors and plots the ratings on a card, which is left with the employee. As the example in Figure 2–6 shows, the six rating points are connected by lines so that the composite rating resembles a spider web. The idea is for the size of the web to shrink—

Figure 2–5. Chukuko Factory Scenes

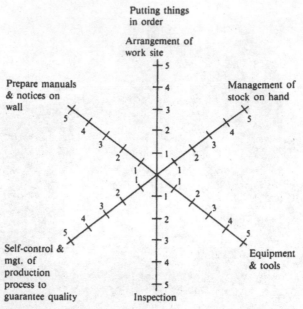

Putting things
in order

Arrangement of
work site

Prepare manuals
& notices on
wall

Management of
stock on hand

Self-control &
mgt. of
production
process to
guarantee quality

Equipment
& tools

Inspection

Figure 2–6.   Chukuko Co. Six-Axis Process Check Diagram

to get closer to "bulls eye" perfection and farther from 5, which is the worst possible. At perfection, there is no web to get caught in.

Ratings for each of the six main factors are averages of subratings for subfactors. Figure 2–7 is a complete list of the subfactors under one main factor. Many of the subfactors, by themselves, seem picayune, especially those like, "Whether or not work area and passage clearly divided by white line" and "Whether or not notices on the wall are properly organized." In combination, however, they add up to a system that stamps out human sloppiness and error. Simple management technique, powerful results.

What if the plant manager himself became careless—or too busy to perform his Friday ritual of evaluation? He wouldn't get away with it. Isuzu audit teams descend upon the Chukuko plant—and Isuzu's other supplier plants—on a regular basis, and they check on the plant manager's diligence.

The Isuzu-Chukuko weekly check helps operators avoid slipups. Some other kind of control is necessary to keep people busy. If employees perceive that no one seems to care, they of course will waste time, run off, and squander chances to contribute to an improvement. The Fort Collins, Colorado, division of Hewlett-Packard has an approach for handling that problem.

Subject	Checking Items	Point
Putting things in order. Arrangement of work site.	1. Whether or not work area and passage are clearly divided by white line.	1.2.3.4.5
	2. Whether or not places for putting uncompleted goods are properly set.	1.2.3.4.5.
	3. Whether or not any unnecessary things are placed around work tables.	1.2.3.4.5
	4. Whether or not trashes and wastes are properly cleaned.	1.2.3.4.5.
	5. Whether or not notices on the wall are properly organized (whether there are unnecessary notices put up or not).	1.2.3.4.5.

Figure 2–7. Production Process Checking Sheet

Keeping People Busy

One of the products at Fort Collins is the HP-9000 computer, which sells for about $50,000 and is made to customer order. A customer can order many combinations of components. With so much uncertainty about which components will be needed next, assemblers sometimes have to wait for work to get done at preceding work station. The waits tend to be fairly long—thirty, forty-five, or sixty minutes—since the operator has to follow a "spec" manual that tells how to make the given component or module. What should an operator do while waiting for a part?

Fort Collins has a procedure for making sure that wait time is used to good advantage. Every time there is a stoppage, the operator logs in on alternate tasks, mostly nondirect labor. Graphics printers produce color charts that summarize numbers of hours spent on alternate tasks. For example, one work group posted 40.5 hours of stop time for a reporting period. Their chart on the wall broke the hours into:

25.25 hours of cleanup, paperwork, typing, miscellaneous
  1.75 hours in meetings
  1.75 hours of rework
  8.50 hours on TQC
  3.25 hours on procedures

In earlier periods, time spent on the last item, "procedures," had been more extensive. The work team had spent several months, in their free time, working with engineers on procedures. They converted assembly instructions from engineers' verbiage to exploded drawings. Now instead of wading through words the assembler can go by a drawing, thumb-tacked at eye level. Time is saved, and errors are avoided.

Note that the activity reports are posted on the walls in the work area. The work group and its supervisor report to themselves and keep themselves alert to opportunities to keep busy on alternate tasks. That is a far better use of reports than the usual Western system, wherein a computer somewhere else transforms data into summary reports, which go to staff people once or twice removed from the action. In that not very effective system, the thinkers delegate the doing to the doers and generally stay away from the action—until a secondary report reveals problems.

Making Data Public

Both Chukuko and H-P, Fort Collins, are notable for making shop data public—putting it up on the walls. There is a substantial benefit from this, aside from the visible control it offers: Information of value to the company does not stay in people's heads. It comes out and is made available so others can learn from it.

One of the top performing manufacturers in North America year in and year out is the Gorman-Rupp Co., a Mansfield, Ohio, maker of pumps and pump accessories. A few years ago machine operators at Gorman-Rupp made the decision to begin "publicly" recording vital operating data—for example, correct machine speeds and feeds, and units completed per shift. The operators also devised a standard form on which to record the data. The filled out forms hang on the machines and are useful for speeding up setups at shift change times and for training new operators. There is always training to do, because Gorman-Rupp has always believed in cross-training people so they can move to where the work is. The company has not laid off anyone in its fifty-two-year history.[3]

Like many skilled people, machine operators at Gorman-Rupp had been in the habit of keeping operating information to themselves. In an information-dependent society, knowledge is power and control, they figured, so why shouldn't we guard our own knowledge?

On the other hand, most of us want to do what is good for our company, and that includes sharing knowledge and data. The trouble is, most companies do not have easy ways to share information. To get the data exchanges going, supervisors need to create project teams and charge them with solving problems. One name for the project teams is "small group improvement activity" (SGIA).

Next best is just putting people into groups and giving them some sort of general charge; that is the typical Western approach to quality control circles. QC circles have not had the rousing successes elsewhere that they have enjoyed in Japan. I think the reason is that we set them up without changing the environment of waste and complexity. Waste, namely excess stock, serves as a way around the problem. That plus cumbersome control systems sap the potential of QC circles or other employee-involvement approaches.

The typical suggestion program is even less effective. In the old Gorman-Rupp program, suggestions went to the suggestion coordinator, probably an engineer whose main job was generating ideas, not looking at the ideas of others. (According to one authority, Western suggestion programs typically yield only one suggestion a year for every six workers. Scanlon plans, which put savings into a growing pool that is then split between the company and the employees, do better: one a year for every two workers.[4] Those miserable rates contrast with a hundred or more suggestions a year per person at top Japanese companies like Hitachi and Toyota.)

Gorman-Rupp threw out the suggestion program and put in a QC circle program. That is when the operators made the decision to post operating data on the machines. Promoting information exchange—especially on quality matters—was the original purpose of QC circles in Japan, and it still is probably the most valuable use of circles.

At Chukuko; H-P, Fort Collins; and Gorman-Rupp, employee involvement happens because of attentive, diligent guidance.

Delegation to a Fault

Some years ago I had a neighbor who managed a field office. Let's call him Joe. Joe habitually went to the office late and came home early; he often came home for lunch and stayed. His superiors came to town on field trips now and then, and as often as not they had to phone Joe at his home. The corporate visitors didn't call Joe on the carpet for not being in the office. He disarmed his bosses by saying in a humorous vein, "Don't you have *your office* organized so you can delegate and not have to be there?"

American business schools have us convinced that delegating authority is good managerial practice, and rightly so. We should value managerial involvement and diligence so highly.

Today managerial diligence is more vital than ever, given the role changes going on in the work place. Let's look briefly at where manufacturing is heading and then drop back to where it is today.

TRANSFORMATION OF DIRECT LABOR

It's 1 P.M., the middle of the second shift. The factory floor is quiet and cool, with bright spotlights in the center creating shadows in the corners. A robotic carrier silently glides down the aisles, between rows of shining, metallic machines. It stops. A silver arm reaches out and grasps a hunk of metal from the bin the carrier holds. The carrier moves on, while the machine cuts the metal into three distinct shapes. A second arm extends and picks up a piece from a conveyor that feeds the machine automatically. Swivelling on its axis, the machine then welds one of the shapes to the new piece, and places all three pieces on a ledge. A crane bends to retrieve them, transports them across the room, and delivers them to a second machine. This machine then combines them with two parts of its own making. In a glass-enclosed control room, technicians monitor the lights and whirring discs of the computers that cover the wall. The people watch. The machines work.[5]

This vision of the factory of the future is fanciful only in extent. There already are some factories like this, and most have some automation in use. When automation is complete, there no longer are any direct laborers. There are only indirects and overhead people. They read dials, program, clean up, perform preventive and breakdown maintenance, and load tools and materials.

Some Hewlett-Packard plants no longer treat direct labor as a separate category. At those locations "direct" labor is only a tiny part of total product cost, not because of automation but because most of the components are bought rather than made. Also, since the assemblers do much more than assemble, it would be a distortion to call them direct labor.

The changes in the roles of shop floor people that accompany each step toward automation are as profound as the automation itself. How many companies have plans and programs in place to make the people transition a good rather than a bad experience? Very few, I think.

No Incentive Pay

For some companies, a nettlesome pay problem stands in the way of smooth transition. I refer to companies that pay incentive wages. There is little or no room for incentive pay plans in a mature WCM plant. I say mature, because many improvements can be put in place before incentive pay becomes a severe obstacle.

Incentive pay can be good (or not bad) in batch production, where the rule is "make as much as you can." It is bad in JIT/TQC, where the rule is "make only what is used, as it is used."

Business school courses generally teach that incentive pay is always bad, but industry knows better. Lincoln Electric Co. was on *Fortune*'s list of the ten best manufacturing companies for 1984 and has been written up for years for its enlightened management and strong competitive position. Lincoln has "always" paid incentive wages. That is not to say that Lincoln has no problems. Their inventories turn only four to six times a year. If Lincoln were to cut lot sizes and convert to the pull system, there would be a reason to abandon individual incentives.

They would not be easy to abandon. A few years ago Lincoln's machine operators' regular pay averaged $17,000 a year, but actual pay, including incentives, was twice that amount. Lincoln would face rebellion if it halted the incentive system by fiat.

The same problem faces hundreds of other companies whose incentive systems have meant much bigger paychecks. One way to make the transition is to phase in pay for knowledge (number of jobs mastered) while phasing out pay for units produced. Lincoln Electric already has a partial pay-for-knowledge system, and so it has flexibility to juggle the mixture of pay sources. (GM and the United Auto Workers have agreed that there will be just *one* job classification in the new Saturn plant and that pay for knowledge will govern pay increases; but in that case the transition was away from too many job classifications and away from seniority, not from an incentive system.)

Another promising approach is to put all wage-earners on salary. That provides more pay stability but offers fewer chances for an occasional big paycheck. In the growing number of companies that have taken this step, labor has tended to support the tradeoff.

Still another approach is to form cells and pay a group incentive. The best group incentive would be one in which the extra pay is for quality, precision, and meeting (not exceeding) the daily quota.

People from some companies have told me that incentive pay is their biggest obstacle, but clearly there are ways around it. For most companies, the people transition problem is more basic.

Not Mere Participation

We need a simple, natural way to wean factory people off a diet of pure direct labor and onto a mixture of direct and indirect duties. The way to begin is with charts and graphs.

Consider the change in self-concept when an employee who has always just chunked out parts takes on data recording duties. Recording disturbances is what managers and technicians have always done, the operator thinks; maybe I am now a part of the management and technical operation of this place. Add to the data recording some time for operators to meet and discuss the results, and you have taken a giant step in altering the unfortunate work culture of them-versus-us.

We have fretted about the bad work culture for years. We have fiddled with it by trying out one people program after another. The common name for the programs of the past is *participation*. From today's vantage point the very word "participation" has a patronizing, indulgent ring to it. The message that went out to factory people was something like this: "In our magnanimity and out of concern for your feelings, the management of Acme Co. will set aside times to listen to you and to allow you to make suggestions and sometimes even to make the decision."

That brand of participation is severely bounded. Acme is telling the operators what the chef might tell the restaurant patrons: You can say how you liked the food, but stay out of the kitchen.

Today participation is out, and *involvement* is the new buzz word. As buzz words go, involvement is a good one.

Involvement

EI, meaning employee involvement, has become, in just the last two or three years, big industry's version of a household word. Surely in many cases the name has changed but the thrust has not.

For all those companies that have their operators doing statistical process control, involvement is a reality. Before SPC, inspectors are in charge of quality; afterward, the operators have that responsibility. Taking measurements and plotting results on SPC charts at half-hour intervals means operators are in on the improvement effort all day long. The same holds true when operators have the authority to stop and slow down production lines, to hit the red or yellow light switches, and to discuss causal data and work out ideas for improvement.

One indication of genuine involvement is the growing number of plants that are sending direct labor people on visits to supplier or customer plants. For example, Omark Industries sent several shop floor operators on one of its study missions to Japan. Hewlett-Packard, Greeley Division, sent two people from its pilot JIT project (the Sparrow project) on an airplane to Lincoln, Nebraska, to tour the Kawasaki plant. John Deere, Ottumwa Works, sent numerous shop floor people on tours of Kawasaki and other JIT plants in other cities.

How do production people react? Do they welcome the chance to be involved? Since no two people think exactly the same way about anything, reactions, of course, vary.

A *Wall Street Journal* article, "Employee Involvement Gains Support," tells about involvement at Aluminum Company of America, Westinghouse, and Bethlehem Steel.[6] The story cites the mixed reactions of one Bethlehem employee to a customer visitation. The employee, Robert Felts, a veteran line operator at a Bethlehem plant in East Texas, leaped at the chance to go to a customer's plant, but he was not enthusiastic about flying on an airplane. "I didn't like that," Felts said. "And they put me on four planes to get me there."

At another Bethlehem plant line operators who were going on visits to customer plants were jeered at by co-workers. The co-workers called them turncoats, taking management's rather than labor's side.

The visits can be hard on people's pride, too. Mill hands at Bethlehem's Sparrows Point, Maryland, facility paid a visit to one customer who was in the can-making business. The foreman in the can factory said, "You guys at Sparrows Point are garbage rollers." The steelworkers have long since recovered from that indignity. Now supervisors and line operators in the can company are in frequent telephone contact with the steelworkers at Bethlehem.

Managers, buyers, engineers, and other staff people have mixed reactions about traveling to other companies, too. But the visits are valuable and necessary. Are visits by production people any less valuable? They are certainly less costly, in view of the lower pay rates of line workers. In some cases, I think, the line operators are actually more effective as emissaries than the staff people.

Table 2–1. Evolution in Employee Skills

Old	New
Machine Operation	
Skill is in the setup	Skill is in simplifying the setup
Sometimes setup technicians or engineers needed	Operators lead projects, technicians & engineers help
Operator watches machine run	Operation is a well-timed routine; operator is busy thinking about next improvement
Assembly	
Assembly jobs were simplified so unskilled labor can perform them	Assemblers acquire: —multiple job skills —data collection duties —diagnosis & problem-solving talents

Regardless of people's reactions, involvement—in SPC, problem-solving, plant visitations, and other non-direct-labor matters—is a necessary WCM element. Without it problems are swept under the rug.

Labor Skills/Skilled Labor

One of the more vital kinds of employee involvement is, in the case of machine operations, setup time reduction. Engineers and toolmakers can be key players in setup simplification, but the most successful programs put the responsibility and the leadership in the hands of the machine operators. The results are as follows: Machine setup is transformed from skilled to mostly unskilled work; the setup person's value shifts from manual skills to mental and problem-solving skills.

Table 2–1 summarizes this ironic but gratifying change in the role of the machine operator. It also summarizes earlier points about assembly work and assemblers: The old division of labor concept was to divide the job into narrow elements; then unskilled people could be hired off the street and learn an assembly job quickly with little training. The WCM concept calls for assemblers to learn multiple job *skills,* data collection *duties,* and diagnosis and problem-solving *talents.*

This chapter perhaps may be summarized as follows:

Take the skill out of the job; develop the skill of the mind.

Chapter 3

Staff as Supporting Actors

Solving problems, continually and rapidly, is everyone's business. Collecting the causal data has been thought of as the front-end, routine part of problem-solving. The vital core, the glamorous part, has been analysis and decision-making, which has required the talents of well-paid staff experts.

Neglect of the front end has been a chief reason why Western industry has done so poorly at problem-solving. The red and yellow light systems, the blackboards, and the SPC charts can provide the causal data the experts have lacked. What is more, the WCM methods of collecting data reduce the need for staff experts and support people. The line operator measures and records problem data. In so doing, the operator naturally reflects on the data and tries to diagnose the trouble. As we ponder, we sometimes come up with obvious, simple, commonsense solutions—the best kind.

Line–Staff Partnership

Some people have said that the Japanese experience shows operators can have an impact on only about 15 percent of all problems; the rest is up to managers and staff experts. Initially this kind of statement had a laudable intent and message: Let's quit blaming shop people for bad performance.

That view has been expounded so often among leading manufacturers that it has become an industrial cliché. Unfortunately, it has taken on something of a paternalistic flavor. The altered view goes something like this: Operators aren't superhuman, and it is not fair to expect too much of them; staff people have to shoulder most of the problem-solving burden.

It's a point of view that will take us right back down the path to mediocrity. The last chapter explained why: World-class manufacturing puts line operators and assemblers in the driver's seat and thereby puts latent talents and potential to use. A central, not a peripheral, role of staff people is to be on call.

Staff "On Call"

Having salaried people (engineers, schedulers, buyers, plant manager—everybody) on call is common in Japan and also seems to be ingrained in Japanese subsidiary plants outside of Japan. The concept was in place at Kawasaki in Nebraska *circa* 1981, when I first investigated its JIT activities. Doug Sutton, chief of scheduling, told me, "Boy, is it ever different at Kawasaki than when I worked at _____. I hardly spend any time in my office."

Doug was out on the floor solving problems much of the time during the work day. Most were probably not scheduling problems. They were problems of all kinds. In the JIT concept, job titles mean little and responsibilities blur. A problem has to be fixed quickly, and everyone must help—as people do when their community suffers a flood, tornado, serious earthquake, or other disaster. When the red light goes on, people come on the run to solve the problem before it *becomes* a disaster. If you do that often enough, chances are you will give up and move your desk down there.

One American company, Hewlett-Packard, has a tradition of having salaried support people's desks on the factory floor, intermingled with work stations. That is part of the fabled "H-P Way." In my judgment Hewlett-Packard is farther along in implementing JIT than any other non-Japanese-owned company except, perhaps, Omark Industries. And why not? H-P had a head start, since the problem-solvers were already located in the right place: next to where the production problems occur.

A 1982 study of thirteen Japanese subsidiary companies in Australia, New Zealand, and Singapore also revealed a pattern of managers and engineers located on the factory floor. The factories in the study were owned, or mostly owned, by Matsushita, Sanyo, Toyota, Nissan, Sharp, and NEC.

Professor Hideki Yoshihara of Kobe University, author of the study report,[1] offers the example of a control center at Australian Motors Industries (Toyota is a major equity holder) that was moved to the plant, but in the past was "in a separate building. . . . When trouble occurs, managers and engineers immediately rush to the site to resolve the trouble. The management is concerned with diagnosing and resolving the cause of troubles."

In another example, Yoshihara states that many of the college graduates in Singapore "prefer work in individual office rooms, where they can work properly dressed with neckties." "We don't hire that type because we have no need for them," says a manager at Matsushita Electronics, Singapore.

The Singapore college graduates are not unique. In most countries it is not only the expectation but the reality that salaried people will reside in another wing of the building or in a separate building. It never has worked well.

It should not be hard to find factory space to which salaried people can move. A JIT campaign frees space where racks once stood. The happy solution for what to do with the space is to move in the engineers and other support people and managers. You could even put the computer (if there's one that supports manufacturing) and computer staff on the floor. Make it another work station. IBM did that at its Lexington, Kentucky, typewriter plant. It is wise to get the support people into the vacated space fast. Otherwise someone will fill it with inventory again when no one is looking.

While the college recruits may expect a quiet office, I do not think many are disappointed if they are thrust into the action of the plant instead—after a sedentary life of study and sitting in lecture halls in college.

Leverage Effects

It may seem that with staff people being pulled to the floor all the time, more staff will need to be hired to "keep the store." That is not the case, because WCM keeps things direct and simple. Simplicity in production is contagious, and it has leverage effects on support staff. Figure 3–1 summarizes.

For the first six staff functions in Figure 3–1, the leverage translates

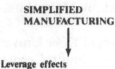

SIMPLIFIED
MANUFACTURING

Leverage effects
on support staff:

* Better support, fewer people
  • Maintenance
  • Accounting
  • Quality assurance
  • Production control
  • Materials mgt.
  • Data processing

* More involvement
  • Industrial engrg.
  • Purchasing
  • Manufacturing engrg.
  • Design engrg.

Figure 3–1. Leverage on Staff

into better support with less people *per dollar of sales.* The improvements, discussed below, make the products more salable. Sales growth, in turn, may keep overall head counts steady or even growing.

1. *Better maintenance with fewer people in the plant maintenance department.* Operators lubricate their own equipment and learn to make adjustments and simple repairs; they come to feel a sense of ownership of the equipment. Operators keep their own work space spic and span.

A chain of attentive, no-nonsense managers, starting with the first-line supervisor, makes sure that the operator comes to adopt this attitude and does not get sloppy. With operators and line supervisors taking over, the armies of people from the maintenance department shrink.

Even though hours of operators' time replace hours of maintenance people's time, the cost of maintenance is less. There are two reasons: One, the operators can fit some of the preventive maintenance, repairs, and cleanup into the wait and delay times that all operators have. Two, the operator who is responsible for the product made will do a better job of keeping the equipment working well than a support person who hasn't the responsibility, so the costs of down equipment and bad production are less.

Shrunk in numbers, the primary roles of the maintenance staff become:

1. Training operators in what to do and how to do it
2. Analyzing data (Component failure data can tell a story that is revealed through statistical analysis—failure-rate distributions, for example; such analysis is a job for staff experts.)
3. Tear-downs and overhauls

This reduced list consists of roles that are, on balance, higher in prestige and commanding of higher pay than before. The maintenance department suffers shrinkage in size but growth in importance and self-image.

2. *Better quality with fewer people in the quality department.* While operator-centered maintenance has not gone very far in Western industry as yet, operator-centered quality has. It appears that nearly all of the Fortune 500 largest American industrial firms have programs for implementing "quality at the source." That means operators inspecting their own work or work from a previous operator, use of process control charts to prevent bad output, and discussing solutions to quality problems.

The results are much like those in maintenance. The legions of inspectors are reduced to just a few. Some will always be needed— for new part numbers and new suppliers that are not yet certified, for example. The costs of quality are much less, because operators can do some of the quality tasks during the work cycle or in delay times, and do it with more care than staff people with secondary responsibility. The quality department's primary role changes to training, auditing, and laboratory testing. The department's status is elevated.

3. *Better accounting with fewer accountants.* When manufacturing is complex, cost accounting and accounting controls are, too. When a good share of manufacturing endeavor revolves around waste, the costs of the waste and all the people who attend to it have to be spread around somehow. Somehow means a burden allocation formula that uses averaging. Rough burden estimates mean that true product costs are unknown. Thus, we use shaky cost estimates in setting prices and making go/no-go decisions.

When line operators take over things like simple maintenance and quality control, the substantial costs of those activities become *direct* costs. Assigning burden costs to products is fraught with error; assigning direct costs is easy.

Accounting is further simplified by some of the JIT production methods. In high-volume production, JIT presses for scheduling and producing to a rate instead of in batches. Batch production requires batch—or job-order—accounting. Rate-based production gets by with simple process accounting: On a periodic basis, just tote up costs and divide into units produced.

Accounting staffs have always been large in low-volume job shops. Studies of job shops show that often more than 90 percent of the process lead time is delay time. Accounting time must be spent keeping track of and categorizing the contributors to waste and delay. JIT wipes out large chunks of job shop delay, which greatly reduces the accounting. Cost validity improves, because more of the costs are direct, fewer are overhead.

4. *Better production control with fewer production controllers.* Production control departments house planners, schedulers, dispatchers, and expediters—the people who mother-hen the work flow in the factory. When work centers are scheduled separately and work is scheduled in batches, the number of coordinators is large (perhaps as many mother hens as there are chicks). When the work centers are closely coupled—the just-in-time way—one schedule can serve many work centers, and eyeball coordination can suffice. The staff group shrinks.

At Hewlett-Packard, Greeley, JIT scheduling led to excess schedulers. Some were moved to the purchasing department, which had its hands full trying to change from an adversarial relationship with suppliers to a partnership.

5. *Better materials management with fewer materials staff* (and also less direct-labor time spent on lifting, pushing, and handling materials). Materials people are supposed to keep the right amounts of stock on hand and keep track of it. That is hard to do well, when there is the typical months' worth of the average item in the factory.

The JIT plants in North America have cut it to weeks', sometimes days' or hours', worth. JIT also fosters strict handling discipline: exact locations, exact quantities in each container. Operators and material controllers can *see* where the material is and when more is needed, and they can count it quickly and often to assure there are no mistakes. Whereas the conventional inventory counting system was the annual physical inventory, which sometimes took three days, some JIT plants count every week. At Hewlett-Packard, Vancouver, Washington, it takes less than an hour to count everything.

Usually a large part of materials management is handling and storage. A WCM breakthrough often comes when the equipment or assembly people are moved close together in cells and flow lines so there is virtually no handling. Stanadyne Diesel Systems now produces about 80 percent of components (by dollar value) in cells, thereby cutting its "headcount" 20 percent, mostly in material handling.

The next best option—automated conveyances to span distances—is not good at all. Automation of the production can have many payoffs; automation of the waste before and after the production makes little sense.

6. *Better information with less data processing.* Compared with the rest of the world, American manufacturers make more use of computers in managing maintenance, quality, accounting, production control, and materials. As we have seen, WCM causes each of these functions to be simplified and reduced. Data processing is cut at the same time. A growing number of production managers, as part of their JIT and TQC efforts, have rid their shop floors of computer terminals. This disconnects them from the central manufacturing computer system, which continues to function as a planner but no longer as a controller. It is no small irony that I hear about this kind of action most often in companies that produce and sell computers.

The computer does have a bright future in the factory. That future is mostly in *direct process control* and not so much in information systems to support staff and management.

Involvement Effects

Many people, especially staff but also line, owe their current jobs to the wastes and delays in the plant. Other staff groups deal more with direct materials, direct labor, and equipment—the value-added elements of product cost—than with fussing over wastes and delays. Those include the bottom four groups listed in Figure 3–1: industrial engineering, purchasing, manufacturing engineering, and design engineering. WCM may not reduce their numbers. Instead the leverage comes from bringing the staff people together and from working with, rather than apart from, the producers on the line.

1. *Industrial engineering* (IE) is responsible for *work study.* Any factory operative or supervisor also can and should perform work study. Flow charting and timing techniques, plus sets of principles and checklists, are easily taught to factory people. In the 1950s *work simplification* programs were popular in many companies, and the programs began with industrial engineers teaching work study techniques to factory operatives. Some of those programs are still around

or have been resurrected, and I understand that Allan Mogensen, the person who inaugurated work simplification training many years ago, still offers that training.

These days the most important type of work study is on setup and changeover time reduction. Few IEs have experience in this, so the first step is to get some: Start by reading Shingo's excellent book on single-minute exchange of die (a good English translation[2] exists); then participate in a couple of studies. After that, back off and focus on training operators to lead their own setup projects.

Shop floor involvement in work study means that much more industrial engineering will get done than if the IE department alone is doing it. It also allows the degreed IEs to spend more of their time on oversight as well as on broader, more complex studies, since the factory floor people will focus on the narrower problems.

A key WCM element is for everyone's job to include uncovering and recording problems and process variation, and then trying to diagnose and solve the problems. Work study—by any name—therefore is a natural element of WCM.

2. *Purchasing* provides first value—the raw materials to which later value is added. The rest of the company often sees purchasing as a source of delay: Acquiring that first value takes too much time, there is too much red tape in getting the *right* purchased materials, and too often the materials turn out to be defective.

Buyers have never relished that rap, and WCM alters purchasing so that buyers no longer need to feel defensive. For one thing, WCM transforms purchasing into a team effort. Product designers, quality engineers, production managers, and even shop floor employees are on the team. It is a good idea for all of them to get to know the people in the supplier companies. Why shouldn't they, since the number of suppliers shrinks to just a few good ones that don't change?

The small, stable supplier base also frees buyers from heavy administrative burdens, which have included rebidding and changing suppliers, writing thousands of separate small purchase orders, expediting thousands of shipments, validating thousands of packets of receiving paperwork, and handling the adjustments when quantities and quality are wrong. Long-term contracts and kanban-triggered deliveries cut out much of the routine work, so that purchasing staff can focus their energies on supplier development.

The number of clerical employees in the purchasing department drops (but not suddenly). The number of buyers may even drop eventually. The number of people dealing with suppliers and the number of hours spent, however, do not drop. When other staff departments, like production control and inventory management, find they can get along with fewer people, there is a perfect spot for them: part of the supplier audit-and-assistance teams. With the "purchasing" function expanded in scope, it may become effective in making money for the company.

3. *Manufacturing engineering.* Manufacturing engineers or process engineers are the equipment experts. They were supposed to find machines that can make what the design engineers design—and make it fast. Today, fast machines may or may not be valued, but quality must always be. Thus the manufacturing engineer (ME) works with and gets a good deal of help from the quality specialists and engineers.

Under WCM, MEs must also work closely with marketing in order to become astute at matching equipment to sales changes.

Perhaps the biggest change of all for manufacturing engineering is getting used to the idea that the best way to make a contribution is found on the factory floor, not in the equipment manufacturers' catalogs. The ME must spend some time with equipment sales reps but should spend more with machine operators, setup crews, maintenance technicians, and supervisors. Most of the tangible wealth of industry is in old equipment that is falling apart fast. Most of it is worth rescuing.

4. *Design engineers.* The engineers who design products in the R&D labs have been outsiders. They are now being brought inside, and the main reason is heightened corporate concern for customers and quality. Quality is fitness for use, we are told, and that means going to the customer to see what uses the customer has in mind. WCM companies must see to it that there are ways for the customer to help the designer design the product right. Marketing is at the interface, and so the designers spend more time with salespeople. It is just as important for the designer to spend time with factory people and processes, getting to know what the factory can and cannot make.

A few years ago designers might have resisted such incursions on the creative processes. Today electrical engineers, chemical engineers, and others in product design are of a different mind. In most cases it is because their companies have shown design people that they are *needed* at both the customer and the factory ends of the business.

Making staff experts feel needed is a key that opens up opportunities—like ways to add value and not merely add cost.

Managing to Add Value

The idea that staff support people should be on call is clearer if we keep in mind this basic manufacturing principle: *Adding value to the product is the true measure of worth.*

In other words, if an engineer or materials specialist is called upon to clear away obstacles and delays so value may be added to the product, the time is well spent. Currently, a good share, perhaps even the majority, of support tasks are *not* of that type. Figure 3–2 lists activities that most Western makers spend a lot of time on. For each one, ask yourself, does the activity add value?

Count, Move, Store, Expedite

Counting, moving, storing, and expediting material, the top three items in Figure 3–2, employ armies of people in industry. Inventory accounting people must keep track of inventory value because of legal requirements on financial reporting. Aside from that, their task, and that of the material movers, stockkeepers, material clerks, expediters, and data processing support people, is a negative one. It is managing the waste, delays, and errors in the system; it depends on failure to make what is needed on time. Clearly those activities add cost, but no value.

Except in the continuous-flow industries, most of the count-move-store-expedite pursuits are directed at work-in-process (WIP) inventories. The common term is "WIP tracking." WIP tracking is closely related to manufacturing lead time. If it takes forty working days to transform the raw material into finished goods, then progress had better be checked about forty times. In other words, enter an inventory

JIT Goal: Add *value*, not *cost*.

Value or waste (cost)?
- Counting it
- Moving it
- Storing it
- Expediting it
- Searching for it (part or tool)
- Taking it out of one container and putting it in another
- Accumulating it into larger make/move quantities
- Inspecting it

Figure 3–2. "Managing to Add Value . . . and Avoid Waste"

transaction into the computer something like once a day per job (for perhaps hundreds of jobs a day).

One approach is for each *move* to require a computer transaction, so that the inventory can be charged out of the sender's records and into the receiver's. At a Rockwell plant near Dallas conversion to machine cells slashed the lead times so much that the computer could not keep up. As Wayne Robinson, a Rockwell engineer, put it, "Now when you go look for a job, it is three work centers past where the computer says it is."[3]

Some plants try to control WIP by sending it into lockable stockrooms. The material may be charged into a stockroom after every operation—and then out of the stockroom when the work gets to the next operation. (If there is just a rack and not an actual stockroom between two work centers, the computer just treats the rack as if it were a stockroom.) Inserting a stockroom transaction between each production operation doubles the number of data preparation and entry steps.

We have done all this to avoid the fearful problems that arise if ever a job is lost or misplaced, which happens all the time in plants that lack production control discipline. Also, we reckon that the system keeps pressure on everybody to move the material forward—since it gets charged off each work center's records when it moves. In some plants the system works so well that nothing gets lost any more. The elaborate system adds no value to the product, however, and it is a system that averts chaos by keeping many fingers in the holes in the dike.

At a few plants (e.g., some Hewlett-Packard and some IBM) WIP tracking had been developed to a high science—but then, through implementation of WCM concepts, the decision was made to dismantle the system and shift the support people to other jobs. WIP tracking became unnecessary when they cut their manufacturing lead time from the twenty-, forty-, and sixty-day range to one, two, or three days. When it takes only a couple of days for the product to make its journey through the plant, there is no need to enter data about its trip into the computer forty or twenty or ten or five times; twice is often enough—once when raw material goes to the floor and again when finished goods leave. Production is under control, because the work is not on the floor long enough to get out of control, and WIP is so small that it may be controlled visually and counted perhaps in minutes.

Taiichi Ohno, one of the masterminds behind just-in-time at Toyota, explains it this way: "If the meaning of production control is truly understood, inventory control is unnecessary."[4]

Pipes and High-Speed Conveyors

The flow industries—powders, pellets, liquids, and gases, as well as bottles, pills, cans, and pouches—have so little WIP that they never did get involved in WIP tracking. Their product flows down high-speed conveyors in an hour or two or through pipes in a minute or two. In those industries the count-move-store-expedite tasks apply to raw material that arrives too soon or too late; the tasks also aim at the huge amounts of finished goods that surge from the manufacturing process in large batches out of "sync" with daily customer demands.

Some liquid and gas processors have sizable amounts of WIP simply because the reactors and mixing tanks are oversized. The material flow through pipes between tanks is swift and automatic, so the moving of the product is not the issue.

Even though the bottlers, canners, and packagers sometimes think of themselves as part of the flow-process industry, their problems are different from those of the liquid and gas processors. Conveyor travel is slow and uncontrolled compared with flowing through a pipe. It doesn't make much difference whether the pipe is 50 feet or 100 feet between two processes. The length of the conveyor on a fill-and-pack line, on the other hand, makes a difference.

Thinking back on the fill-and-pack lines I have studied over the years (assembly lines are a bit different), I am ready to conclude that in about every case, the conveyor *lengths* are twice as long as they ought to be. There may be a hundred units (trays, pouches, bottles, cans) on the conveyor between a pair of work stations. Why not put the stations closer together so that there are only, say, ten units between? The WIP in transit might be cut from an hour's worth to a few minutes' worth.

The value of the inventory saved may be of little concern. There are other, more serious, wastes: Cans on a can line get damaged by chafing against each other and against the side rails. Paper cartons and packages get torn, snagged, and bent on conveyor lines. Shortening the conveyor reduces those wastes.

Many who tend automated fill-and-pack lines are there to trouble-shoot, to throw away damaged packages, to clean up messes, to make product changeovers, and to check and tweak the processes. Some of those support people would not be necessary if the conveyors were shortened. For example, if a conveyor length is halved, the total floor space occupied by the line would be reduced by perhaps a third. That is one-third less space to clean, and if the product is food or drugs, cleaning is frequent and costly. Another gain is that, with filling and packaging stations closer together, each line tender is able to cover more ground; that is, each can handle more of the between-station trouble and perhaps monitor more than one station.

Low-Speed Assembly Conveyors

Most of these points apply to assembly lines as well as to high-speed fill-and-pack lines. For example, at Kawasaki's motorcycle plant in Nebraska, a roller conveyor originally ran along the fuel tank fabrication line for about half the length of the building. In 1983 the conveyor length was halved, and the presses, welders, grinders, and other machines were shoved closer together. Shortening the line made it possible to get by with fewer people manning the line when demand falls off. With the longer conveyor, an operator tending more than one station would spend as much time walking and pushing fuel tank pieces as running machines.

At another company, I observed a JIT line making microcomputer modules that, for a different reason, had too much conveyor and too many units on it. About ten robots did the assembly, but they weren't small assembly robots. They were large industrial robots usually used for jobs like welding or moving heavy metal parts or tooling. The big robots required 15, maybe 20, feet of "elbow room." So the robot assembly stations were separated from each other by conveyor spans of 15 to 20 feet.

The correct number of work units and feet of conveyor between processes is not necessarily zero. Just a little "slop" in the system can keep downstream processes going when the machine jams, the robot comes up empty-handed, or the assembler fumbles. Usually progressive conveyor reduction, not sudden conveyor removal, is the goal.

Invisible Inventory

The manufacturing cycle entails more than making the product itself: Engineering produces pieces of paper that are sold to manufacturing,

manufacturing makes and sells products for accounts receivable, accounting exchanges invoices for cash. All are producers and sellers. All have the same delay problems.

Some companies call the premanufacturing (order booking, design, and ordering) and the post-manufacturing (invoicing) *invisible inventory.* One diversified manufacturer took a close look at its invisible inventory and was shocked to find about the same amounts of operating cash tied up in each of the three components of the total manufacturing cycle; that is, about one-third tied up in premanufacturing, one-third in goods manufacturing, and one-third in accounts receivable. I have since learned of other companies that have found somewhat the same thing.

The shock effect has been even greater in plants like one that slashed manufacturing lead time to the point where order entry time was greater by a factor of two or three.

Emptying the In-Baskets

It is not yet common, but there are a few companies that have extended JIT into the realm of the invisible inventory. In one company the first major project was to cut order entry and engineering time, which had been twenty-two days. Study revealed only thirteen hours of "costed" work. By cutting out unnecessary steps and changing the method, the work content could be cut to six hours. A plan, to be accomplished before the end of 1985, would reduce the order entry and engineering lead time to just one day (instead of twenty-two).

Sure-fire evidence of long lead times in office work is piled-high in-baskets—just like racks and conveyors full of parts in factories. Unlike factories, the stacks sitting in the delay mode in pre- and post-manufacturing do not arise from batching. Each order entry, engineering, work order preparation, or invoicing task is a separate job. Long lead times occur because of backlogging, poor methods, "cherry-picking," and "diversions." Each is briefly discussed here.

- The backlog is the orders in the in-basket. Backlogging means too many orders are in the system for the order processors to handle.
- Factories do not have a corner on bad methods; in offices methods are at least as poor. A common example is checking the document at the end rather than during the process. Error rates are high in offices, and rework is too.

- Cherry-picking is looking through the in-basket to find the "friendliest" job. The nasty ones keep sinking lower in the stack. The result: Urgent jobs are often put off in favor of jobs that are not urgent, for example, jobs with far-off customer due dates or stock-replenishment jobs.
- Office employees are also adept at finding diversions: telephoning home, writing personal letters, working crossword puzzles on company time, shooting the breeze. Compared with factory folks, office employees find it easier to pursue diversions, because their work and their inventory—a piece of paper or an entry into computer memory—is not very visible.

Factory techniques are usable for emptying the in-baskets and shortening the lead time: Set up a flow line. Use kanban squares and allow no more than one document on the square between processes. Use under-capacity scheduling, and the day is not done until every job has been completed. Cross-train so that it is easy to move labor from where backlogs are gone to where they are getting worrisome. Use temporaries and use supervisors, managers, and people from other departments when the day's schedule is unmakable. Use statistical process control to reduce errors. Keep all tools and materials precisely located or filed and in perfect working condition.

The list goes on. Not all are usable in every case, but in every case some are useful. Sometimes special lead time reduction techniques may need to be devised. In engineering work, for example, there is the "carry-on-ban" technique.

Carry-on-Ban

Assume that ten R&D projects are under way. They involve design and process engineers, machinists, test technicians, buyers, and others. A plan in the form of an arrow diagram exists for each of the ten projects, but the arrow diagram does not show all the small coordination steps that can speed up the projects. To make sure there are no delays, everyone has sets of coordination cards, called "carry-on-ban"; the cards direct the person to carry rough work or completed work to those who perform the next steps.

For example, the plan may call for an engineer to rough-sketch a design for a tuner in a radio, then carry the sketch to the designer of the enclosure and also to a prototype shop to make a sample tuner.

The engineer hand-carries the sketches without delay—because two carry-on-ban cards tell the engineer to do so. The engineer goes back to work refining the design, and the designer of the enclosure and the prototype shop are also hard at work. The latter may have carry-on-ban instructions to carry their results right back to the tuner engineer. Figure 3–3 shows the plan.

The term "carry-on-ban" is a play on the Japanese word *kanban*. Kanban is the Toyota-devised card that tells a maker to make and deliver more of a certain material to a user. Since in engineering makers produce a unique piece of paper, not more of the same material, kanban cannot be used. Carry-on-ban can.[5]

Carry-on-ban is just one technique aimed at getting projects done fast. It helps keep in-basket piles low and delays short; it also reduces opportunities to cherry-pick. There are many carry-on-ban variations. For example, the cards may be produced only for urgent steps or projects, in which case they serve as a priority system.

The Broad View

The invisible inventory—the staff support people—are inclined toward a narrow view, a tendency the WCM company must forever combat. Part of the weaponry to fight overspecialization is what has been mentioned: removing sources of delay so staff employees have nothing secondary to work on—only customers and products. More weapons are needed in the battle, namely a total program for moving people from one specialty to another.

It is a travesty for a buyer to be a buyer for an entire career, for a scheduler to be a scheduler for a career, for an accountant to spend

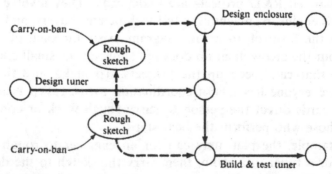

Figure 3–3. Coordination with Carry-on-Ban

a lifetime in tax accounting. When that is allowed, people's vision narrows. Late in their careers, the company encourages their early retirement. With more experience, people should be more valuable to their company, not less. Virtually every book about Japan comments favorably on the Japanese practice of moving people across specialties, which is a way to develop generalists. Even computer programmers in Japan stay in that specialty only seven years on the average.[6] Then it's off to the factory or perhaps into the sales organization.

Is our tight-fisted attitude toward training the reason why we haven't developed the broad view? Or is it lack of awareness of the consequences? Whichever one, we now know it's time for change.

The molding of all-arounders—both line and staff—has been the subject of this and the previous chapter. The all-arounder manages the resources at hand—time, methods, tools, equipment, work space, and information—with a broad view of their purpose. But the equation is reversible: Time, methods, tools, equipment, space, and information shape the behavior of the people, too. The next three chapters show how the inanimate resources manage their masters—with bad or good results.

Chapter 4

Overstated Role of Capital (Automation in Slow Motion)

"We were the best in our industry when I started working here twenty years ago. Ever since then we—by that I mean corporate—took cash out of the business. We got rid of engineers—we have no process engineers any more; and we chopped the equipment maintenance budget. Our plants are old and run down. But last year we finally came to our senses. We have the green light to spend $50 million on equipment."

The speaker is vice president of manufacturing in one of North America's large chemical companies. The details will change, but the basic tale of neglect is common and probably the norm in Western industry.

The neglect comes in many forms—process engineering and equipment maintenance, for example. Most of our industrial leaders, economists, and political leaders, however, see the problem as lack of investment in new equipment. Automation and robotics, to offset high labor costs, head most people's needs lists.

Nor are they just wish lists. American industry spent more in 1984 on capital equipment than it had in the previous twenty-eight years. After two decades of seeing Japan outspend most of the rest of the industrial world roughly two to one on capital equipment, it's about time. Japan has raised itself from a primitive state to rough parity in equipment with other countries (more modern equipment in some industries, less in others).

Are our recent and future increases in capital spending likely to close productivity gaps where they exist? Unless we learn some lessons about how to spend equipment money wisely, the answer is no. *Spending our way to cost reduction* is a flawed solution.

Smothered by Capital

If large amounts of capital were available at low interest rates, what would industry spend it for? Some likely candidates are computer systems for sending shop floor data to planners, controllers, and middle managers; automated inspection equipment; automated storage systems and large holding tanks for material staged between processes; or conveyors to move materials faster.

To the world-class manufacturer those must be viewed as dubious investments. One of the messages in Chapters 2 and 3 is that charts and blackboards on the shop floor can make a good information system. Automated inspection may just put off the correct response: improving the process. Automated storage and distance-spanning conveyors are no good (except in distribution centers for finished goods), because they add cost, not value, to the product.

If not automation of information processing and automation of storage and handling, how about the manufacturing itself, where the value *is* added? Process automation includes robots, automated transfer lines, and computer-numerically-controlled machines. It also might include a bigger, faster model of a current machine, one with all the latest bells and whistles.

Process Automation

Automation is worthwhile if it improves upon the performance or the cost of humans. But comparing a person with a machine is not straightforward. In the complex conventional factory, local changes have hard-to-predict global effects. Equipment feasibility studies use only the obvious numbers, and they rarely consider the many ways of doing much better with the people and equipment on hand.

Being antiequipment makes no sense, and later we shall examine why manufacturers who are able to improve rapidly will end up with the most automation. But first let us better understand the idea of making the most of equipment already owned. Toyota's No. 9 Kamigo engine plant is a case in point. John McElroy, editor of *Automotive*

Industries magazine, says that it is "probably the most efficient engine plant in the world."[1]

Engine Plant No. 9

The No. 9 Kamigo plant is equipped with twenty-year-old machines from America: machine tools from Cincinnati Milacron, and both Ex-Cell-O and Cross transfer lines.

Over the years the machines have been retrofitted so they don't miss a beat. Limit switches and electric eyes check, count, and index. If a machine makes a bad part or breaks down, the giant overhead electric *jidoka* signboard lights up and summons help to fix the problem right away. Quality problems are nipped in the bud, so there is little rework to do and little need to keep buffer stocks just in case of bad quality.

As is true nearly everywhere in Japan, the plant runs just two shifts, and preventive maintenance goes on between shifts and during the one-hour lunch breaks. When a machine is scheduled to run, it runs right.

Most machines can be set up in one or two minutes, so there is no reason to run large batches. The plant makes and delivers a variety of engines to the nearby assembly plant hourly.

With no large batches, there are no large storage areas or large-capacity storage and handling equipment. Their absence allows machines and processes to be jammed into a small space. One operator can run several machines with little time wasted walking, and with all the machine improvements, like automatic loaders and checkers, the operator has only brief duties at each machine. So why put in robots? There are none at the No. 9 plant.

Kamigo No. 9 is compared with Chrysler and Ford engine plants in Table 4–1. When adjusted for volume, the American plants are more than three times larger with six times more material, and it takes about six times more labor per engine than at the Toyota plant.

Toyota's methods are now well known in the world's auto industry and in many other industries as well. There is nothing surprising about the report on Kamigo plant No. 9, except that the plant happens to be one of Toyota's oldest. If asked about how such old equipment can yield such good results, a Kamigo manager might say, "After twenty years, shouldn't we know how to make the machines run right?"

Yes, you may say, but my plant is already so hopelessly run down

Table 4–1. Comparison of Engine Plants

	Toyota Kamigo No. 9	Chrysler Trenton	Ford Dearborn
Products	2.4 L4-cyl. 2.0 L4-cyl.	2.2 4-cyl. incl. turbo	1.6 L4-cyl. HO; turbo: EFI
Plant size (sq. ft.)	310,000	2.2 million	2.2 million
Hourly employment	180	2,250	1,360
Line rate (per day)	1,500	3,200	1,960
Labor-hours/engine	0.96	5.6	5.55
Shifts	2	2	1 assembly 2 machining
Inventory (average)	4–5 hrs.	2.5–5 days	9.3 days
Wages	$11.35/hr.	N.A.[a]	N.A.[a]
Robots	None	5	N.A.

[a] Industry average is $12.50 per hour, excluding fringes.

SOURCE: Adapted from McElroy, "Quality Goes In Before the Part Comes Out," *Automotive Industries,* November 1984, p. 52.

through years of neglect that we might as well open the purse strings and buy new equipment. Why not buy the most automated while we're at it?

The rest of the chapter deals with that question and a few others. Let's start with robots, since they have seized the public's imagination and industry's attention.

Robots

People used to react emotionally to robots. Technologists couldn't wait; humanists and labor leaders angrily or fearfully denounced them. Now robots are being installed at a steady pace, and for the moment with few voices of alarm.

Some companies are trying hard to make sure their uses of robots cause sales to grow so much that hiring rather than layoffs is the result. IBM is one such company. The IBM personal computer is a product, assembled with the aid of robots, that has led to hiring, not layoffs. But the PC is a marketing phenomenon—from zero to $5 billion sales in less than four years. Who can say what contribution the robots made? The same question may be asked about Apple's highly robotized factory that produces the Macintosh, which is a marvel of design if not a marketing phenomenon.

59

High-Volume, Low-Cost

IBM seems to be modeling other products after the PC success. Like many companies, IBM releases operating information reluctantly, but IBM has opened one of its newer products to public scrutiny. It is the 3178 logic unit, a module that combines with different keyboards, display units, and other peripherals.[2]

The 3178 is made in Raleigh, North Carolina, in what is called a "project management center" (PMC). The PMC has freewheeling authority, and the management team decided to make a just-in-time commitment, except that IBM calls it "continuous-flow manufacturing" (CFM) instead of JIT.

With CFM as the means, the desired outcome was a high-volume, low-cost (HVLC) product. That sounds like automation. More specifically, it sounds like assembly by robots, and that is the manufacturing approach IBM adopted. Most of the assembly, testing, and packing operations are done by several robots grouped in a compact area largely devoid of inventory and delays.

Any experienced visitor can see that the 3178 *is* a high-volume, low-cost product. Most visitors are likely to go away thinking that the robots are the key in the HVLC success. But are they?

Here, in my opinion, are the main reasons why the 3178 is a low-cost product:

1. *Design.* The 3178's predecessor was made "any way you want it," a product strategy that raises havoc in manufacturing and for the outside suppliers of component parts. The havoc was averted by making the 3178 a vanilla product—no features or options. That's not all. The engineers in the laboratory designed the 3178 for ease of manufacture. It has a very small part count compared with its predecessor and hardly any screws. Assembling it is mostly push-and-snap.

2. *Quality at the source.* Most of the component parts are bought, not made in IBM fabrication and subassembly shops. The purchased parts do not need to be inspected when received (except on an audit basis), because IBM spent the necessary up-front time to certify the quality capabilities of its suppliers. The number of suppliers is small—most suppliers appear to be sole-source—so it was not an impossible job to go to the suppliers to assess needs and help with quality assurance.

In short, the preproduction planning was outstanding. Could the product fail to be low-cost with such a fine head start? Most surely it could. If it were produced in the old way, the conventional way that the Raleigh plant once followed, it would have taken weeks to assemble, test, and pack. Any product that takes that long to manufacture collects large indirect and overhead costs and ends up being high-cost.

Instead of the conventional way, where the product travels to work centers scattered about the plant, all the work is done in a compact cell. It takes only hours instead of weeks to transform the raw materials into fully packaged finished goods. With so short a flow time, low cost is virtually guaranteed.

The method of manufacture may not have much effect on product cost. The robots don't receive wages, but they cost hundreds of thousands of dollars. The robots themselves are not nearly that expensive, but a large group of manufacturing engineers had to be hired to plan it all, and a large group of equipment technicians had to spend a long time on installation and trouble-shooting.

What if all the robots were replaced by humans? Robots sometimes have capabilities to make consistently good products that humans cannot match. Producing the 3178, however, does not appear to involve exacting tasks that humans would be unable to do right repetitively. Fail-safe devices, thought up by the work group itself, could catch the little mistakes that humans are bound to make.

With robots, the unit cost of the product turned out to be low because the high startup costs are amortized over a large sales volume. If human assemblers were doing the job, there would be higher variable cost, lower fixed cost. The total cost per unit could be higher, but who knows?

One thing is certain. If humans were building the product, they could diagnose and solve problems. They could be moved easily to other work if 3178 sales tapered off or fluctuated wildly. More humans could be inserted if more output were needed. A human work force could adapt easily to a new product when sales on the 3178 fade. *Robots are several orders of magnitude less flexible than humans.*

Low-Volume, Low-Cost

Companies that do not sell the massive quantities that IBM does cannot even think about early automation. I take it back. They can *think* about it, and should, but cannot afford to do much of it.

The following example is from Hewlett-Packard's Personal Office

Computer Division in Sunnyvale, California. In 1983–85 they made the HP-150 personal computer. H-P had not had much experience in mass consumer markets, so the 150 was a product that would test the waters—and perhaps even make a splash. We shall see how the 150 and its successor could perhaps make money even if sales were not large. A bit of background will help to show how the division lowered its break-even point and planned to keep it low through cautious automation.

The HP-150 is the one with the touch screen. Its predecessor was the HP-120 personal computer, along with nineteen other desktop computer products.

The 150 was planned for just-in-time production. The previous products required 30,000 square feet of plant, whereas the 150 took only 7,500 (a building was vacated). There had been some 2,000 suppliers; for the 150 it was to be two hundred suppliers. The number of part numbers was cut from 20,000 to 450.

Material requirements planning (MRP) had been used to schedule production, which was planned in lots of 500 for end items and in lots of 100 to 500 for printed circuit boards. Under JIT the computer issued a single work order per month, expressed as a daily rate; MRP was used to schedule the suppliers and for little else. Work orders were not needed, because the work centers were laid out in one long serpentine flow line, so that a visual (kanban) system could pull work from preceding work centers just-in-time for use.

The successor to the 150 was to be released in 1985. It would be an even better JIT product, because it was *designed* for manufacturability. The number of part numbers was to be only 150 (versus 450), and there were to be only thirty suppliers (down from two hundred). Work-in-process inventory was expected to be just one day's worth.

The designers of the product spent time on the shop floor with a six-axis IBM robot that was in use experimentally. The idea was to find out what the robot could do—what it could lift, how far it could reach and with what turn angles, what grippers it could use, and so forth. Then the designers went to work designing the new computer for assembly by robots.

How many robots were on order for the new production line? Zero. The designers did what was necessary to be ready for robots. Then, the idea is, don't put any robots in—don't spend the money—until experience shows where they really can pay off. Experience will reveal the tasks that a human operator cannot do the same way in the same invariable cycle time with dependably high quality all day long. (The largest uses of robots in the world so far are in painting and welding, which tend to be difficult for humans to do the same way over and over.)

Pre-automation

The design engineers were doing their part in what we call *pre-automation:* making it possible and making it easy for a mindless machine, robot or otherwise, to do the work. Other aspects of pre-automation are up to production people and process engineers. They must do the following:

1. Shorten reach distances.
2. Shorten flow distances.
3. Put all tools and parts nearby and in exact locations.
4. Design packages, containers, racks, and fixtures so that every part and every tool is correctly aimed and easy to grasp.
5. Design simple automatic checking devices that catch common errors—sometimes called fail-safe devices (*pokayoke,* in Japan).

The merits of pre-automation are many. Lee Rhodes, production manager, points out that when a product is designed so that a robot can assemble it easily, it is also much easier for humans to assemble.

During my own tour of the plant, I suggested taking that common-sense notion one step farther: Maybe they should have bought a small pick-and-place (three-axis) device to experiment with instead of the full-function six-axis robot. If the engineers could design the product for the limited motions of the pick-and-place robot, I said to Lee, the product would "*really* be easy for humans to assemble."

Probably the engineers at H-P Sunnyvale could have fashioned a convincing robot proposal based on labor cost displacement. They could do so by comparing *present* labor costs against robots and ignoring the lowering of labor costs and variability that come from pre-automation. As Hayes and Wheelright put it, "Any project can be made to look attractive if it is compared against something sufficiently unattractive."[3]

The usual way we justify equipment, including robots, is by some variation of a return on investment (ROI) analysis—this sort of formula:

$$ROI(1) = \frac{\text{Labor cost savings}}{\text{Installed cost of equipment}}$$

That type of analysis is not nearly sufficient. Equally important, but not so easy to measure in numbers, are the benefits and costs in this variation of the ROI formula:

$$ROI(2) = \frac{\text{Benefits of reduced variability}}{\text{Costs of reduced flexibility/mind power}}$$

The managers and engineers at the Sunnyvale plant made decisions that seem consistent with this way of justifying equipment expenditures. The result is, I expect, a low break-even point for H-P's personal computer, because (1) little capital was needed for plant space and equipment, (2) jobs were simplified so that labor costs per unit were lowered, and (3) mental capacity is still available on the line, and the environment is conducive for line people to keep suggesting improvements.

Machine Vision

I have emphasized the value of the robot to decrease variability. Advanced robots have a feature that does not decrease variability but instead reacts to variability. That is what the vision systems, or robots with eyes, are equipped for. What is their proper role?

My own rule-of-thumb on vision-equipped robots is that they make sense for process control where human eyes are deficient. Visitors to Apple Computer's Macintosh factory in California have been impressed by one such device. A robot inserts a 256K RAM chip into a printed circuit board, and a vision device underneath the board checks all the leads to make sure that each is bent at the proper angle. That is a complicated check, and a human could not do it well. Some of GM's planned uses of vision systems for checking welds and for seeing that no parts are missing are also sound.

Factories that are advanced in uses of robotics, such as the Macintosh plant, IBM's typewriter factory in Kentucky, and some of GM's assembly plants, are eager to press on. We hear of plans to add vision systems for finding a part in a jumbled location and turning it so that it is presented properly for assembly. While that is the kind of task any child could do, the enthusiast would argue that the vision-equipped robot can do it cheaper. That might be so, if we were stuck with the problem of jumbled boxes of parts. We are not. Pre-automation concepts apply: Have the parts packaged so that a standard machine, a robot, or a human assembler can find the next part easily. (Unless there is a breakthrough that causes machine vision costs to tumble, the home robot will remain a fanciful idea, because whose home is so neat that a robot could navigate or find anything?)

There is still much to learn about robots, new as they are on the manufacturing scene. IBM and Apple have had explosive demand to contend with and have been willing to pump in money to buy capacity quickly and to learn about robotics. H-P's Sunnyvale division had less certainty of revenue and took a more cautious approach.

At the other end of the spectrum is an older kind of automation in which different kinds of equipment are fashioned into linked processes. JIT modifies some past beliefs about such equipment.

Linked Processes

What if you were to buy a machine for your home that peels potatoes? You acquire another one that slices potatoes into the shape of French fries. A third machine, a cooker, fries them. You are so good at it that you go into selling cooked and quick-frozen French fries. Now you want the peeler, the slicer, and the cooker right next to each other. You may engineer some devices that grab a peeled potato and feed it into the slicer and grab the slices and feed them into the cooker.

What you have created is a form of automation. It is a production line that links machine tools together; the automotive industry calls it a transfer line. Transfer lines have been around for years, especially for transmissions and engines.

Today many industries that make panels out of metal are investing in their own versions of transfer lines. The panels are used for steel doors, file cabinets, desks, partitions, and so forth.

It usually begins with roll-forming equipment, which straightens coiled steel or aluminum. Next the straightened coil is cut into panel shapes. Benders, trimmers, grinders, stuffers, welders, drillers, perforators, and other processes may follow. The old way was to locate each of the processes apart from each other one and to transport material between them. Inventories, lead times, and floor space were high— definitely not the just-in-time mode of manufacture. The new way is the transfer line approach, which yields some JIT results. Some of the lines are even equipped for quick setup of a new coil and quick adjustment of cutoff widths and lengths. There are also problems that negate some of the JIT gains:

1. The lines cost a lot.
2. They take six to twelve months to install and debug.
3. They are immobile; the different stages in the line must be carefully aligned and then bolted to the floor.
4. When (if) they can be made to run right, the best we can expect is an average up time of perhaps 80 percent, and the day-to-day variability of up time is high: maybe up for all but fifteen minutes on one shift, then down during the next—for five days.

Undependable, highly variable output is destructive of a JIT campaign.

When the transfer line is running well, and it may do so for several days in a row, it really pumps out product. In the days of conventional manufacturing, such a string of productive days brought smiles to everyone's faces. The work team, the maintenance people, and the supervisors might celebrate by going out for a few drinks after work.

In the JIT mode such days of high output are bad and not allowed. The goal is to make only what is needed by the next process each day. The term for this is "make to a number." If the daily schedule

"We may turn out things in half the time with this new machine, Mr Barr, but we have to. It's down the other half."

Courtesy of AMERICAN MACHINIST, February 1983

is met early, stop the line; use the extra time for problem-solving sessions and for preventive maintenance aimed at lengthening the string of days without breakdown.

Most of the companies that are putting in these lines of linked machines are in fast-growing industries or companies; they generate earnings to reinvest, and they need more capacity. The office furniture industry grew so fast in recent years that most, maybe all, of the leading companies in the industry have put in high-volume linked lines: Steelcase, Herman Miller, Haworth, Houserman, and others. There is another way to get the volume, a way that supports rather than clashes with JIT objectives.

The other, usually better way is to put in two or more low-capacity, mostly unlinked lines made up of equipment with a record of high reliability. Each line might have a roll-former, a conventional press brake to cut sheets to size, semiautomatic welders, manual debur, and other processes. With more than one line, each can be scheduled to run a different size or model. If one line goes down, the others still produce and perhaps can run extra shifts so that no sales orders are late. Within a single line, it is safe to link any pair of the processes together *if the first of the two can run without breakdown.*

The tortoise and the hare come to mind. The high-volume transfer line is the hare. It can hop awfully fast, but it is forever stopping to talk with members of the opposite sex or for a short beer. Two or more low-volume unlinked lines are like two or more tortoises. They plod along, but they are dependable.

No Tolerance for Down Time

In conventional manufacturing, down time is a serious problem only for bottleneck equipment. A bottleneck machine runs full blast and forwards work to the next process just in time. If it breaks down, it's just too late.

Only a small fraction of a plant's work centers are bottlenecks. The bottleneck work centers hog the time and attention of engineers, technicians, and supervisors. One effect of buffer stock removal, a JIT technique, is to turn *all* work centers into bottlenecks so they receive problem-solving attention. That spreads the staff experts thin; operators must be the first line of attack on the problems that pop up when a buffer stock runout causes a work stoppage.

Operator-Centered Preventive Maintenance

Many of the problems are machine malfunctions and breakdowns. Operators can learn to adjust machines, but we cannot expect operators suddenly to have the expertise to fix them when they break down. Therefore, with all work centers potential hot spots, the operators need to cool them off with daily regimens of preventive maintenance, simple things like adding lubricant, checking for wear, listening for the telltale whine or tick that suggests a serious problem.

An example of that approach is at the Indianapolis plant of Detroit Diesel Allison, a division of General Motors. The plant makes diesel engines, power shift transmissions, and related products. The plant employs about seven thousand people, represented by the United Auto Workers. Detroit Diesel was one of the first plants in the North American auto industry to achieve impressive within-plant JIT results, namely, sharp cuts in manufacturing lead time.

Joe Gossman was named coordinator of Detroit Diesel's MAN (material-as-needed) group in 1982. One early action of the MAN group was to send survey forms out to the manufacturing employees at the plant. The form asked, "What do you think is the major reason for machine down time?" About 70 percent answered: inadequate lubrication.

That answer provided the opening for Gossman's group to go back to the operators and say, in effect: You are complaining about the job the maintenance department is doing on lubricating the machines. We are going to give that job to someone we *know* will do it right—*you,* the machine operator.

For about the next year the maintenance department had a new job: training the operators in how to lubricate the equipment correctly. Barrels of lubricants were placed out on the shop floor so that operators had ready access.

After that the maintenance department had another new job: training the operators in how to do simple repairs. That could include changing and tightening belts, replacing oil seals, maybe even changing a motor or a bearing.

Harley-Davidson's engine and transmission plants in Milwaukee have gone through a similar transition. At Harley, machine operators, in taking over the lubrication, discovered some fittings that had *never* been lubed. At first maintenance people went around checking to see if the lubrications were done right. The operators squawked until maintenance backed off. That put operators on their own, except for having to turn in lube checkoff sheets to supervisors. Again the operators objected: "What's the matter? Don't you trust us?" Now the operators check off and sign the lube sheets but self-post the sheets instead of turning them in.

The concept practiced at Detroit Diesel and at Harley is for the machine operator to feel a sense of ownership: I own the machine. If anything goes wrong with it, I feel personal responsibility. I do not blame the maintenance department. I should not only lube it but also wipe it down several times a day so that if there is a leak somewhere, the excess fluid will not disappear into a pool but will be obvious; then I get the seal or gasket or other trouble fixed *before* it causes a work stoppage.

It is a natural step for the operator to keep the area, as well as the machine, tidy and clean—no outside custodians. Special machine setup crews become unneeded as the operator comes to know all about the machine. At the same time, world-class manufacturing companies are rapidly shifting away from quality inspections by inspectors; the operators control the process and perform any necessary inspections themselves. Routine machine maintenance, area cleaning and arrangement, quality control, tool changing, tool care, and machine loading and unloading all become duties of the operator. They are not seen as a collection of different kinds of duties. The differences blur and become one job.

Making Time for Maintenance

With all this tender loving care by the operator, the machine is going to work better and last longer. *Total preventive maintenance* is that and more. The machine still needs attention from talented experts out of the maintenance department. They need to perform higher-level preventive maintenance, and to do so often. The problem is finding free time when the machine is not running.

In *Japanese Manufacturing Techniques* I told about two-shifting. This plan allows a maximum of two shifts per day, with two maintenance shifts between. While many of the Japanese techniques for stamping out waste and eliminating problem causes have a strong foothold in North American industry, this one has only a weak foothold. The U.S. auto industry is about the only one that is massively abandoning a three-shift tradition. (Some countries in Europe have never had a history of three-shift operations. There are social policies and even laws that mostly rule out three shifts; for example, Germany, like Japan, has laws against having women work in factories past a certain evening hour.)

Industries in North America that are mostly hanging on to three-shift scheduling (in times of high demand) include chemicals, rubber, food, weaving, paper, molders and extruders, sheet coaters, and most of the metal fabricators. Those are capital-intensive industries. Labor-intensive industries, such as light assembly of electrical and electronic products, can easily accept two-shifting, because not running a third shift avoids that much wages. Equipment, unlike labor, must be paid for whether operating or not. So aren't the bottom-line-watchers right in their view that plants full of expensive equipment ought to run three shifts?

Available for Use

The answer is no. Costly equipment deserves our best care, not our worst. You might be able to prove by a cost analysis that running three shifts saves money, but you would get that answer only by using *average* down time data and also by ignoring time when defective product is being produced. High average down time is costly, but it is high down time variability and bad quality that can be fatal. Figure 4–1 demonstrates.

Part A of the figure shows what many plants on three shifts experience. In the twenty-four-hour period the machine (or line) is up sixteen hours and down eight hours. Some of those eight bad hours might be times when the machine is running but producing product that is unacceptable and has to be scrapped—which is worse than not running at all. The net *good* utilization of the equipment is 67 percent, as is its availability to produce good product.

We see that the longest down/bad time in the twenty-four hours was between hour 18 and hour 21. That means there must be a three-hour buffer stock before the next process, Y. Y's down/bad duration, in turn, determines the buffer stock before Z. Actually, the buffer stock would be based on the longest down/bad time in recent memory—and that could be weeks!

Part B of Figure 4–1 shows how the problems melt away with two-shifting. There are frequent heavy doses of PM from hours 8 to 12 and 20 to 24 each day. (Besides PM, the scheduled down time may also be used for such things as training, overtime, prototyping,

A. Three-shifting, work-center X: 67% up time; 67% availability.

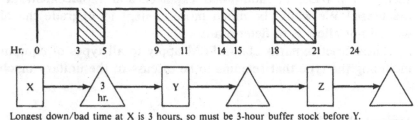

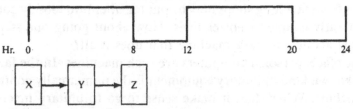

Longest down/bad time at X is 3 hours, so must be 3-hour buffer stock before Y.

B. Two-shifting, work-center X: 67% up time; 100% availability.

No down/bad time at X, so no buffer stock before Y.
No buffer stock, so no racks or space; processes right next to each other.
Note: Spaces containing diagonal lines stand for repair or bad-production time.

Figure 4–1. Three- Versus Two-Shifting

machine warmups, and complicated setups.) The machine does not cause trouble any more. Its up time is the same as in A, 67 percent, but its availability for use when we want to use it now is 100 percent. With no breakdowns, there is no need for buffer stock. With no buffer stock, the machines need not be separated with racks or pallets of material and bulk handling equipment between. The machines are back to back.

If total preventive maintenance (TPM) sounds like the old term "life cycle management" of capital equipment, it is just that. However, our life cycle management notions revolved around buying equipment and then replacing it when its maintenance costs get too high and its performance gets too bad. Equipment policy for the world-class manufacturer must be to keep maintenance costs from getting high and to keep performance from deteriorating. TPM and statistical process control to detect abnormalities are the means.

As companies adopt TPM and SPC, they should end up with a substantial shift in the way they spend capital for equipment, a shift toward the Japanese pattern of expenditures. According to one report, in 1980 the majority—about 60 percent—of Japanese equipment spending "was devoted to upgrading the capabilities of *existing* equipment and processes." In contrast, the report says, most U.S. companies spend 75 percent on additional capacity and replacement of old machines.[4] We would be much more content to upgrade the old if we did not allow it to deteriorate.

These brief remarks about TPM apply to all types of equipment, including the type that remains to be discussed: the unitary machine.

Unitary Machines

Machines from far-flung shops may be put together into loosely coupled cells or tightly coupled transfer lines. How about going one step further? How about a unitary machine that does it all?

In the office, personal computers are such machines. In the factory, the best-known kind of unitary equipment is the numerically controlled (NC) machine. When does it make sense to go to unitary machines? Two examples, one office and one factory, help shed light on the question.

Back-Office Efficiency

Citibank, headquartered in Manhattan, grew fast in the 1960s—so fast that a paper-processing disaster was waiting to happen. Huge computers and a backroom staff of 10,000 by 1970 did not defuse the bomb. Customers raged about errors and delays, and paper and data processing costs were growing by 15 percent a year.

Citibank hired Robert B. White, whose experience was in the auto industry, to straighten out the mess. White announced that he did not know banking, but he did know about assembly lines. "Show me the assembly lines," he told his staff.

The search was on to find out how documents got processed, where they flowed from and to—and why. White did not find assembly lines. Instead he found that each transaction passed "through many hands. The backroom was organized by function: All check encoding was done in one place, all computer entries in another. Responsibility was lost; errors couldn't be corrected."[5]

The many hands that touched the transactions had to be linked. White's team set up assembly lines according to customer types: one line for local businesses, one for large corporations, one for other banks, and so on. The organization structure was flipped 90 degrees. One manager was now in charge of each line.

Those changes led to simplifications and cuts in labor, but a problem cropped up: Different customers had to deal with different assembly lines.

The solution was to assign each account to a single person. The large IBM mainframe computers were not well suited for this. Out they went, and computing was decentralized. Citibank bought hundreds of video display terminals for the people who now had responsibility for whole customer accounts.

To summarize, Citibank did not settle for the large improvement in efficiency and quality that came from organizing flow lines or cells. They took the last step—unitary machines and work stations—which allowed a variety of transactions to be processed at one place.

While the unitary approach seems to suit Citibank and information processing, how about factory work?

Gear Boxes

The Cushman Division of Outboard Marine operates a large plant in Nebraska. Cushman's golf cart business, which it was once known for, was lost to Japanese competitors years ago. Cushman has a full product line of golf course maintenance equipment that has stayed profitable. The company plans to ensure that the product line stays healthy by putting capital into the business. For example, it installed several numerically controlled machines at prices in the $350,000-to-$400,000 range each. With NC machines, work-in-process inventories and lead times plunge. The example of a gear box shows why.

It used to take a month to manufacture a gear box. A typical first operation was to mill surfaces of the raw casting; more than one milling operation meant more than one setup and sometimes a move from one milling machine to another.

Next the work traveled across the plant for drill and tap operations. After waiting for a time in a queue, the work piece went into a fixture for mounting on a drill press and then into another machine for tap operations. Alternatively, both drill and tap might be done on a radial drill press with a "magic chuck" for quick tool change.

The third step meant a trip back across the plant for boring operations and a likely wait in another queue of orders stacked up. An Excello boring machine would work for a smaller gear box; a horizontal boring machine was used for a larger one. Several boring operations required several setups.

To summarize, making a gear box required many setups, plus two major moves across the plant. It would not do to make and move only one. A lot that would fill a whole wire basket of that gear box model is more likely.

Now at the Cushman plant an NC machine can make a gear box in one hour, and the lot quantity can be just one. For a quantity of one on a unitary machine, there is no need for a wire basket, for transit inventory, for fork lifts to transport across the floor, and for queues in different work centers. The unitary machine seems to be the answer to a JITer's prayers.

Lest we go overboard in our enthusiasm for NC equipment, we should ask ourselves if there is any other way to slash the lead time. There is: Create cells by bringing scattered equipment together. Cell A, for small gear boxes, might have one or two milling machines, a drill press, a tapping machine, and an Excello boring machine. Cell B, for large gear boxes, would have the same, except for a horizontal boring machine. The cost of moving present equipment is a fraction of the $350,000 cost of an NC machine.

There will, of course, be a setup delay for the whole cell each time a given model of gear box is run, and the setup time dictates that the lot size be larger than one—perhaps a dozen. The flow time through the cell will be several hours, not just one hour. The net result is slightly less of a JIT accomplishment than with the NC machine, but the cell approach has a bargain price.

On the other hand, some NC equipment is remarkably trouble-free. That is true of Cushman's NC machines. Comparing the old conventional machines with the new NC machines is like comparing a high school performance of "Fiddler on the Roof" with Broadway's version. We know that those kids are trying hard and we admire their efforts, but they are not in the same league with the Broadway troupe.

The decision to NC or not NC really boils down to a question of model variety and volume. If the variety of models is high and the volume of each is low, the NC machine is the logical choice. If there are a few dominant models of gear box, then the cell of loosely coupled older machines is probably best: Set up the cell for a run of eight of one model, then set up for perhaps fifteen of the next, then three of the next. Either way—unitary machine for low volume or cell for higher volume—gives excellent JIT results, compared with conventional practices.

The Merits of Automation

We have seen, through a few diverse examples, how equipment policies can hamper or enhance a JIT/TQC effort. Some general principles emerge.

Principle no. 1. Do not put in equipment simply to displace labor. Equipment cannot think or solve problems; humans can. Our past failures to use shop floor people as problem-solvers have shaped the view that labor is a problem. The WCM view is that equipment is a problem, and labor is an opportunity.

Principle no. 2. The main advantage that equipment has (over people) is to decrease variability: uniform motions, uniform cycle times, uniform quality.

Corollary A. Employ TPM to make present equipment completely reliable so it can do a job in a uniform, dependable cycle time with no question about quality.

Corollary B. Employ pre-automation to eliminate search time and thereby make the operation cycle time shorter and more uniform.

Corollary C. Link machines together only if the feeder machine is reliable.

Corollary D. Buy small, simple machines one by one as demand grows instead of large, complex machines. Smaller machines are easier to maintain, and several instead of one provide protection against a disastrous failure. Other reasons for small machines in multiple copies have to do with refinements on the old economy-of-scale concept, a topic in the next chapter.

If the two principles and the four corollaries are negative about equipment, it is because there have been so many years of equipment neglect, and there are so many wrongs to be righted. In the past the machine tool manufacturers were not asked to produce totally reliable machines; if they had, the equipment users would not have been willing to pay the price.

We do ask that airplanes be totally reliable and not fall out of the sky. By and large, the airframe industry, together with the airline maintenance people and the pilots doing preflight checkouts, are able to meet our expectations. Making manufacturing machines run right is not nearly so hard. In the competitive world of manufacturing today, reliable equipment is becoming necessary, not just nice to have.

Letting machines run down is part of a broader recent problem of societal preoccupation with things financial and delegation of things technological. Western industrial leaders once were good managers of capital equipment. In companies whose managers reacquire that skill, we may expect to see more problem-pull automation and less of the money-push or technology-push variety. Where there is skill at managing equipment, there is reason to press for automation at a faster pace, because world-class manufacturing demands the capability of machines and automation to reduce variability.

Chapter 5

Economy of Multiples

WCM offers new thoughts on not only types of equipment but also size of equipment, be it robots, transfer lines, unitary machines, or an ordinary machine tool. The size issue has been neatly resolved in the past by the economy-of-scale concept, which usually leads to picking the biggest machine in the catalog. The engineers call the concept the six-tenths rule: A machine with twice the capacity has six-tenths of the unit cost of output.

The rule has proofs to back it up. If the proofs are valid for traditional manufacturing, they surely are not for world-class manufacturing. The obvious costs—the amortized cost of the machine and the labor to operate it—only scratch the surface. WCM requires paying heed to some other machine capabilities—which together overshadow the surface costs:

- How fast the machine can be set up
- How easy it is to maintain the machine and keep it making good product
- How easily the machine may be moved
- Whether the machine's speed can be adjusted up and down to match up-and-down use rates at next processes and up-and-down final demand rates
- Whether the machine's price is low enough for multiple copies of it to be bought over time, matched to the growth of demand

Machines Dictating Policy

The last point, matching capacity growth to demand growth, is a key concept of capital investment for the world-class manufacturer, and it fits well with the JIT ideal of producing only what is sold every day. While industry has always tried to add equipment as demand grows, the additions have generally come in large gulps that have proved hard to digest. A typical equipment cycle—we might call it the *supermachine cycle*—is as follows:

1. Marketing projects growth in demand.
2. Decision is made to add capacity.
3. Engineering searches machine tool manufacturers' catalogs; selects large machine—enough capacity for three to five years of projected demand growth. In the name of the six-tenths rule, two or more identical smaller machines are rejected in favor of the larger one.
4. Machine is installed and debugged, which takes several weeks or months, owing to the large machine's complexity and needs for special utility hookups and perhaps a reinforced-concrete base.
5. Machine is mostly underused in its first two or three years.
6. Demand growth catches up with machine's capacity. Machine finally is fully utilized—three shifts a day—in the fourth year.
7. Three-shift operations allow little time for maintenance; neglect results in only about two shifts of up-and-good production.
8. Machine's capacity and reliability are inadequate; time to buy another supermachine—and repeat the cycle.

In times of fast demand growth the cycle is much shorter. Whether the cycle is long or short, the demand projections are often wrong, which magnifies the problems in the machine's life cycle.

For example, let us say that a capacity shortage seems just around the corner for machine center X, and the finance committee gives the green light to add capacity. A $400,000 supermachine is no sooner bought and installed than demand takes a nosedive. The supermachine's utilization rate plunges. Everyone is nervous, because "that machine that we just paid $400,000 for is idle." Now the problem is too much capacity. Furthermore, the $400,000 is tied up in yesterday's technology, and retained earnings are not being generated to pay for tomorrow's advanced equipment. Marketing is under pressure to mount an advertising campaign, cut prices, sell something that will keep the supermachine busy. The machine has become the master, dictating policy.

Machine-Taming

The supermachine is like the lion in the zoo. It demands to be fed on a regular basis, and it eats a lot. The lion needs taming.

In the summer of 1983 I had the pleasure of spending some time with Randy Thom and Jane Peterson, manufacturing engineers at Tektronix in Oregon. Thom and Peterson were buying equipment for the "color-shutter" project, a new product offering, and they devised an equipment strategy that avoids the depressing supermachine cycle.

High-Risk Strategy

To set the stage properly I'll describe an earlier Tektronix product, one no longer marketed. It was a precision video display product used with oscilloscopes. Market surveys indicated that the product was likely to be a hit in the market place. On that basis Tek was off and running to manufacture the product in high volume. Since bad quality can kill off demand, funds were not spared in getting the best component parts and equipment. For example, two or three large clean rooms were constructed at great expense.

The high equipment expenditures were partly offset by avoidance of costly delays and inventories between process stages. Production was laid out in a serpentine flow path with short distances, and there were scarcely any places where buffer stocks could build between processes. Short lengths of conveyor kept the product moving from machine to machine in the large two-floor facility. The manufacturing engineers had done their part in improving the chances that the glowing market surveys would come true. Market response times (lead times) would be short, and quality would be high. Even though the equipment was expensive, unit costs would be low if the product sold as well as expected.

It didn't. If sales had met the forecast, the facility would have been operating three shifts by midyear 1983. It was not even running half a shift. The product was a failure, and a costly one at that. Some of the equipment could be used elsewhere, but much of it could not, and the clean rooms were immobile—part of the structure.

That kind of disaster occurs in every company (and is in no way a negative comment about Tektronix, which is among the leaders in implementing WCM concepts). Those who study such things tell us that two out of three product introductions fail. Probably in the high-tech sector the failure rate is higher. Let us see what Thom and Peterson did to ensure that, if the color-shutter product were a market failure, it would not be a financial disaster.

Low-Risk Strategy

The Thom–Peterson plan was to buy capacity in small increments, that is, add more increments as demand grows. A representative example (not the real figures): Buy enough capacity for eight to twelve months' projected demand growth as the first increment. Install it, start producing, and place orders for a second increment. If demand is less than expected, slow down deliveries of the equipment; if the product is a market failure, cancel the equipment orders and kill the project.

If the product sells well for several years, new machines arrive and go into production every eight to twelve months. Each new increment becomes a separate flow line inside the factory. If a key machine in one of the lines goes down, only that line stops producing. Its labor, cross-trained and versatile, can help out elsewhere, perhaps on the other lines, which keep running. The other lines may run overtime or weekends to make up for the lost production on the down line so that no orders are late, no sales are lost. Figure 5–1 summarizes the capacity concept that Thom and Peterson originally came up with (the concept, but not the exact details).

There are several models of the color-shutter product. If changeover time from model to model is very short, each line has the flexibility to run mixed models. Alternatively, if some machines resist quick changeover, line 1 may be dedicated to model A, line 2 to model B, and line 3 to model C. Either way—mixed-model or dedicated lines— some of every model is produced and is available for sale every day. That gets marketing off the hook; it does not need to guess correctly the model mix that customers will be buying.

If Thom and Peterson had planned equipment for the color-shutter product in the usual way, there would be a single large, costly, high-capacity line. Model-to-model changeovers would take hours or days. That would dictate a long production cycle: model A made this week, B next week, C the third week, and D the fourth. Marketing would

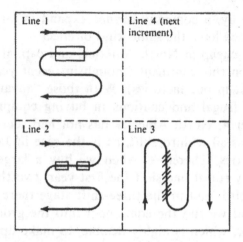

Notes:

Flow line 1 has enough capacity for 8-12 months of projected demand growth. The machines are the smallest in the catalog—providing the small ones have a high quality and performance capacity. The engineers see no way to avoid a large, costly, inflexible, clean room. The serpentine layout makes the production area compact. Processes, people, and even shipping and receiving are close together. The flow line can be managed largely by sight.

Flow line 2, added later, is like line 1, only better. Some machines have become available that are cheaper, more reliable, and easier to move and set up than their predecessors. Owing to better procedures and components, the clean room is no longer necessary; modular clean tunnels will do.

Flow line 3, added still later, is still better, cheaper, and more flexible. Quality improvements permit use of laminar-flow benches instead of modular clean tunnels.

Flow line 4, added if the product is a hit, is better yet, and even cheaper and more flexible. Line 1's performance is not up to par and may be torn down.

It is likely that one or more types of equipment will cost too much and have too great a capacity to buy in multiple copies. So be it. Buy one and put it in the center to be shared. While this forces the product to come out of the flow lines and incur large transport and batch production costs, sometimes there is no reasonable alternative—at least in the short run.

Figure 5–1. Adding Capacity in Increments at Tektronix

have to try to guess the sales rate weeks or months out—at the far end of the production cycle. Large finished goods inventories (FGI) of every model would be needed to protect against underestimates. More FGI, a good deal more, would be heaped up in distribution centers to guard against production stoppages, which are a certainty when there is only one large, complex production line instead of several small, simple ones.

Adding Fixed Capacity the Way We Add People

The equipment concept that Thom and Peterson followed was not theirs, nor is it mine. It is common enough in most countries where space is very expensive (Japan and Singapore) or countries that have severe shortages of capital (the underdeveloped countries). If capital is hard to come by, a company *cannot* expand in large increments; high costs of space have the same kind of effect.

Space is still cheap in North America, and capital has been relatively plentiful on this continent (though in recent years we did not spend much of it in our factories). With those "advantages" we did not learn to be frugal and cautious in buying equipment. Also, as noted in Chapter 4, North America has not had social policies that make it hard to staff a third shift, as is the case in Japan and some European countries. Therefore, when we buy a large increment of capacity, we may run it one shift the first year, two the second year, and three the third; and in the three-shift stage there is no time for maintenance, and we run the equipment into the ground. We use— or misuse—labor, which is highly flexible, to make up for the equipment inflexibility that comes from installing single large-capacity production facilities instead of multiple small ones.

This discussion may be summed up in the form of two lessons:

1. *More than one team, cell, line, or machine is better than one.* Two teams and sets of equipment making the same product or product family are in friendly competition for results when things are going well. They back each other up so that sales need not be lost when things are not going so well.

2. *Add fixed capacity the way we add people: in small increments as demand grows.* The lesson applies not only to single machine types and cells but also to whole product flow lines, manual or automated, and even whole factories.

Whole Factories

Toyota's Kamigo engine plant no. 9, mentioned in glowing terms in Chapter 4, is an example of adding whole plants in small increments. No. 9 is one of a string of engine plants that Toyota has built side by side as demand has grown over the years. Toyota could have just enlarged the original plant and replaced low-capacity transfer lines with larger-capacity lines. Not doing it that way spares Toyota from hodge-podge and from having "all its eggs in one basket."

Heat-Treat

The small increments concept applies to nearly any type of equipment. Heat-treat equipment is a common example, and experiences at Omark Industries serve to illustrate.

Omark's Guelph, Ontario, facility, which makes saw chain, is one of North America's most advanced JIT plants. In November 1982 its lead time to produce a lot of saw chain was twenty-one days, and the flow distance was 2,620 feet. About six months later the lead time was three days, and the flow distance was 850 feet. There was not much further reduction for well over a year.

The problem was heat-treat. After the saw blades were formed—in small amounts through cells and flow lines—they had to be sent to the large central heat-treat oven, which processed blades in large batches. If a large oven heat-treated a thousand blades per batch, a thousand would come out at a time. Then 999 of them would have to sit waiting to be siphoned off one at a time for assembly. That adds to manufacturing lead time, carrying costs, potential scrap/rework, and all the other ills of inventory retention and process lead time.

The first plan was to install small laser heat-treating stations on production lines all around the plant. That plan fell by the wayside. The next proposal was to get rid of the large central heat-treat oven and buy about twenty small ones to disperse around the factory.

While the story might have stopped there and neatly illustrated the multiple small machine concept, the Guelph plant went one step further. Purchasing found a pretempered type of steel that did not need to be heat-treated. In going to no heat-treat at all, the lead time was cut from three days to one day, and the flow distance dropped from 850 to 173 feet.

While JIT mostly aims at chopping delay (non-value-added) time, cutting the process (value-added) time has the same happy results. The overall lead time drops, problems get solved to sustain the drop, and competitiveness increases. Omark, Guelph, did not just cut the heat-treating process time, it eliminated it.

A Side Issue: Toolmaking and Machine Tools

A side comment on Omark seems appropriate. Why has the company been so successful in its WCM efforts? One reason, I think, is Omark's strong toolmaking capability. People in the company say they think they have the best toolmaker in the land, a fellow who has taught the toolmaking art to others. Omark had to have that capability years ago when it got into the manufacture of saw chain; it couldn't go out and buy saw-chain-making machine tools. Omark retained that strength. It came in handy when the company embarked on its first significant JIT thrust, which was quick machine setup projects. The toolmakers could quickly make any machine modification that engineers or operators could think up. A WCM trait is moving the most innovative machine operators into the tool room—for higher pay and prestige.

Omark is exceptional in North America for not phasing out its toolmaking strength. One can envision this, more typical, kind of reasoning going on in industrial America in the 1960s: Why not cut back on the toolmaking department, which is costly, and buy from the experts, the very capable U. S. machine tool industry? Now the U. S. machine tool industry is not so strong. Hayes and Wheelwright suggest that by experiencing no pressure from their industrial customers to innovate, the machine tool industry grew stale. In Germany, by contrast, "producer's emphasis on making their own capital equipment seems to have *strengthened* the German machine-tool industry."[1]

The best policy may be something like this: Make your own equipment wherever possible, because (1) it shortens the lead time, (2) you can produce small-capacity machines and add more as demand grows, (3) you can design for your own narrow needs and perhaps keep costs lower, and (4) you retain the expertise so that you can keep improving and "foolproofing" the equipment. Buy from outside when you need advanced, state of the art expertise—which the machine tool industry should be able to provide.

Wave-Soldering

Returning to the discussion of adding machines incrementally, here is an example for a common type of equipment in electronics. Today in North America, most towns of more than 10,000 people have at least one printed circuit board assembly plant. Most of those plants own a machine for soldering the leads on the underside of the boards. A good wave-soldering machine has been costing above $100,000. Except in some of the high-volume board shops, the capacity of the machine is usually far greater than needed.

In 1984 I became aware of a company that makes small, inexpensive wave-solderers that do high-quality work (for certain types of boards, so they tell me). Lately I have been seeing those small machines in more and more board shops as a part of their JIT operation.

For example, the UNIVAC 1170 mainframe computer, now produced in an impressive JIT facility (see Chapter 4), uses the small wave-solderer. There is an even smaller degreaser (which cleans the board after soldering)—on wheels—right next to the wave-solderer. The 1170 is one of many electronic products that Sperry makes in a single large building. It may now be feasible for each of the products to have its own wave-solderer, which slashes delay time in each case.

While the small wave-solderer is an excellent example of a "JIT machine," many of the 5–10–20s listed in the Appendix that are electronics manufacturers do not yet have one. They already own a large one that works well, and the "sunk cost" of the large machine inhibits change. Perhaps the best approach for those companies is to keep the large one for a while and dedicate it to one product family in one part of the plant; buy one small machine and dedicate it to a second product family in another part of the plant. Continue to add small ones over time. One of the benefits of this sort of strategy is that it creates factories-within-factories, which is the topic of the next chapter.

Perhaps in a few years the used-equipment market will be glutted with high-capacity heat-treat and burn-in ovens, wave-solderers, cleaning and etching tanks, holding tanks, mixing tanks, cooking vessels, carousel storage systems, powered conveyor systems, and forklift trucks—to name only a few kinds of equipment affected by JIT.

Learning

Do these practical observations about capacity invalidate the economy-of-scale concept? No. It is still true that when sales of a product rise, its unit costs drop. That is why quality is so important. It gives more consumers a reason to buy the product.

That starts the engine. Fuel must be added to make the engine go faster and not stall. The fuel is not bigger machines and plants. It is *learning,* and the *learning curve* will never be invalidated. Retained earnings from early success for a new product can be reinvested in human talent and in product and process improvement: more and more hours of talented people's time spent on simplifying the product design, making the process more capable and dependable, finding better sources of material, working with suppliers to raise their level of performance, and taking the pulse of the consumer so that the product may be improved and its life extended.

The learning that comes from this kind of improvement cycle cannot be bought with money. Competitors cannot succeed unless they go through the learning–improvement cycle themselves.

To summarize, the economy-of-scale concept correctly identifies the opportunity that greater sales offer. Learning on a large scale, not equipment and plants on a large scale, explains how the concept works.

Slowing Down the Machine

The principle of adding fixed capacity in small increments as sales grow is easy enough to put into practice. Much of the time, however, sales are not growing but are going up and then down. Manufacturing is not world-class unless it is able to respond well to sales ups and downs, and that means flexible production rates: Match the production rate to the up-and-down use rates at next processes and to up-and-down final demand rates. This concept, producing to the use rate, applies to the ups and downs from week to week, day to day, hour to hour, and minute to minute.

We are not used to the idea. Instead, the Western way has been to run flat out—to see the machine smoking and throwing sparks—until there is no more raw material or no more space to hold the excess production. Stated that way, it sounds like madness. Actually the reasons for that mode of operation seemed to make sense in an earlier era. Before considering those reasons, let us look at an example of slowing down a machine to the sales rate.

Dialing Down

At a seminar I conducted at one of the large pharmaceutical companies, I was talking about equipment and carefully developing each concept. One fellow in the audience couldn't wait for me to get to his favorite topic. He said, "Don't you think we run our equipment way too fast in the United States—our high-speed packaging lines, for example?"

"Everybody runs their packaging lines too fast and hard," I agreed. I told about a fill-and-pack line at a frozen food plant I had studied. The line had been running at the equipment manufacturer's maximum rated speed for years, and somehow over the years the number of maintenance people and frequency of scheduled maintenance had dwindled. The line jammed and was stopped briefly many times per shift, and the average total down time was one to three hours per shift.

By that time people in the audience were grinning and nudging each other, because, they explained, it sounded just like their lines, which put tablets or capsules into bottles or flat packs.

Plant-level people *know* about the folly of running fast only to cause more stoppages. This message is finally reaching the decision-making echelons so that something can be done about it.

Slowing equipment down is resisted the most in the continuous process industries, where there often are acute startup problems. An example that comes to mind is a factory that produces a bimetallic material for thermostats. The product is made on a large "bonder-miller" that uncoils two different types of metal, bonds them together under pressure, and mills the bonded material to the right thickness. It was not economical to run less than twenty-four hours a day because of the large cost of heating up and starting the machine. Demand had been slack in recent months, and the machine was run ten days and shut down twenty days each month.

The monthly buildups of raw materials and finished bimetal coils were huge, and just-in-time solutions were sought. Could the machine be run more slowly—specifically, at one-third speed? The answer was yes. Would it run better—produce better-quality product—if it ran at one-third speed? The answer was probably. Would it be easier to maintain on the fly if it ran more slowly? The answer was yes. Were there any reasons not to run it slowly? Not really. The machine operator, a versatile fellow, could adjust to a different work pattern: monitor several pieces of equipment at the same time rather than ten days of scrambling trying to keep the bonder-miller working, followed by a similar stint at another machine.

Work Rules

The labor to operate the bonder-miller was nonunion, and there were no restrictive work rules. In contrast, Honeywell's Consumer Products Division in Minneapolis is union. The division's first high-performing JIT project involved an air cleaner that goes into home furnaces. Most of the many production processes had been arranged into a long serpentine flow line, and the line was "cut over" to pull production in October 1984. Packing at the end of the line issued the initial pull signals, and prior stages responded. There was little inventory or time delay between stages—except for the first stage, cutting metal panels from coil.

The only large machine in the process is a roll-former, which straightens steel coil and then cuts it to length and width to form the cut metal panels. The roll-former was at the front of the JIT line but was not a part of it. Many carts full of cut steel panels were staged between the roll-former and the aircleaner line.

Questions arose: Why all the carts of cut panels? Was the machine unreliable? Was it down for repairs a lot? No, it worked very well, so the carts of panels were not used as buffer stock protection. The answer seemed to revolve around the skilled operator of the roll-former. In the past the operator just ran the machine and made as much as possible for a whole shift. Now, under JIT, the roll-former should be turned off and on to produce only as many panels as are being used, hour to hour and day to day. Producing as much as possible per shift to keep the operator busy does not make sense, especially since the carts full of inventory looked as if they might be worth more than the operator's monthly—maybe even annual—pay.

Tony Lipari, JIT manager for the air cleaner, and his staff concluded that the carts of stock were not needed. The excess was used up, and the roll-former was integrated into the JIT pull system.

What about the operator? Honeywell's contract with the union includes some of the standard work rules that limit moving operators to other jobs. Rules of that sort have not been the obstacles to JIT that we might have expected. In many unionized plants, like Honeywell's Consumer Products Division, the work rules crumble (or are winked at) when there seems to be good reason. The past approach—stay at your machine and produce, even if the stock rooms are already full of parts from your machine—was wasteful.

Today we see, and the enlightened union member can easily see, that those wasteful practices are bad management. Since bad management leads to shuttered plants and lost jobs, union opposition to relaxed work rules is melting. There is, of course, normal fear of change and fears about learning new jobs. Those fears are best combated by training; all parties need to see the merits in and requirements for labor flexibility in the present era of rapidly improving factory management and tougher competition.

Frequent Speed Changes

We may now review why, in the past, we preferred to run machines at full speed. The idea of frequent speed changes would have given rise to four concerns:

1. What is to be done to keep the machine operator busy if the machine is stopped or slowed down? WCM demands that operators be versatile, able to move to where the work is. In the short run, hour to hour, there is often enough work, other than making parts, right there at the work station. Chapter 2 offered explanation: The operator is much more than a maker of parts. Potentially more valuable are the operator's mental contributions. There is also plenty of training, machine maintenance, cleanup, and other work of an indirect nature to be done. Planned machine stops are welcome in that they provide needed time for employee involvement in such things.

2. How can changes in usage rates be communicated back to the maker? JIT advises the pull system: Signal the need by kanban squares, cards, empty containers, empty shelf space. That is management by sight, and it is made eminently possible when the feeder machine and the user machine are right next to each other.

3. *Can* the machine be slowed down? It is no problem with standard machine tools that make or test discrete parts—lathes, grinders, test equipment, and the like. They can make a part, stop; make a part, stop. Extruders, chemical reactors, continuous mills, can-fillers, dial assemblers, and hundreds of other more automatic machines are a bit different. People often have doubts about running them more slowly. In some cases machine adjustments would be required, which is usually a rather minor problem. In a few cases there seems to be an ideal speed for quality reasons. The best approach to that obstacle is full study of the reasons why. On the whole, there are few cases of severe obstacles to varying machine output rates. Where there is a severe obstacle, inform the machine's manufacturer that the next machine you buy must have more flexibility.

4. We are measured on machine utilization, and to look good, don't we have to run full blast? That is the tail wagging the dog, but the concern is real. The utilization issue bears careful scrutiny.

Utilization

The tight reins on output rates that are becoming necessary for the world-class manufacturer make machine utilization appear to be a useless, even destructive, measure. It is not quite that bad. Utilization patterns have always helped to signal when to buy more capacity and when to sell off excess equipment.

Utilization has never made sense as a measure of management

performance. Yet it has come to be used that way, and that leads to bad decisions.

One such bad decision is to overproduce in order to make this quarter's utilization statistic look good. Next quarter's output will have to be cut, but we often do not look that far ahead. We *hope* for a sales upturn that will use up excess inventory and keep capacity busy next quarter.

A worse decision is always to run jobs on the fastest machines. Then we set aside the slower ones and try to get them declared as excess. Sell them off so that total capacity falls and overall machine utilization goes up. Revenue on sale of the machine, tax writeoffs, and space savings add to the feeling that a good decision was made.

The reasoning is unsound. Small, slow machines—added in multiple copies—are, if they work well, world-class JIT machines. A large, fast one is not. I don't think it is necessary to repeat all the reasons. Instead, let us see how JIT affects capacity utilization.

Equipment Hours

Table 5–1 compares capacity utilization under common and JIT production. For reasons just reviewed—running big machines at maximum speed and selling off excess equipment—conventional manufacturing may show high utilization of equipment *hours* (or rated capacity). JIT may show poor utilization of equipment hours, since the JIT concept calls for stopping rather than making product before it is needed or making it wrong.

Utilization of equipment hours or rated capacity, however, is a trivial concern. Utilization of equipment *dollars* is the real issue. By the dollars measure, JIT policies shine.

Equipment Dollars

To illustrate, let us consider one of the JIT projects listed among the 5–10–20s in the Appendix (I'll not identify the company). Part of the JIT project was to replace one large $130,000 wave solderer (to solder printed circuit boards) with two small ones costing $10,000 each. The two would produce the same amount of product, but on two flexible JIT lines instead of in batch processing.

If the single large machine were in use six hours out of an eight-

Table 5–1. Capacity Utilization

	Equipment Hours	Equipment Dollars
Conventional	High	Low
Manufacturing		Costly equipment; a lost
Large-lot production		hour is expensive
High-capacity general-		Complex equipment, so
purpose machines		much debugging, down
		time
		Large machines not fully
		utilized early in
		product life cycles
		Queuing effects; cycles of
		overtime and underuse
JIT	Low	High
Small-lot production		Low-cost equipment; a
Low-capacity, special-		lost hour is minor cost
purpose machines		Simple equipment, so
		little debugging, down
		time
		Small machines added
		one by one as sales
		grow
		Regular schedule, steady
		use of capacity

hour shift, that would be 80 percent utilization. The two small ones would each run only three out of eight hours, which is only 37.5 percent utilization each. How do they compare on utilization of equipment dollars? To find out we might divide use time by dollar value. We'll use minutes of use in the numerator and thousands of dollars in the denominator:

$$\text{Big solderer: } \frac{6 \text{ hrs.} \times 60 \text{ min.}}{\$130,000} = 2.8$$

$$\text{Small solderer: } \frac{3 \text{ hrs.} \times 60 \text{ min.}}{\$10,000} = 18.0$$

The indices, 2.8 and 18.0, have no particular meaning, and I would not recommend their use. But they do show the magnitude of advantage that the small JIT machine has over the large one. (Actually, there are common measures of merit that may be used instead of the artificial one just concocted. One is asset turnover: annual cost of goods sold divided by annualized cost of the asset. Another is return on investment.)

The lesson is clear: Capacity utilization should not be used as a measure of plant management performance. It is misrepresentative and destructive.

The last of the reasons for the sudden unpopularity of larger machines is that they are not easily moved. Why should the world-class manufacturer have particular needs for movable equipment? Let us see.

Movability

Stereo components—that's what was on my son Clay's last birthday list. Nothing else. My wife and I went with Clay to the stereo store, which was stocked with the latest technology. Clay was almost more interested in showing us a sensational Bang & Olafson turntable than in having us pay for the medium-priced sound system that he had picked out. The Bang & Olafson turntable rides on a shock-resistant cushion of some sort. The salesman takes delight in banging on the turntable's frame while the record is playing and noting that the needle does not bounce or skip.

Industry should have such equipment. It is becoming more and more common for manufacturing plants to have at least one machine so temperamental that it has to be mounted on a special shock-resistant platform. Its location has to be carefully selected, because that machine is likely to stay there.

Life Cycles and Sales Volumes

The desire for movable equipment is not new. We have never valued immobility. The machine tool manufacturer who offered self-contained, shock-resistant properties has always had an edge.

Today movability is much more important. Product life cycles are being compressed, we are told. Therefore, we will be starting up new products, which means moving equipment around, more often than ever. Actually, the Naisbitts and the Tofflers who tell us these things often fail to point out that sales volumes for each product offering may be enormous—short time duration, but very high volume. Sanyo VCRs, Toyota Celicas, Chrysler minivans, copies of *In Search of Excellence,* IBM PCs, Pampers, Campbell's Tomato Soup, 3M's Post-Its—the list of mass-marketed products is endless. With such product successes, does it matter that the plants making them are inflexible? Steven Jobs, cofounder of Apple Computer, says of the Macintosh factory: "Because it was designed to last only thirty months, we can tear the line down, sell the metal for scrap, and build a better one."[2]

Move to Improve

No, the shortening of product life cycles is not the reason why movability is so important to the world-class manufacturer. The reason is that a plant cannot be world-class if it does not achieve *continual and rapid improvement.* Rapid improvement is part of the WCM definition, and rapid improvement means frequent change, including changing the locations of equipment.

In the recent two decades of Western industrial neglect, a factory was counted as a success if it stayed in business. We may forget that definition of success and go back a bit further. In the 1950s success was cutting costs and nonconformities (defects) by, say, 2 or 3 percent a year. In Figure 5–2, I translate that rate of cost improvement into JIT/TQC terminology: nonconformities, lead time, and WIP reduction (which lead to cost reduction on a much broader scale than just direct costs).

When measured against WCM standards, 2 or 3 percent annual improvement is poor. A factory with that modest performance will be driven out of business by its world-class competitor, which might be improving at a 50 percent annual rate. A reminder: The 5–10–20s listed in the Appendix cut their lead times at least fivefold in,

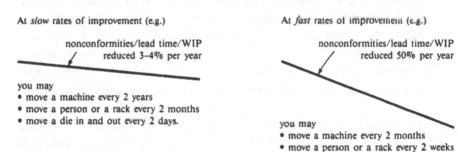

At *slow* rates of improvement (e.g.)

nonconformities/lead time/WIP
reduced 3–4% per year

you may
• move a machine every 2 years
• move a person or a rack every 2 months
• move a die in and out every 2 days.

At *fast* rates of improvement (e.g.)

nonconformities/lead time/WIP
reduced 50% per year

you may
• move a machine every 2 months
• move a person or a rack every 2 weeks
• move a die in and out every 2 minutes.

Figure 5–2. Why Movable Equipment?

typically, a year or two. Quality improvements are just as impressive in many of those and other plants. Since our Japanese competitors have managed to sustain high rates of improvement for many years, there is no reason to think that we will not do as well using nearly the same concepts and techniques.

Figure 5–2 shows the impact on movable resources. At slow rates of improvement, we may need to move a machine every two years, a person or rack every two months, and a die every two days. At fast rates, we may need to make those kinds of moves every two months, two weeks, and two minutes.

Movable Racks

Our die racks—and our racks for molds, base plates, fixtures, inserts— used to be rigid; in WCM companies many are now on wheels. Toyota was storing dies in carts in the 1950s.

Racks for component parts are sometimes on wheels as well. The Tennant Co. in Minneapolis now stores many of the parts for its industrial scrubbers and floor sweepers in "WOW carts" (warehouse on wheels). The obvious advantage is that the rack can do double duty as the transporter. Furthermore, as problems with quality, with machines, with setups and changeovers, with product designs, with supplier deliveries, and so forth are solved, needs to store material evaporate. Racks, a few at a time (and conveyors and forklifts, too), need to be pushed out. Smaller racks replace larger ones.

For a while, in my tours of plants with JIT successes, I snapped a picture when I saw a rack that had been emptied. That became so routine that I quit taking pictures. The best stories—alas, no pictures— are the ones about removal of, or cancellation of a project to install, a $2 million or $5 million or $10 million automated storage/retrieval system. For example, Oldsmobile removed an AS/RS with 3,300 storage locations in one of its sixty-jobs-per-hour car assembly plants. FMC Corp. had two AS/RSes stopped before they got built, one in its ordnance plant in San Jose and the other at their Stephenville, Texas, plant that makes fluid control devices for the petroleum industry.

The initial plan for Apple's Macintosh plant called for storing fairly large amounts of purchased components. Mac's buyers and engineers have since stepped up their supplier development efforts, working with suppliers to improve their reliability. Every gain in supplier performance lowers the amounts of raw materials that need to be stored as protection. With topnotch suppliers, direct dock-to-line material flows often become possible. At the Mac Factory, however, an obstacle stands in the way of cutting raw materials and storage space and streamlining the flow for dock-to-line movements: There is a long, tall tote stacker in the heart of the plant (see Figure 5–3).

Tote Stackers

The tote stacker at Macintosh is by no means unique. A number of high-volume assemblers use tote stackers, especially in the printed circuit board business.

Figure 5–3. Tote Stacker at Macintosh Factory

One printed circuit assembly plant has *three* tote stackers. Its JIT task force has grappled with exactly what to do with them. Here are some of the options the task force has debated:

1. No change. Use the stackers as a big storage-and-handling system. This option is out, because storing and handling adds cost and delay, not value.

2. Run them empty, but use them as a transporter to move printed circuit boards from one type of insertion machine to another. It could forward components only in response to a pull signal from a machine. There are several board types, numerous components, and several of each type of equipment (e.g., DIP inserter and axial-lead inserter), and the stacker may be programmed to take materials from anywhere and send them to anywhere.

3. Cluster cells of machines along the length of the stacker, as in the symbolic (not representative) sketch in Figure 5–4. Cell A would process one type of board through three types of machines; the "square" machines are slower, and so two are needed for balance. Cell B runs board B, and so forth. The stacker would receive, store, and forward components, and it would send assembled boards onward to board test. (Intel, Puerto Rico, uses a tote stacker this way—but for microcomputer assembly, not printed circuit assembly. The stacker was approved and was going into operation about the time when a JIT task force was deeply involved in training and some JIT pilot projects. The material manager, who was in charge of the stacker's operation, was cheerful about his task: "I will have to get the stacker up and running—and then figure out how to get rid of it.")

4. Get rid of it. This is my own choice. Option 3 is workable, and the stacker can move materials in and out quickly enough with minimal WIP. Using a tote stacker as a material mover, however, is like using an eighteen-wheel semi to deliver Domino's pizzas around town.

"But we paid $2 million for the stacker, and we haven't gotten much use out of it yet." Never mind, that's sunk cost. In rational

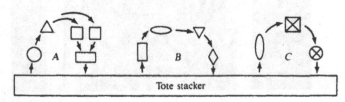

Figure 5–4. Tote Stacker Serving Machine Cells

decision-making, old costs don't affect new decisions (except for tax-loss effects). Don't look over your shoulder. March forward. Tear out the stackers. Sell them to your competitors.

AS/RS and FMS

Is the need for tote stackers and automatic storage/automatic retrieval systems going to dry up totally in our WCM factories? Perhaps so in the high-volume shops, like the Mac Factory, but what about plants that have flexible manufacturing systems (FMS)?

Those who write about the "factory of the future" usually describe FMS cells making parts and forwarding them to an AS/RS, which later forwards parts to another cell. AS/RS should *not* be part of the formula, unless the material storage and handling industry devises small movable AS/RSes or stackers. The present types bolt to the structure and are themselves supermachines that dictate policy.

Flexible automation requires nothing so elaborate. A special issue of *Iron Age* magazine describes eighteen of the world's prominent FMSes (total FMSes in the United States in 1985 were about fifty).[3] While most have an AS/RS, some apparently do not. Most do have automated *tool* storage, and that is proper, since tools are reusable. A few of the FMSes cited in the magazine have the ring of world-class manufacturing; I'll mention just a few:

- Vought Corp. in Dallas operates a $10 million FMS that produces "531 different parts, usually in batches of one." There is no need for automated storage when you make just one, because you wouldn't make it unless you intended to use it right away. Art Roch, Director of Industrial Modernization, refers to the cell's capability for "serial production," which means make one and use it, make one and use it—the JIT concept.
- Yamazaki Machinery Works has installed its third FMS facility, a massive one with eighty-eight machines and thirty-two robots, in Minokamo, Japan. Work awaiting a turn on one of the machines sits on an indexing pallet station right beside the machine. Work between machines, or in transit to the subassembly department, rests on a robot cart; the cart carries a circular pallet with spaces for eight workpieces. This FMS also follows the JIT concept of using the parts, not storing them.
- General Electric's Erie, Pennsylvania, locomotive plant includes a highly publicized $16 million FMS that makes motor frames

and gear boxes. The system is said to have cut production lead time from sixteen days to sixteen hours.

- Harris Graphics Corp. in Fort Worth, Texas, produces printing equipment in an FMS that fits many of the WCM concepts to a tee: Raw metal passes through several cells in becoming finished shafts and cylinders (700 part numbers in five families); standard off-the-shelf machine tools are used, a few manual machines as well as programmable ones; a cell may be run in the manual mode whenever there are problems; and Harris people write their own software and are not dependent on outsiders. The consultant John A. Maddox, who guided development of the FMS while employed at Harris, sought ways to ensure that people could manage the system rather than the other way around.

- Ex-Cell-O Corp.'s U. S. and European engineers have developed a modular, expandable FMS they call the FlexCenter. A customer may start with a stand-alone machine and add to it. Finally it is a cell that may be incorporated into flexible transfer lines.

- Daimler-Benz, Stuttgart, Germany, makes a variety of exhaust manifolds in its version of a flexible transfer line. This is not exactly an FMS, but its variety—200 different types of manifolds—is impressive. The flexibility comes from movable fixturing rather than from the machine tool spindles.

North American transfer lines became so inflexible in recent decades that reacting quickly to market changes—for example, six- to four-cylinder auto engines, and back—was impossible. In some people's minds, a flexible manufacturing system is a step in the world-class direction almost by definition, because an FMS has fast response to the customer as its chief claim to fame. It is hasty to confer WCM status upon a definition, however. The high cost of an FMS must be justified, and one of the justifications is using the FMS in the JIT, not the batch mode. Another feature that a "good" FMS ought to have is simple parts transfer and automatic guided vehicles (AGV), not rigid overhead or floor-embedded chains. (No FMS facilities are in the 5–10–20s list in the Appendix, because their high costs make their worth hard to judge.)

The authors of the FMS stories in *Iron Age* observed that with the "arrival of new buzz words like computer-integrated manufacturing (CIM) and artificial intelligence (AI), FMS fell out of fashion" for a time.[4] Their correct implication is that CIM is a bit too fancy and futuristic to warrant all the press it gets (and the term is used so loosely as to have lost commonly accepted meaning). FMS is all we can handle for the rest of this century.

Of course, we must begin to plan in the twentieth century for the realities of the twenty-first, and therefore may keep full-blown CIM in mind as a far-off target. The CIM factory, it seems, will have automated design cells feeding automated cutting cells feeding automated fabrication cells—all the way through to outbound freight. Host computers will oversee and direct the whole works. There will not be much to store, since the host computer will direct a provider cell to go into action only when a user cell is about ready. Cell-to-cell coordination won't ever be perfect, so there will be some need for racks. They will not be of the large, central AS/RS variety.

(Note: John Deere's highly publicized automated tractor works in Waterloo, Iowa, has been called an example of CIM, up and running in this century. It also was designed with flow-through JIT production in mind; yet it has five high-rise AS/RSes. Deere people say that if they had it to do over again, they would not put in the AS/RSes. In fact, one of them broke down and had to be bypassed for a time. No problem; production appeared to go more smoothly with the high-rise out of service!)

Quick-Change Artistry

When the racks go, the equipment moves together to fill the gap. That is why the ideal machine or work bench is also on wheels or is light enough to pick up. In touring plants I look to see if machines are bolted down, dug in, or otherwise immobile. While the racks and conveyor systems at Apple's Mac Factory are quite fixed, the machines are fairly movable. Even the utility hookups look rather simple and minimal.

When I think of movability, the feats of a stage crew come to mind: complex scene changes in minutes. I don't know of factories that can move work stations around in minutes, but I know of one that can do it in a modest number of hours. It is the assembly plant for Hewlett-Packard's Personal Office Computer Division, located in Sunnyvale, California. On my tour of that plant, Lee Rhodes, production manager, took pride in pointing out that "most of the equipment is on casters." Furthermore, the material-handling equipment was simple and lightweight, because inventories between processes were very small and flow distances were very short.

At that time the plant produced the H-P 150 personal computer. The 150 was not a big sales success. What if the product had been a winner and they had needed to ramp up production in a hurry? The flexible plant configuration minimizes the problem. A central final assembly line was sandwiched between two identical serpentine printed-circuit assembly (PCA) lines. Adjoining space that had contained desks and support people could be cleared out, and another production module (two PCA lines with final assembly between) could fill the space. Helter-skelter layout would be avoided. Rhodes estimated that it would take only six weeks to double capacity.

Size for Performance

In this and previous chapters, outsized machines have been raked over the coals. The fact that supermachines are detrimental to the WCM cause does not mean that "small is beautiful" (the title of a book popular in the 1970s).[5] Where equipment is concerned, small is not beautiful; we shall not go back to hand tools and cottage industries.

By human standards, there are few machines that are not large. Machines and automation offer means of performing tasks with precision and invariability that far exceed the capabilities of humans. Giant-size equipment usually does not yield more precision and invariability—indeed, it often yields less—than normal-size equipment. In acquiring equipment, the commonsense rule-of-thumb is this: Buy for performance, not for volume.

Chapter 6

Responsibility Centers

It is insane for the operations to be planned this way:

. . . the people to be organized this way:

. . . and the jobs to move among machines and assembly stations this way:

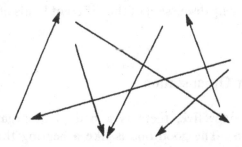

Now we also see the insanity or, to put it more mildly, the ineffectiveness of having process engineers design the work process, general managers design the organization of people, and industrial engineers design the equipment layout. Each suboptimizes; it is no wonder that the result is a bad mismatch.

The two preceding chapters treated some of the process, people, and equipment issues, but not how to organize the three as a coordinated set. That is the task of this chapter.

Tight Linkages

The three terms—process flow, human organization, and plant layout—identify with the disjointed, independent ways of the past. Designing a tightly linked set, the WCM way, deserves a term that can dissociate itself from the old narrow approaches. The term that seems to fit is *plant organization*. (In *Japanese Manufacturing Techniques,* I used *plant configuration,* but that term is only somewhat broader than plant layout.)

WCM requires organizing for quick product flow and tight process-to-process and person-to-person linkages. The overriding goal is to create *responsibility centers* where none existed before. When responsibility centers are operating, the procrastinating, finger-pointing, and alibiing fade; the stage is set for conversion to a culture of continuous improvement. Management and the staff groups then have the job of channeling the improvements and speeding up the improvement rate.

Most plants worldwide (including Japan) are, for many reasons, badly organized. It may take a long time and some money, too, to change the plant organization. What can be done in the meantime to make the best of a bad plant organization? Some answers are included in the following discussion of the different kinds of plant organization.

Bad/Good Plant Organization

From a WCM perspective, there is a bad plant organization, and there is a good one. The good one is like a bearing that is properly greased: The wheel turns fast and effortlessly. The bad one lacks grease, turns slowly with great consumption of energy, and even freezes up sometimes. The one with the grease is a *flow* organization. The one that lacks grease is plant organization by *clusters.* While flow and clustered organizations have subtypes, we should look first at basic bad and basic good.

Clusters

The clustered organization is the one that puts all the lathes and lathe operators together in one place, all the welders together in another, all the motor assemblers in another, all the engineers in another, and so on. The clustering is bad for the obvious JIT/TQC reasons: extended product flow time, much handling and delay, losses of evidence of defect causes, bad coordination, and high level of potential scrap and rework. Clustering by common processes has those bad effects for several reasons.

One is geography. If you and your machine or work station are near to others of the same type, it is a geographical impossibility also to be near those that send work to you and receive work from you.

Another is obstructions. The long distances from process to process require saving up enough work for an economical transport. The saved up work goes into containers and racks, and large-capacity handling equipment—fork trucks, conveyors, elevators, and the like—are needed to budge it. The containers, racks, and handling gear take up space themselves, which puts even more distance between the maker and the user of a certain component or assembly. The maker and user often cannot *see* each other, because of the distance and also because of the storage and handling obstructions in the way.

When we are bent on clustering, we like to carry the idea to its illogical conclusion: Put each cluster into a separate room with walls and doors. That makes coordination between makers and users even worse.

Clustering causes not only space separation but, worse yet, time separation. What the previous process makes today I may not work on for several more days or weeks. The carefully developed schedules, resource plans, cost estimates, maybe even product configurations would have begun to unravel by then, requiring a new set. The customer's mind may have changed, too.

Perhaps the main drawback of the cluster concept is that it places people into something akin to *gangs*. Enterprise gangs have some behaviors in common with street gangs. They include defensiveness, blaming other gangs (or "the system") for troubles, and sitting back and letting someone else make the decision or take the action. We may expect regression, not continual improvement.

Flows

Organizing by flows has opposite effects. The nearest people and machines are the maker of parts you use on one side and the user of parts you make on the other. You are part of a serial flow line, not part of a gang who do the same thing. You are close to the source and destination of your product—geographically and in time. You answer right away, not next week, to the user of your product. If you don't do it right, you could cause the next person to have to shut down.

The people at the Building Products Division of American Standard like to tell this story. The product was steel doors. For years one of the door assemblers complained about a burr on end channels (for door frames) made on an automatic roll former in another building. The burr was a minor flaw, but it tended to tear the flesh of the assembler handling the end channels. More than once an engineer was dispatched to try to solve the problem. No help; the burrs persisted.

Finally (for a reason unrelated to JIT) the roll former and the operator were moved into the assembly building, very near to the door assembler. The assembler and the machine operator were now going to coffee together.

It only took one day for the machine operator to solve the burr problem. The operator explained: "I couldn't stand listening to that guy gripe about the burr."

Putting the assembler and the channel-maker together created a flow-line segment, which behaves as a mini-responsibility center. The maker of the frames was now directly and quickly responsible and could not blame another operator, another shift, another person's machine, or lack of knowledge for something like a burr. More important, the operator had to get along with the user of the part.

Linking several flow-line segments together creates a larger chain of people and work centers that are mutually responsible for results. Positive results—fast action to solve problems—are to be expected. Once responsibility centers are created, only inept management can stop the problem-solving.

Plant Organization: Subtypes

Clearly the ideal is plant organization by product flows rather than by clusters. Now let's get realistic. Sometimes the plant is organized wrong and cannot be changed except at great expense or over a long time. Also, the direction of change is not simply from clustered to flow. There are several subtypes of plant organization, and the right subtype depends on the situation.

Six subtypes are listed in Figure 6–1, along with a few schematic illustrations. Each is explained below.

1. Clustered, jumbled
   - Clusters of generic work stations
   - No attempt to organize by product flows
   - No easily identifiable flow path, or organization contrary to flow path

2. Clustered, flow-line
   - Clusters of generic work stations
   - Organization by product flow

3. Cellular
   - Unlike work stations grouped into cell to produce a product family
   - Only one work station of a type, except where more needed for balance
   - Cell-to-cell organization by product flow

4. Unitary machine or assembly station
   - Complete module/product made at one machine, station, transfer line

5. Dedicated flow line
   - Unlike work stations grouped into flow line
   - Only one work station of a type, except where more needed for balance
   - Organized by flow of a single product or a regular mix of products

6. Combined
   - Mixture of any of above for a product or group of products

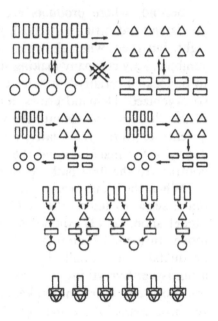

Figure 6–1. Plant Organization Subtypes

Clustered, Jumbled

The clustered, jumbled plant organization is the very worst and also probably the most common type—in offices as well as factories. Clustered, jumbled occurs in two situations.

First, there may be no easily identifiable standard flow path for the products made. In machine shops, for example, different jobs require different machines, and so jobs take a variety of paths or routings around the shop. There are always some standard flow paths, but until recently we did not know how to identify them in the jumble of the job shop environment.[1] So all the lathes and lathe operators went over there, and all the milling machines and operators came over here.

Second, where products are more standardized (e.g., consumer goods and industrial materials), the plant organization may start out right, but then, when the plant expands, it degenerates to clustered, jumbled. Any company making standard products *wants* the processes to be located serially—in "clustered, flow lines"—and new plants are so organized. Demand grows, and a wing is added to the plant; one of the clusters expands into the wing—and out of the serial flow line. Twenty or thirty years later, after several expansions—growth "like Topsy"—the machines and the people end up located and organized contrary to the flow path. Most older factories are like that.

When the plant organization is contrary to the flow path, it may make sense to tolerate it, if (1) the plant is very small, (2) it is a model shop, or (3) equipment is in the wrong place but costly to move. In a model shop (which produces prototype versions of new products) or any small plant, location of people and machines is not a big issue. Everything is fairly compact anyway, transport distances are short, and users and makers often can see and talk to each other. In those cases, where the "bad" plant organization is tolerated, the question is: How can its operation be improved, short of moving equipment and people?

Small job shops and model shops tend to have the most waste and delay, the longest lead times, and the largest inventories. No one blames the craftsmen, journeymen machinists, and other skilled people who do the work there. It is simply the nature of the highly variable work and unpredictable mix of jobs—we thought.

One combination model shop and small production shop where I consulted makes advanced, state of the art aerospace products. They range from helmets for space vehicle pilots to "black-box" test equipment. Lead times and inventories were on the order of a year or more. Piles of printed circuit boards were everywhere. There were far too many jobs in process.

That is a common phenomenon, and a couple of generations of production control books have offered the same good advice: Cut the WIP, cut the lead time, and release new jobs to the factory only as other jobs are completed and capacity is freed. JIT/TQC offers three ways to carry out the advice:

1. *Overlap production.* Overlapping is possible when a job order is for more than one of something. Overlapping means spreading a job out so that it is in process in several stages of manufacture at the same time. For example, wire a board and forward it, wire another and forward it, and so on. Don't wire ten boards and then forward them as a group to the board test area, because that lengthens the flow time many times over. (Conventional production control practice is to overlap only the hot jobs; the JIT concept is to make overlapped production the norm for all jobs at all times.)

2. *Slow for problems.* A companion to overlapped production is to slow or stop production if the user downstream is having problems. It is futile to make faster than the user is using; go to other jobs or other work centers and do something that needs to be done now. In the aerospace model shop, many of the problems were defects requiring rework. Setting a maximum number allowable in rework was the natural solution. For example, allow only two circuit boards to be in rework, and control that by having only two red rework cards ("rework kanban") in the system.

3. *Make only what is used.* This rule is partly, but not completely, covered by the slow-for-problems rule. In the aerospace model shop, completion times were unpredictable and work did not balance well from one stage of production to the next. (It might take two hours to wire a board and four days to test it as part of an assembly.) Here is what *not* to do: (1) Try to keep plenty of work ahead of each work center so that the operator can stay there and keep busy. (2) Use estimated lead times to control the flow of jobs on the floor. The better way is to control the flow of jobs by signals (some form of kanban) from the downstream work center.

The three "rules" just listed apply not only to model shops but to any job shop or a larger plant temporarily stuck with bad plant organization. For example, one of the more common sights in medium-size plants producing consumer and industrial products is lengths of conveyor before each stage of assembly. My rough estimate is that the average length of assembly conveyor holds about twenty units, which means twenty idle units for every one in process. In most cases two units would be plenty. Allowing no more than two idle units instead of twenty *forces* overlapped production; for example, a work order for twelve units would be overlapped in four work centers, each having two units on deck and one in process. At the same time the tenfold reduction in excess stocks forces closer time linkages from one work station to the next. Slowing for problems and rework becomes unavoidable. Making only what is used is also unavoidable, because the next length of conveyor is short and will hold only two units, not twenty. (Note: My comment in Chapter 3 on conveyors concerned their use on high-speed fill-and-pack lines, not assembly lines.)

Clustered, Flow-Line

Look around your house, your office, or your shop floor. Most of what you see was manufactured in plants organized in the clustered, flow-line manner, type 2 in Figure 6–1.

In type 2, the clusters are not jumbled but organized, to one degree or another, by product flows. The figure shows two flow lines; one line might make mufflers and the other tail pipes. Half of the process clusters fit into one flow line, and half fit into the other. Alternately, both flow lines could make exactly the same product and compete for results, as well as back each other up.

The type 2 plant organization is not world-class, but it surely beats type 1. The least offensive use of type 2 is when it makes odds and ends: special orders, low-use options or service parts, prototype work, and the like. Those products may be the trivial many that remain in the clusters after the important few are taken out. (Where do the important few go? Into plant areas organized as type 3, 4, or 5.)

Type 2 is also a haven for certain types of automated equipment, namely *unitary machines.* A unitary machine is one that performs several diverse kinds of operations and makes a whole complex product. A numerically controlled (NC) machine and a dial assembly machine are examples. Each machine absorbs and eliminates several moves, delays, queues, transit quantities, and setups.

An NC machine may cost several hundred thousand dollars, and keeping it busy is a worry. Therefore, a tendency develops to organize an NC machine cluster and backlog some work before the cluster in order to get high utilization of the machines. If the cluster were broken up and the machines were dispersed so as to be close to feeder and user work centers, would the costly machines be utilized less? Probably so, and therefore the clustered, flow-line organization is easier to tolerate for such machines. (For reasons presented in the previous chapter, however, utilization numbers are a poor basis for a decision.)

Clustered, flow-line—with kanban. With rare exceptions the thousands of plants that are of the clustered, flow-line type perform miserably. Typically they turn their inventories only three to six times a year.

It is instructive to see how at one plant, while staying with the clustered plant organization, inventory turns were improved from 7.5 to 45.6 in the space of nine months. That took place at Hewlett-Packard's desktop computer division in Fort Collins, Colorado. The entire production sequence for the H-P 9000 Series 500 computer was included: assembly and test of all the printed circuit boards; assembly and test of major modules; and final assembly, test, and packaging of the full computer system. The 9000–500 is a sophisticated computer made to customer order, most customers being scientists and engineers. By one estimate, the product could be ordered in 6 million different configurations.

An early improvement was reorganizing assembly from clustered, jumbled to clustered, flow-line. That shorted flow distances, which made the next giant step possible: eliminating work orders and converting to visual shop floor control.

The visual system begins with an exploded customer order; that is, the computer explodes the major modules into components. The final assembly and test people need a copy of the exploded listing. The assembler picks tested modules (e.g., a keyboard) from a kanban rack; the empty space in the rack is the pull signal (or kanban) that directs the module test department to test another of the same type. The test equipment operator pulls an untested keyboard from a rack, which leaves an empty space; that space tells the module assembler to build another. The pull signals wind backward all the way to raw stock. Purchasing orders more raw stock based on what the customer orders are calling for.

The turnover rate of 45.6 means that a few days' worth of the average module, subassembly, or part is on hand. Only a few of each part number are there, but that is enough to make it possible to complete and ship most orders fast.

The purpose of the pull system, then, is to replenish: make another of what was just used. That makes it likely that the next customer order will also be completed fast. It is vital not to lose track of any item or to have to spend any time searching for the right part. It is also vital that no assembler or machine operator get bogged down working on part numbers that will not be needed for a long time. H-P, Fort Collins, employs these pull concepts to make sure that everything is under control in the shop floor:

Concept	At Fort Collins
1. Minimum container sizes and transit quantities between clusters	Usually hand-carry just one or push a wheeled cart of components for just one
2. Minimum lot sizes	Usually just one
3. Minimum setup times, so that a small lot size is economical	Most setup times are negligible; IC insertion machines are stocked with tubes or taped strings of components, and a new floppy disc executes a change
4. Small allowable number in rework	Stop primary production and do the rework when the small number of rework kanban are used up
5. Mimimum number of stock points	Completed unit goes into nearby kanban rack or onto kanban square right away

These pull concepts are correct for all companies in all lines of work, but they are particularly valuable in making the best of the clustered, flow-line plant organization. Furniture manufacturers and window and door makers should be naturals for emulating the Fort Collins approach.

The last of the five pull concepts has received rather little attention in industry. In fact the only plant I know of where "minimum stock points" is a formal goal is an Intel semiconductor assembly plant in Penang, Malaysia. P. L. Lai, managing director of the plant, had minimizing the number of stock points on his list of seven key measures of success in the plant's vigorous JIT implementation campaign.

Informal pull. Formal rules and kanban-like signals (limited numbers of cards, containers, spaces, conveyor lengths, and so on) are excellent for making the pull system operate automatically. Good results are also possible without the formal signals.

For example, people at a semiconductor wafer assembly plant near

Paris found a simple non-kanban way to cut lead time in half. The wafers (which later are sliced into memory and logic chips) go through many processes as layers are built up. The lead time had been about fifty days, and six months later it had been cut to about twenty-five days. The method: a daily meeting of supervisors of each work center (oxidation, several photo lithography processes, test, etch, and others). If an etch machine went down, the supervisor alerted the other supervisors in the next daily meeting. The policy was for the others to slow down production in their work centers, too, especially those directly before and after etch. That policy kept the other work centers from putting more wafers into the flow than could be etched. In the wafer industry WIP inventory is particularly bad, because exposure to the elements (dust, chemicals, static) causes yields to plunge.

Cellular

We have seen ways to make the clustered plant organization operate well, given its inherent limitations. The best solution of all is find a way to break up the clusters. Atom smashing comes to mind: Bombard the atom and regroup the particles in ways that are beneficial to mankind.

In manufacturing, when you break up the process clusters, where do the particles go? They go into cells or dedicated flow lines. We call it a cell if it makes a family of products; we call it a flow line if it makes just one product. (We don't know which to call it if it makes just one product but in different shapes and sizes.)

Figure 6–1 lists characteristics of cellular organization (type 3). Unlike machine or assembly stations are grouped into a cell, and there is only one work station of a type (for example, only one drill press), except where more than one are needed for balance. Naturally, if a plant has incurred the cost of moving the resources into cells, the cells themselves should end up arranged by the flow of the product family; a chain of cells is the result.

Product families produced in cells. A product family is *not* a sales catalog family; it is a production family. The products in a production family often look similar to each other, but not necessarily. More important, they employ common materials, tooling, setup procedures, labor skills, cycle times, and, especially, work flow or routing. In other words the processes are quite repetitive, even though the products in the family differ somewhat.

The discovery of cells by the world's manufacturing experts was like the apple falling on Issac Newton's head. *Ergo,* high-variety, low-volume manufacturing is repetitive; we simply failed to organize it that way.

Another name for cellular organization is *group technology* (GT). The writings that exhaustively treat GT (one of the hot topics in industrial engineering in the 1980s) prescribe computer sorting to put products into families. The advice was based on good intentions, but it set back progress several years. The reason is that the method requires all part numbers to be coded in such a way as to permit computer sorting. The coding itself normally takes a few years.

One of the leaders in organizing cells is a Rockwell plant, Telecommunications Division, in Richardson, Texas. In 1981, when it started planning cells, part numbers in its computer files were not coded for GT sorting. Its method of grouping parts was to examine route sheets. Part numbers that followed about the same route were a family. The next step was to clear out an area and move in the machines to make that family of parts.

Rockwell's first cell made a family of wave-guide parts. Figure 6–2 shows the process flow on a floor plan before and after the cell was formed. The arrows in Figure 6–2A designate the long flow pattern "before." Figure 6–2B shows where the cell was located on the floor plan. Figure 6–2C shows, in blown-up scale, the short, clean flow lines in the cell after it was up and running.

Several more cells have been organized at the Rockwell plant since that time.

Cellular organization made sense at the Rockwell plant because (1) distinct product families existed; (2) there were several of each type of machine, and taking a machine out of a cluster therefore does not rob the cluster of all its capacity, leaving no way to produce other products; (3) the work centers were movable, being mostly standard machines tools—heavy, but anchored to the floor rather simply.

These three features apply in every business and are therefore general guidelines on *where* cells make sense.

How many industries meet these guidelines? The answer, I think, is an enormous number. It might not be hard to arrange a list of industries by suitability for cellular organization. Rather than having a go at developing such a list, I'll just make a few comments.

First of all, the industry most suited to organizing cells is light assembly. Most jobs are fairly easy to learn, and equipment is quite movable. That helps explain why the electronics industry is hogging

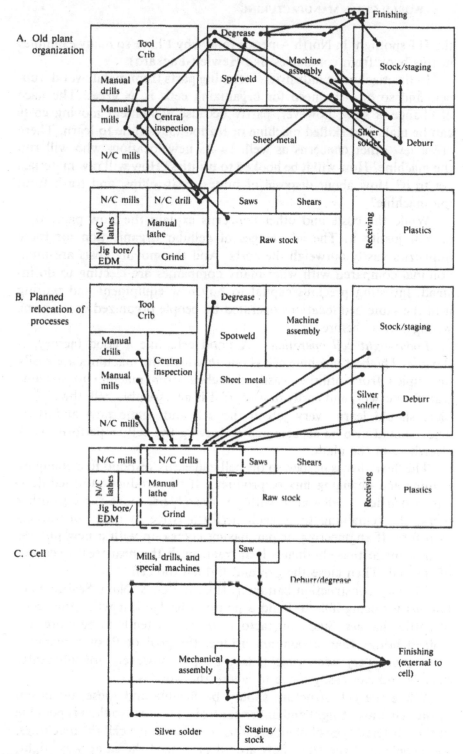

Figure 6–2. Developing a Cell to Produce Wave-Guide Parts

A. Old plant organization

Tool Crib
Degrease
Finishing
Machine assembly
Stock/staging
Manual drills
Spotweld
Manual mills
Central inspection
N/C mills
Sheet metal
Silver solder
Deburr

N/C mills | N/C drill | Saws | Shears
N/C lathes | Manual lathe
Jig bore/EDM | Grind | Raw stock
Receiving | Plastics

B. Planned relocation of processes

Tool Crib
Degrease
Machine assembly
Stock/staging
Manual drills
Spotweld
Central inspection
Manual mills
Sheet metal
Silver solder
Deburr
N/C mills

N/C mills | N/C drills | Saws | Shears
N/C lathes | Manual lathe
Jig bore/EDM | Grind | Raw stock
Receiving | Plastics

C. Cell

Mills, drills, and special machines
Saw
Deburr/degrease
Mechanical assembly
Finishing (external to cell)
Silver solder
Staging/stock

the JIT spotlight in North America (and why I have so many examples in this book from companies like Hewlett-Packard).

In the machining industries—forming parts from metal, wood, rubber, and so on—the need for organizing cells is as great. The pace of change is slow, however, partly because equipment moving costs can be high, and skilled machine operation takes time to learn. There are a few other concerns as well. In its new location, who will run the machine? How will it be hooked to utilities? How will raw materials get to it? How about disposal of fumes, heat, chips, and trash from the machine?

While the costs and other concerns explain the slow pace, they do not justify it. The advantages of cellular organization for these industries vastly outweigh the costs. And the moving costs are often nominal compared with what many companies are electing to do instead: investing precious capital to buy new equipment and putting it in the same bad locations operated by people organized in the same wrong way as before.

Loose–tight cell operation. A good cell, like a good factory, is *flexible.* The best machine cell is one in which the machines are easily uncoupled from utilities, easily detached from machine-to-machine transfer devices, and easily moved. If it is an assembly cell, the assemblers should learn every job in the cell and rotate now and then. They should also be accustomed to leaving the cell to perform work elsewhere in the plant.

The flexibility is needed so the cell can easily respond to a changing volume and changing mix of products. If the production schedule is cut in half for a cell staffed with six assemblers, move three to other work; the remaining three each perform twice as many operations as before. If engineering or purchasing comes up with a new process or new metal that eliminates heat-treat, push the heat-treat oven out of the cell. Then close the gap and tighten the cell.

Military construction battalions (like the U. S. Navy Seabees) are famous for being able to build a pontoon bridge fast when the scene of battle changes. Since our factory equipment tends to be more like a fixed bridge than a pontoon bridge, the goal of flexible machine cells is not very achievable today. People, however, are inherently flexible and can easily move to where the work is.

While the cell structure should be flexible and loose, operation of the cell must be tight and under control—far more so than is possible in the clustered type of plant organization. Since in a cell the machines, the people, and the work flow are all organized the same way, tight, controlled cell operation is not hard to attain. The cell leader and the cell members have control of most of the factors that affect product quality, cost, lead time, and flexibility. They will feel responsible for most things that go wrong and are in such close contact that they can act to fix the problem fast.

That is not to say cell members will automatically become aggressive problem-solvers. Cells will perform well only if the rest of the enterprise is organized for local control. Other chapters have explained local control, which means, briefly: Data are captured on the spot whenever there is a disturbance; cell members are charged with using the data to diagnose problems and have time most days to do so; staff experts are quick to respond when asked for help; supervisors put people into project teams to solve problems; and managers spend time on the floor talking with cell members about the data and the projects.

Unitary Machine or Station

The second subtype of the flow organizations is the unitary machine or work station, type 4 in Figure 6–1. Like a cell, the unitary machine or station performs several serial operations in building a complete module or product. Unlike a cell, the operations take place at one rather than several machines or stations. (Unitary is actually a special case of cellular organization.)

The unitary type includes numerically controlled (NC) machines, which can fabricate a complete part (perform several metal-forming operations). Unitary also includes transfer lines and autonomous assembly stations, which can assemble a whole module or product, like a motor. On a transfer line the motor is passed automatically from one assembly device to another. In autonomous assembly a single assembler builds the motor at one work station.

The unitary type of organization works best in these conditions: (1) The machine, transfer line, or assembly station is located close to previous or next operations, or both. (2) There is more than one machine or station of a type; this provides flexibility and backup when something goes wrong. (3) Setups or changeovers are simple and quick. (4) The equipment is movable. (5) The equipment is highly reliable.

Some of those issues were addressed in prior chapters—with regard to equipment, but not human assembly. When assembly work is mostly manual, the inherent flexibility of humans enters the picture. Should the assembly be autonomous (unitary—sometimes called "generic"—work stations) or progressive (flow lines)? Or does it matter?

Autonomous assembly has job enrichment benefits: total responsibility for results, pride of accomplishment, and task variety. Companies that have been experimenting with JIT/TQC have found there are also disadvantages: In autonomous assembly, build times tend to be long. That means interactions with people at prior and next work stations are infrequent, which offers few occasions to discuss improvements and lack of peer pressure to do so. For those reasons the WCM scales are tipped slightly against unitary and in favor of cellular or flow-line organization of manual assembly.

Dedicated Flow Lines

The third of the flow-line types is the dedicated flow line. As Figure 6–1 indicates, it is dedicated to one product or a narrow, regular mix of products. Like the cellular type, the full flow line is composed of unlike work stations arranged by flow of the product. There is only one of each type of work station in the flow line, except where more than one are needed for balance. For example, if testing takes twice as long as the other operations, the test work station ought to have two test stands instead of one.

Dedicated lines are suitable in these conditions:

1. The product is made in high volume or under a long-term contract. An aircraft manufacturer, for example, could have a three-year contract with the Air Force to deliver one plane a month. That kind of stability over that long a time period is likely to justify the effort to set up a flow line.

2. There is more than one line making the same product (or capable of making it). The need for flexibility to adjust when something goes wrong on one line is a reason, and it has been repeatedly mentioned. Another reason is the benefits of having one line compete with others—seeing which can achieve the highest rates of improvement.

One model or a mixture?   Is it better for a flow line to be dedicated to a single model or a mixture of models? The common view, that making a single model is more efficient and therefore better, is flawed. Even if the volume of a given model is thousands per day, it is, at least in principle, better if the flow line making it is capable of intermixing models. The simple reason is that in about every case the demand volume and the model mixture change all the time, and the best manufacturer is the one that is so flexible that market changes don't matter.

To be sure, there are a number of high-volume industries in which no company is able to run mixed models (camera A runs on line 1, and camera B runs on line 2). Sometimes it's because the machines are not flexible enough. That simply shows there is room for improvement. At Kawasaki in Nebraska, the managers were cocky enough about their flexible people and equipment that they set up a single line to run two models of dirt bike and one type of jet ski as a repeating mix: for example, dirt bike A, dirt bike B, jet ski, jet ski; bike A, bike B, jet ski, jet ski.

A mixed-model line has little appeal if the mixture varies from day to day, because an irregular mix has ripple effects on all the providers of materials, tools, and services. The public and the experts, too, have misunderstood the repetitive assembly line concept perfected at Ford in the 1920s. The big gains were not in human efficiency. They were in providing a regular rate that could govern all providers so that everybody's activities match up with those of everybody else. The coordination benefits apply just as well to the line that runs a regular mix of models as to a line that runs a regular number of "basic black" Model T Fords.

Human error and boredom. There is still another advantage of mixed-model production. In plants that have tried it, like the Harley-Davidson assembly plant in York, Pennsylvania, prevailing opinion is that people on the line make fewer errors. Apparently the mixture of models keeps people on their toes and less likely to get careless out of sheer boredom. When the assembler has the authority to slow or stop the line to "get it right," the assembler's attentiveness is called upon, and boredom is further reduced.

It does not work out that way, however, unless the number of models is small, so there are not too many variations to learn and so they repeat often enough for assemblers to remember the right way. Three or four models might be ideal; ten might be too many.

Combined

In companies that are moving along the WCM path, there may be a long transition period from poor plant organization (clusters) to the ideal (flow line). A mixture of clustered and flow line, the *combined* type, is common during transition.

Food industry example. Let us consider an example of how to begin, what to pull out of the clusters and into a flow line first. The example (made up but realistic) is from the food industry, a canned food plant. The volume is 100,000 cases a day, a hundred different products are produced, and the plant runs three shifts. At the input end of the plant are the fresh and frozen raw materials: corn, peas, mushrooms, potatoes, meats, and many others.

Plant organization is entirely clustered, flow-line. There are six clusters, and the clusters are arranged the way the product flows: (1) preparation—on several washing/slicing lines, (2) blending—twenty blending kettles, from 300-gallon to 700-gallon capacity, (3) filling—ten filling machines, where the product goes into can bottoms, (4) sterilizing—ten sterilizers, where canned product goes through steam sterilizing/cooking and top of can goes on, (5) labeling—ten labeling machines, where cans are labeled and cased, and (6) palletizing—ten palletizers, which stack cases on pallets. The pallets go into finished goods inventory (FGI) warehouses.

Average flow time, raw material to FGI storage, is twelve hours. Four are spent in actual processing, which leaves eight hours of work-in-process inventory (WIP) between stages. Compared with other industries, eight hours of WIP is negligible (eight weeks of WIP is more typical). What, then, can the canning plant gain from plant reorganization into flow lines? The answer is huge reductions in FGI, and probably a lot less raw material as well.

First change—dominant products. The first step, phase 1, is to select a few dominant products to pull out of the clusters and put into flow lines; let us pick 303-size cans of corn, peas, green beans, and tomatoes. Those four account for 15 percent of sales. Corn sales average 10,000 cases a day, and the other three average 3,000. The numbers look just right for organizing two flow lines:

• Line 1 is a dedicated flow line; it cans corn two shifts a day (with seasonal fluctuations); plenty of time is left for daily preventive maintenance. The corn line has six stations: prep, where the corn is cut, washed, and sorted; blending—two 300-gallon blending kettles; filling—one filling machine; sterilizing—one sterilizer; labeling—one labeling machine; and palletizing—one palletizer. The flow line is serpentine and looks like this:

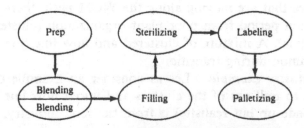

• Line 2 runs peas, beans, and tomatoes, all three every day, with this typical schedule: five hours making 3,000 cases of peas, two hours changeover; five hours and 3,000 cases of beans, two hours changeover; five hours and 3,000 cases of tomatoes, two hours changeover; a final three hours of complete cleaning and preventive maintenance. Line 2 has the same equipment and layout as line 1.

The before-and-after effects on FGI are displayed in the accompanying table. The flow lines keep the four high-volume products from having to get in line with the ninety-six low-volume products; the four don't have to wait their turns to be cycled through the clustered processes. Pulling those four out also allows the ninety-six other products to be cycled more often through the clustered processes.

	Before	After
Frequency of a production run, corn	Weekly	Daily
Frequency of a production run, others	Every 2 weeks	Daily
Average corn FGI in distribution system[a]	25,000 cases (½ week)	5,000 cases (½ day)
Average peas, beans, tomatoes FGI in distribution system[a]	50,000 cases (1 week)	5,000 cases (½ day)
Net FGI for all four	75,000 cases	10,000 cases

[a] Does not include quality-hold stock, transit stock, and buffer stock.

There should be modest reductions in the raw material pipeline as well, since the suppliers of the corn, peas, beans, and tomatoes can put their delivery schedules on a even keel.

While the inventory reductions are amazing, the greater benefit is in creating responsibility centers. Flow lines 1 and 2 each have a single manager with complete responsibility for quality, cost, problem-solving, and other results. The operators are organized into teams, not gangs.

Continuing the reorganization. In phase 2, do the same thing again. Pull the next most dominant products out of the clusters along with some equipment. More flow lines and responsibility centers and teams are created.

Phase 2 may also be the time to improve phase 1. Line 1, the corn line, can be improved by making two lines out of it, but some new, smaller, simpler equipment is needed. Six 100-gallon blending kettles replace the two 300-gallon vessels so that smaller batches may be blended. If smaller new machines replaced the large one for the other five processes, there would be the chance to organize more than one line for each product.

Two lines are always better than one for reasons that have been mentioned: providing a way to meet the schedule if one key machine goes down, providing competition between lines, and putting equipment into the plant that is more flexible and movable.

Extensions to other industries. The food industry example incorporates key concepts from earlier chapters, and it presents a way to get moving. The same general approach applies in many other industries, for example, tires, semiconductor assembly, motors, pumps, wire and cable. In the mainstream discrete goods industries, there will be large cuts in WIP, not just in FGI; otherwise the results and the methods are much the same.

Buildings

Sometimes there is little that can be done to reorganize a plant because the building gets in the way. Industry has many buildings similar to the one described next.

Multistory Building

Weyerhaeuser Co. has an architectural door division that operates out of an ancient five-story ramshackle building, which is to be demolished and replaced. The sagging floors are topped by large sheets of steel plate that distribute the loads of heavy machinery; the load-bearing members holding up the floors had to be reinforced to carry the heavy sheet steel.

The plant is the largest of its kind in the world, and it's still a profitable business (which says something for the workmanship) despite the problems presented by the building. The most visible problems are the high WIP—as many as 50,000 doors in process—and long lead time; the lead time is weeks, while the actual processing time is just a couple of days (not counting finishing and drying). About fifty people do nothing but push "jimmies" of doors into and out of elevators and across floor space.

In the new one-story building the lead time, WIP, and human material shufflers should be halved even if the organization is clustered, flow-line. If it is set up as cellular or dedicated lines, the reductions should be fivefold or better.

Equipment could be moved into cell segments or flow-line segments in the present five-story building, but it is hardly worth doing. There are too many permanent obstacles, like floors. Such a building needs to be torn down.

It is true that our world has some worthy manufacturing plants in multistory buildings. Most of the good ones are in Singapore, Hong Kong, Taiwan, Manila, and perhaps Seoul. Not in Japan. Even though land sells for twenty-five times more in Japan than in the United States,[2] top Japanese manufacturers build one-story or two-story plants.

What explains the differences in the Far East? Labor costs. Wages are high in Japan, very low in Singapore, Hong Kong, and the others. With low wages, why not pay people to push carts in and out of elevators in space-saving high-rise factories?

Mezzanines

Food processors like to put filling machines on mezzanines or second floors. Then they can roll the peas or slide the chicken Cordon Bleu or squirt the mashed potatoes and the gravy downward onto pans on the fill lines below.

I've seen a better way. It is a one-story food plant that has its filling machines on wheels. At changeover time—changing from, say, green beans to pudding—the filling machine's drive chains are detached from the main drive shaft. Maintenance people wheel the machines away for thorough cleaning and, I hope, preventive maintenance.

There are a host of advantages to running fill hoses and pipes downward from mezzanines. Light, mobile, flexible filling machines are better, however.

Open Factories

The vision of people shooting material downward from an upper floor reminds me of kids on roofs dropping water-filled balloons onto pedestrians. We shake our fists at them, but that only relieves some frustration. We are not in control.

Factories have too many chances to get out of control. The open

121

factory concept helps combat the problem. Multifloor plants cannot be controlled easily, because people in different stages of the flow can't see each other, communicate and coordinate easily, and jointly attack the day's little problems.

Too many walls and too many rooms present the same problems. One plant manager showed me several substantial interior walls. They had been exterior walls, but business grew, and new walls enveloped old ones. One of his next plant improvement projects was to tear out a few of those inside walls and open up the factory. He would not mind, however, if there were one wall that divided the plant into two factories-within-a-factory, because he has two distinct product lines.

The open office concept has received publicity. Some office people— those who have to be creative—will argue for solitude and private cubicles. Except for environmental control—clean rooms, cold rooms, hot rooms, and the like—private cubicles in factories have no merit. The benefits of open factories greatly exceed the usually large benefits of open offices.

Team Building

It has taken quite a few pages in this chapter to present a simple idea: The plant should be organized to get processes, people, and equipment aligned.

One more summarizing point needs to be made: The reorganization and realignment yield substantial lead time and waste reduction gains, but the greater benefit is in getting the people into teams. Perhaps the human resource department specialists, presuming they really do believe in team building, should be put in charge of plant layout. More practically, processes, human responsibility structures, and plant layout should be jointly planned by a task force steeped in WCM concepts.

It's okay to start small. Two stations back to back make a two-station cell; two assemblers serially linked make a two-person team.

Chapter 7

Quality: Zeroing In

Quality is like art. Everyone's for it, everyone recognizes it when they see it, but everyone defines it differently. Unlike art, nobody takes violent exception to someone else's definition of quality.

All the definitions—fitness for use, meeting the customer's requirements, right the first time, reduction of variability, and others—are just fine. They aren't in conflict. We'll take them all.

Quality: Competitive Weapon

Not long ago the first few Western companies took quality vows, then a few more, and before long whole bunches. Pledges to make quality "our basic business principle" or "the foundation for the management of our business" can have a hollow ring, like New Year's resolutions. But the training that has followed the quality proclamations has been substantial. So have factory floor implementation efforts.

That is remarkable. Before the ferment of the 1980s, quality in Western industry had gone through thirty-five years of stagnation. Yes, we did change the name of the quality function: quality assurance department instead of quality control department. Slogans like "quality is everybody's business" appeared, too. It was talk without action. In Japan there was talk *and* action. An American, Armand Feigenbaum, wrote a book called *Total Quality Control,* which proclaimed that all functions must unite in *building quality in. Inspecting quality in* by sorting the bad ones out—the "death certificate approach"—was outmoded. Large Japanese manufacturers seized upon the Feigenbaum message and even adopted the title of his book as the name for their quality movement: total quality control (TQC).

There were many minor players in Japan's ascendency as an industrial power. I think there is no question about the star player: quality. The world's consumers would pay more for a Sony television because they were convinced it was better. The scrap and rework avoidance and the simplifications that came from continual improvement of quality quickly drove costs down; then people elsewhere in the world could buy a superior Japanese product—and pay less for it.

It is my impression that in the 1950s top-level executives in Japan were serious enough about quality to demand concerted action from line and staff subordinates. In other words, quality was delegated. The results, after ten years or so, were astonishing growth in sales and productivity. That signaled the beginning of *managing quality in.* That is, quality came to be thought of as a strategic weapon, a matter for daily attention by senior management.

Quality Strategies

Competing with quality has alternate paths. David Garvin[1] identifies eight dimensions of quality and gives a few examples of how certain of the eight may be pushed to the forefront to gain market share. The eight dimensions are (1) performance (acceleration for a car, brightness on a TV), (2) features (push-button windows), (3) reliability (failure rates), (4) conformance (lack of defects), (5) durability, (6) serviceability, (7) aesthetics, and (8) perceived quality.

One of Garvin's examples is Steinway & Sons. A Steinway piano is known for even voicing, sweetness of its registers, duration of tone, long life, and finely polished wood. Those appear to be performance, durability, and aesthetics dimensions of quality; Steinway continues to enjoy its high reputation for them. Yamaha has become a large-scale piano seller by focusing on reliability and conformance. Leading Japanese manufacturers in many industries have made their mark along those two quality dimensions.

Some experts look at examples of this sort and conclude that there is room for all sorts of quality strategies. For example, maybe there is room for more kinds of piano companies. How about one that focuses on pianos that are highly serviceable or that have features like automatic page-turners?

That conclusion is utterly wrong. Steinway's and Yamaha's quality strengths are not to be sneezed at; the same goes for their weaknesses. Yamaha's opportunity for rapid growth in profits and sales is to build its own reputation for pianos with even voicing, sweetness of registers, long life, and finely polished wood. I would bet it is working on some of those by plowing retained earnings into research. Steinway's challenge is to do everything it has always done but mount a companywide campaign to achieve statistical control of all processes—in supplier plants as well as its own. Steinway has the easier task, since the way to process control is known and sure.

The niche concept is bad medicine. One reason is that the quality dimensions are not in conflict with each other. Another is that quality tends to fall into place along several of the dimensions all at once by executing WCM concepts whose main costs are "soft": coordination, training, data collection, and problem-solving.

> *The world-class manufacturer always goes after the next class of customer by making the product attractive in one more way.*

Process Control

Gaining control over the process, Yamaha's strength, is founded on measurement and study. Voluminous written material is available on how to improve a process, and now many of our colleges, as well as consulting firms, offer short courses and seminars on the subject for industrial audiences. I'll confine my remarks to a few summary points and examples.

Process Analysis Tools

Continual and rapid improvement requires a never ending succession of projects. The project leader often is a machine operator or assembler. The project team zeroes in on a process improvement by using one or more tools of process analysis.

A process analysis may be as simple as using a gauge. First- and last-piece inspection using a gauge is a common and valued technique for small-lot production, especially in machine shops. A more complete study may employ the following six primary tools of process analysis (and perhaps some others as well):

1. Process flow chart: Track the flow of the product through all steps and stages.
2. Pareto analysis: Plot disturbances (like defects, machine stoppages, late deliveries) at every point in the process flow; select the worst case (longest bar on the Pareto chart) for further study.
3. Fishbone chart: Make that "worst case" the spine of a fishbone chart. Secondary causes become secondary bones connected to the spine. Tertiary causes connect to secondary causes. Begin experiments on extremity "bones."
4. Histograms: Sometimes it is useful to measure a process characteristic—perhaps one of the extremity bones—and plot the measurement data on a histogram. The shape provides clues to causes.
5. Run diagrams and control charts: In many cases it is valuable to plot measured process data for critical characteristics on run diagrams and SPC charts.
6. Scatter diagrams and correlation: When the process is in statistical control, it is time to consider improving it. One way to investigate things to be improved is by changing something and seeing what happens. The changes and the results go on scatter diagrams, to be checked for correlation. A good correlation is a "hit"; it identifies a likely cause and candidate for improvement.

Teachers and Users

Those six tools are more thoroughly treated in Ishikawa's 1972 book, *Guide to Quality Control;*[2] numerous other books now include them as well. Here is a small paradox: The tools are easy for staff people with a bit of math education to learn but hard for them to make use of. The tools, at least the more mathematical ones, are harder for the average shop employee to learn but easy to make use of. The not too subtle point I am making is that staff people are naturals as teachers; line operators and assemblers are naturals as users of the process analysis tools, since they take the measurements and possess the data.

The six tools are mostly not for design engineers and quality engineers. Design engineers may have a need for higher-order statistical analysis, particularly design-of-experiment methodologies. Quality engineers may need to use multiple regression techniques to investigate complex causal patterns; a homely example is what happens to bread dough under the enormous variety of possible combinations of amounts of flour, yeast, water, salt, butter, heat, time, and humidity.

Fishbone charts and Pareto analysis are well suited for use by production employees—if they are used right. What constitutes right and wrong use of the tools? An example can help answer the question.

During my hurried tour of the Hewlett-Packard Greeley plant in the fall of 1984, one of the shop assemblers, Gerald Forbes, quickly briefed me on their use of Pareto charts. In fact, Mr. Forbes ran off a copy of one of their Paretos on a nearby graphics printer and presented me with it.

I hope my disappointment did not show. The Pareto chart (see Figure 7–1) looked almost useless to me. The chart displayed "interruptions that prevent linearity" (linearity is their word for meeting the

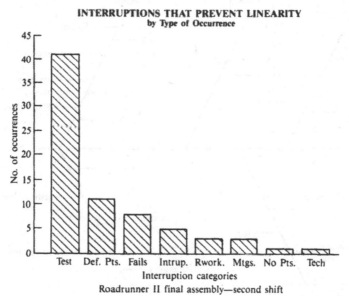

INTERRUPTIONS THAT PREVENT LINEARITY
by Type of Occurrence

Roadrunner II final assembly—second shift

Figure 7–1. Pareto Chart

production rate every day). Reasons for interruptions included "test," "defects," "rework," "meetings"; each looked so general as to tell nothing of value.

A week or so later I received a packet in the mail from Mr. Forbes. It contained a fishbone chart showing a more complete picture of possible causes of nonlinearity (see Figure 7–2) for the product that Forbes and his associates were producing. The assembly team developed the fishbone chart in brainstorming sessions. I was beginning to be impressed.

Among other sheets in Forbes's packet was one that contained hard data: number of occurrences of each category of problem and number of minutes of delay time for each. The sheet (Figure 7–3) shows that the greatest delays—41 occurrences and 217 minutes—were in testing. I was more impressed.

The last sheet in the packet (Figure 7–4) got closer to the kind of detail necessary for problem-solving. The team had attacked the worst problem, testing delays, and had come up with a list of likely causes: "KO button not being pressed promptly," "training in 4th

CAUSES OF NONLINEARITY

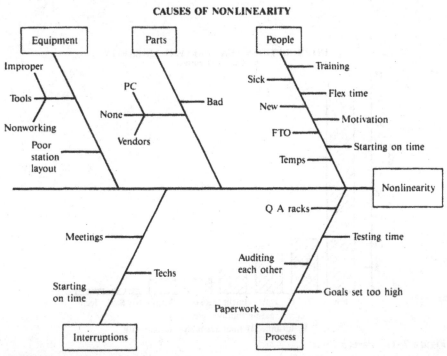

Figure 7–2. Fishbone Chart

NONLINEARITY:
COLLECTING THE DATA

Category	No. of Occurrences	Time (Min.)
No. parts	1	110
Def. parts	2	61
Meetings	3	210
Training	0	0
Interruptions	5	157
Testing time	41	2J7
Failures	8	55
Paperwork	3	12
Tech.	1	15

Figure 7–3. Problem Occurrences and Delay Times

position is poor," and others. The next steps were to isolate one or more of those causes and conduct a finer investigation, perhaps using highly detailed Pareto analysis and other tools. I finally realized that their approach was sound. I had sold them short.

Now the whole plant is caught up in a TQC effort using the basic approach just described: Break a problem down into finer and finer detail until the easy fix has been unearthed.

While Pareto and fishbone charts clearly belong in tool kits on the shop floor, like wire cutters and wrenches, what about SPC charts?

Formal SPC requires control charts with upper and lower control limits at a statistically set distance from the center line or average. There are quick-and-dirty methods that may substitute for, or precede, full SPC in some conditions. Let us take a fast look—not to rehash well-known SPC concepts but to contrast them with the simpler alternatives.

TESTING:
WHY DOES IT TAKE SO LONG?

- KO button not being pressed promptly

- Failed unit being removed and taken to techs rather than setting it aside until new unit is on the tester in its place

- Training in 4th position is poor

- Poor organization

- Poor coordination with packaging

Figure 7–4. Detailed Causes

Run Diagram

Quick-and-dirty no. 1 is the *run diagram*. It is a chart of individual measures, whereas full SPC plots averages of samples on x̄ and R charts. Figure 7–5 shows a segment of a run diagram and an SPC pair. Arrows between the run diagram and the SPC charts show how an occasional sample of five measured diameters would plot as a single point if the two SPC charts were used instead of the run diagram. One point, the average, goes on the x̄ chart, and the other, the range, goes on the R chart.

On the surface, the run diagram and full SPC appear to have different uses:

• The run diagram *seems* to be just a way to sort out the bad ones through 100 percent inspection. The run diagram (Figure 7–5, part A) has the desired diameter as its center line. The top and bottom lines are the customer's upper specification limit (USL) and lower

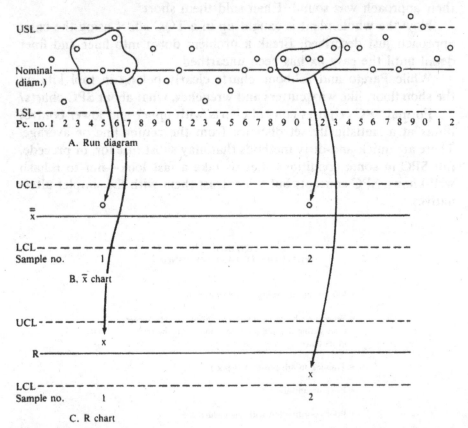

Figure 7–5. Run Diagram and SPC Charts

spec limit (LSL). Any diameter that is above the USL or below the LSL is a defective. The twenty-ninth diameter is bad, since it plots above the USL; it must be rejected. For this limited example the reject rate is one out of thirty-two, about 3 percent.

• The use of x̄ and R charts is to control the process, not to sort out defectives. For one thing SPC uses sampling and thus could not catch very many of the bad ones. For another, the center line and control limits are not goals but simply refer to the way the process has behaved in the past when in statistical control. The x̄ and R center lines are the past averages of the process, and the upper control limit (UCL) and lower control limit (LCL) are simply three standard deviations from the center line. If points plot outside the UCL or LCL, the process is straying from normal. The reason may be tool wear, bearing wear, or another problem that you want to catch right away and correct.

To summarize, the SPC charts have the excellent purpose of giving statistically valid notice when something in the process has changed. It is the process talking to us.

But wait. The run diagram talks to us, too! The one in Figure 7–5, part A, tells us the process is straying off on the high side. In fact about the last half of the diameters are at center line or above, and the twenty-ninth went over the limit. The run diagram does not talk in a statistical language, and thus it could falsely alarm or lull us once in awhile. Still, it is easy to understand and requires no staff statistician.

Run diagrams might be preferred over SPC charts in many cases were it not for one problem: the cost of inspecting and plotting every unit. The method could be modified to check just a few now and then and plot them on USL/LSL charts, but that would be silly. If only a few are going to be checked, average them and put the averages on statistically correct charts: x̄ and R.

When may the run diagram make sense then? For small lots, say, fifty or a hundred pieces and, often, for the first fifty or one hundred pieces of a new part number that is to be made in large quantities. Use it to weed out special causes, and then graduate to SPC sampling.

Precontrol Chart

Quick-and-dirty no. 2 is the *precontrol chart*. The chart has colored zones, green, yellow, and red, for easy use. Precontrol starts out like the run diagram. The operator sets up and begins a new run and inspects and plots on the precontrol chart. That continues until five consecutive pieces are in the green zone, as shown in Figure 7–6. That signifies the setup is right. Then, at random times during the following production run, the operator inspects and plots two pieces. The rules are:

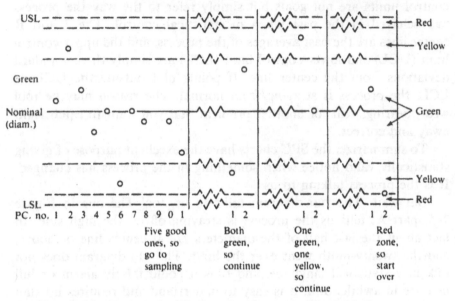

Note: The precontrol chart is easy to construct: Make the green "target" zone equal to 50 percent of the tolerance, set the yellow zones on either side at 23 percent each, and set the outer red zones at two percent each. For precontrol to be effective, the actual process spread (three standard deviations above and below *x*) should be no more than 75 percent of the tolerance spread.

Figure 7–6. Precontrol Chart

1. Okay to continue if both green, or one green and one yellow.
2. Stop, adjust the process, and start over—continuous checking until there are five straight in the green—if both yellow, or either red.

The Materials & Controls Group of Texas Instruments has had machine operators using precontrol for years. Because it is a simple way to suggest (not guarantee) statistical control, "our goal is to maximize the use of . . . precontrol," according to Neil MacKinnon, quality assurance manager at the TI Group's Attleboro, Massachusetts, location.[3]

Precontrol is not in the standard kit bag of quality aids in Japan.

It was developed at Jones & Lamson Machine Co. by Dorian Shainin and others, who at that time were industrial consultants with Rath & Strong. Jones & Lamson produced an inspection device called the "optical comparator," and that device inspired some of the thinking that led to the precontrol technique.[4] The simplicity and ease of use of precontrol fits well with other manufacturing concepts that have come out of Japan.

Ratings, Audits, and Awards

Statistical controls and visible measures provide for controlling the process; they also serve as the basis for rating suppliers, auditing both suppliers and your own production, and passing out awards.

Supplier Rating

Supplier rating systems have been around for many years. What makes today's rating systems different is that the rating factors have been juggled. Price does not get 100 or 75 or 50 percent of the weight any more.

As an example, consider Uniroyal's supplier rating program, which was announced at the American Chemical Society, Rubber Division, meeting in 1979. Suppliers were told that from that point on Uniroyal would grade all incoming shipments. The advertised grading criteria assigns penalty points for specific deviations from specifications. A vendor quality rating (VQR) of 100 is perfect and declines as penalty points are assigned. If a VQR falls in the 50-to-70-point grade level, the supplier must allow an in-plant audit in order to remain a supplier. A VQR of less than 50 points disqualifies the supplier.

The VQR, in turn, is a factor in Uniroyal's overall vendor service rating (VSR). Here are the factors and weights that make up the VSR:

Factor	Points	Basis
VQR	40	Numeric parameters
Price	25	Numeric parameters
On-time deliveries	20	Numeric parameters
Service	15	Buyer's judgment
Total	100	

While Uniroyal is pleased with the results of the VQR/VSR rating system, it was based on inspection. As of March 1983, all of Uniroyal's approximately three hundred suppliers were doing some statistical process control.[5] As the suppliers' SPC efforts take hold, Uniroyal will be able to wind down its inspection function. Inspections and an inspection-based VQR will need to be used only for new suppliers or part numbers.

Quality Audit

When SPC takes over and inspection drops off to just new items, audits come to occupy the largest part of the quality department's time—and a good share of the time of buyers and engineers as well. The quality audit can consist of a mixture of methods.

The most important ingredient in an audit—including the "audit" involved in selecting a supplier—is process capability. The maker should have evidence of capability of meeting specifications. In other words, the supplier should be able to provide data from a *process capability study*.

Hy Pitt has authored a fine article in *Quality Progress* on the ins and outs of process capability studies.[6] Pitt notes that SPC comes first: Assure the process is in statistical control—special causes have been cleaned out—and then see if the process also stays within the spec limits. Of course, the process may be in statistical control but not capable. If so, there are several options: (1) Engineer an improvement to the process (change a bearing, get more uniform raw materials, train the operators); (2) broaden the specification limits—sometimes (often) they are set without great thought as to need; (3) keep on chunking out parts and sort the bad ones out by 100 percent inspection—not a happy solution, but it may have to do for a while.

Some companies, Ford and General Motors, for example, require suppliers to show statistical control as part of their evidence of process capability. Other companies have accepted "as-is" capability data, which at least is better than nothing.

Where supplier plants are located all around the globe, some companies are turning to independent quality consultants who can conduct audits and perhaps assist on process capability studies. The consultants serve a geographical area or specialize by kind of product. I have heard good reports from some companies that have used such services for remote-site audits.

In the quality audit, inside as well as outside, process capability is the foremost concern. The audit also may include checking on quality training, measures to improve design quality, use of value analysis, use of control charts and diagrams and process analysis tools, quick response to correct problems, quality costs, and recognition and awards for successes.

Those factors define a quality audit in the narrow sense. In the broader sense the audit may delve into all of the JIT and TPM measures: rates of reduction of lead times, inventories, flow distances, design quality, space, setup times, and machine down time. The audit may also address asset turnover, competitive analysis, and employee attitudes.

The best recognition and awards are simple: a place of honor on a prominent awards board, notices in the house organ, use of a reserved parking place, free lunches in the plant lunchroom for a week, an ice cream or pizza party for the whole team, a beer bust for the whole plant. Effective recognition must be fast, that is, be awarded soon after the good deeds. Profit-sharing schemes, including the Japanese system of large semiannual bonuses, do not qualify as recognition; their purpose is to endear people to the company, not to a certain company goal.

Thus far in this chapter, quality has been treated, for the most part, as an independent issue, but, of course, it isn't.

Quality/JIT Interlink

Someone asked me once what the connection is between quality and JIT. I said, "Two peas in a pod." It was a dumb thing to say. I should have said one pea in a pod. Figure 7–7 summarizes the quality/JIT interlink (see page 136).

Variability, Buffers, and Quality Costs

The first point in the figure is well understood. Buffer stock exists partly to protect against quality variability. Therefore, making quality consistent opens the door to a JIT opportunity: Cut buffer stocks. If we stop right here, we might decide that JIT can't be done until the quality is right. It is a limited view, but some hold it.

The first goal of quality improvement is *satisfying the customer;*

1. How quality enhances JIT

Fact	JIT/quality effect
Variability in quality is major reason for buffer stock.	Control variability to justify buffer stock cuts.

2. How JIT cuts cost of quality

Scrap/rework/damage costs of quality linearly related to raw and in-process (RIP) stock.	RIP reduction cuts scrap/rework/damage costs to same extent.

3. How JIT improves quality (reduces variability)

Time destroys evidence of causes of variability.	Effective process analysis requires fresh evidence in period of limited changes—provided by vigorous JIT.
JIT shrinks lead time & • keeps evidence fresh • limits no. of changes to check	

Figure 7-7. JIT/Quality Connection

QUALITY COST

To the quality community, quality cost has a special meaning, one quite different from what a layman might guess: It is any cost of manufacturing or service that would not have been incurred had the product been built exactly right the first time.* It includes: (1) direct costs of prevention (planning and training), appraisal (inspect and test), internal failure (scrap and rework), and external failure (warranty and liability claims); and (2) derivative costs of keeping buffer stocks and excess capacity as protection against quality uncertainties.

Many Western companies now calculate quality costs; since most do not include the derivative costs, they underestimate. On the other side of the coin, those that include prevention costs probably shouldn't. Prevention costs are a proper part of everyone's job. (Every animal, including each human being, devotes every waking moment to staying alive—preventing death. Similarly, it is the job of everyone in a factory to devote full time to preventing the death of the product. Our systems of checking on the life functions—appraisal costs—deserve to be reduced, leaving the life-extending pursuits intact.) Computing quality costs is rare in Japan, probably because the years of quality-driven growth have removed doubts about the value of continual quality improvement; no need to keep proving it.

* J. Campanella and F. J. Corcoran, "Principles of Quality Costs," *Quality Progress*, April 1983, p. 17.

the quality cost gains are a bonus. The reasoning is the same with JIT: First benefit is *fast response to the customer;* a bonus is taking out the inventory and therefore the potential scrap, rework, and damage elements of quality cost. Thus, quality improvement and JIT serve together in attacking quality costs. This is the second point in Figure 7–7.

Cause Analysis

Lowering quality costs does not deal with the cause of the quality problem, however. Isolating causes is where JIT really shines.[7] In slashing lead times JIT creates a permanent *early warning system.* That is, when a problem is found in a later process, little time has passed. As the frontier tracker might say, the trail is still fresh; only a few process changes could have occurred. Tracing the cause is not so difficult. In fact, in ultimate JIT the next work center tries to use a part right after it is made. If the part is bad, the maker stops and often *knows* the cause.

In ultimate JIT, the short time interval between cause and effect opens the door for the operator to carry on simple process experiments all the time. Here's an example: Perhaps operator X makes the same part all day, and operator Y joins it to another part right away. At 10:30 A.M., after 250 successes, operator Y finds the 251st won't join. X quickly stops and knows the cause. It is the *one thing that changed* from the 250th part. It might be a change in a machine setting, a new tool, or a new lot of raw material.

The notion that time destroys evidence is not new. Western Electric's classic, *Statistical Quality Control Handbook,* states: "It is an axiom in quality control that the time to identify assignable causes is while those causes are active." Further, "Delay may mean that the cause of trouble is harder to identify, and in many cases cannot be identified at all."[8]

Early Warning

Statistical process control reveals problems in the feeder process, but SPC is fallible. Even 100 percent inspection does not catch all the nonconformities because of the well-known inspector fatigue factor. Therefore a later process, later plant, or final customer will find things that are not right—that SPC or inspection cannot or does not catch.

It is up to the early warning system to record and feed back the user's complaint.

Japan awards an annual Deming Prize for quality. The number one criterion for a company to receive the prize is having a good early warning system. A good system gets the information to the designers and makers quickly, unfiltered by marketing or the chain of command. The number two criterion is taking quick corrective action on problems the early warning system uncovers.

One U. S. example of early warning is GE's redesigned dishwasher. GE recorded who bought the first thousand units and did a thorough aftermarket survey of those customers. Designs and processes were changed based on the survey results.

Pontiac came up with a novel early warning approach when it introduced the Fiero. All factory people were invited to survey Fiero buyers. Each volunteer received names and phone numbers of five owners; they were to use their home phones—the company paid the phone charges—to call the Fiero owners every ninety days. The feedback went right into the factory.

Let us say that SPC or inspection *does* catch all nonconformities. An early warning system is still necessary, because there are and always will be problems in trying to find out what customers want in the first place; often *they* don't know. Zero-defect production is for naught if the product is designed with unappealing features.

Design Quality

Compliance quality has been reduced almost to a science. Design quality is still largely a black art. Design quality can never be reduced to systematic procedures, because even the customer does not know exactly what is good quality and what is bad—without trying the product. More on this issue in the next chapter.

Nevertheless, some science *is* being injected into design and development. The Western quality and design community has been jolted by its belated discovery of "the Taguchi methods," named after the works of Dr. Genichi Taguchi of Japan. *BusinessIndia* magazine went so far as to title a story on Taguchi's methods, "Japan Does Away with Quality Control."[9] With the assistance of Dr. Taguchi, his co-author Dr. Yu-In Wu, and Taguchi's son, Shin, the American Supplier Institute (ASI), a Ford Motor Company spinoff, has been offering technical seminars and executive briefings on the methods.

The Taguchi method has as its basis *value for the customer*. To define "value" Taguchi devised what he calls the *loss function*. To design products that minimize losses to the customer, Taguchi prescribes use of low-cost off-the-shelf materials whenever possible, materials that work over a wide range of use conditions, and statistical experimentation. We may briefly consider each of the concepts.

Loss Function

Taguchi illustrates the loss function by referring to the Japanese bullet passenger train, the *Shinkansen*. The train was a functional breakthrough, but it operates poorly in snow, is noisy, and shakes the surrounding community as it passes through.[10] Those are losses to its customers, the Japanese public. If a train designer could develop a train that had the *Shinkansen*'s speed and reliability but without all the noise, vibration, and weather limitation, the designer's company would surely reap rewards in the world market for passenger trains.

I made the same sort of point with regard to pianos early in the chapter. It applies to all design work and all products in all industries. That may seem roughly like common sense and not very profound. Taguchi makes it profound by the way he defines quality and also by his mathematical expression of the loss function. The Taguchi definition of quality is:

"Quality is the loss imparted to the society from the time a product is shipped."[11]

The loss is measured by the loss function, which is the "loss constant" times the variation of the process. Say, for example, that a defective sheet of vinyl, used in making a greenhouse, has an average cost of $40.[12] This could be warranty cost, or it could be the cost to the greenhouse owner if a sheet breaks or is too thick to fit in the frame. Assume the thickness allowance for a sheet of vinyl is ± 0.2 mm.; it breaks if it's thinner, and it won't fit if it's thicker. The constant, k, used in the loss function, is:

$$k = \frac{\$40}{0.2^2} = \$1,000$$

The variance of the process equals square of the tolerance (twice the allowance) times the standard deviation. Assume the vinyl-making process has a standard deviation of $\frac{1}{6}$. Then the loss per vinyl sheet, caused by variation, is:

$$L = k \times \text{variance} = \$1,000 \ [(0.4) \ (\tfrac{1}{6})]^2 = \$4.44$$

Let's see what happens if the process variation can be cut in half to $\tfrac{1}{12}$; for example, use a grade of raw material that does not expand or contract much with changes in heat (low coefficient of expansion). Now the loss from variation is reduced to:

$$L = \$1,000 \ [(0.4) \ (\tfrac{1}{12})]^2 = \$1.11$$

Assuming monthly production of 50,000 sheets, the savings from reducing the variation is 50,000 ($4.44 − $1.11) = $166,500.

The enemy is not merely defectives; it is variability. Taguchi points out that a failing exam score in school might be 59, but a passing score of 60 is hardly better. We are surrounded with products that do not quite work right because two or more components that met tolerances nevertheless had too much variation. Perhaps one of the keys on my keyboard is loose and comes off because the metal prong is on the low end of its allowance and the aperture in the plastic key is on the fat side of its allowance. Perhaps I dump an aspirin from a bottle and it falls on the counter and breaks into powder because all of the aspirin ingredients were on an extreme side of their allowances. The phenomenon is called tolerance stackup.

There is a problem with the loss function. It requires placing a cost on defectives. Defectives can cause loss of life, pollution, accidents, wasted time, and mere annoyance. We have never been any good at costing such things, and there is no chance that we will suddenly learn how. The loss function has value, however, even if we don't calculate it. It creates the proper mind set, and that is important even in mundane R&D tasks like selecting materials. Let us see how the job of selecting materials is spiced up by thinking about in the Taguchi way.

Materials

My plant seals cartons with glue from an automatic gluer, and I, the engineer, must select the right glue. The manufacturer of the gluer recommends a commercial glue from Acme Corp. selling for $2.00 per ounce. But my name is Genichi Taguchi, and I have noticed Elmer's Glue in retail stores all over North America; Elmer's sells for only about $0.20 an ounce. Alma's glue is also available in some retail stores at $0.20 an ounce.

In testing the gluer and Acme glue, there have been problems: The carton does not always seal well, and the problem is traceable to the nozzle on the gluer. It deposits just a trace of glue sometimes, an even amount at other times, and a big glob at other times. Everyone suspects the cause to be things like changes in room temperature and humidity and amount of glue in the tank. I'd rather not check all those things. I would prefer to find a glue that seals the carton well whether a trace or a glob of glue comes out. I try Elmer's, Alma's, and Acme.

The results of my tests of the three glues are in Figure 7–8. The vertical scale is the loss (cost to reglue by hand) when the carton does not seal right. The horizontal is the amount of glue I applied in my experiments.

The graphs show why Acme costs more. It has the lowest loss, the least chance of a need to reglue. That result is obtained only if the right amount of glue is applied, however. Acme doesn't stick well at all if too little or too much glue goes on. Alma's has the second lowest loss, and it works well if the amount of glue is just right or a lot. Elmer's is a bit higher on the loss scale, but it does all right regardless of the amount of glue applied.

Elmer's glue wins hands down: (1) It is cheap; (2) it operates well over a large range; and (3) its performance midpoint is also the performance midpoint of the gluer. Each of those three points is a Taguchi design principle.

It might be better to make the experiment more elaborate. Try Elmer's for each amount of glue and also (1) with high, medium,

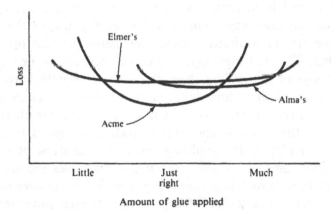

Figure 7–8. Glue Experiment

and low room temperature; (2) with high, medium, and low room humidity; and (3) with much, average, and little glue in the tank. That creates a three-level-by-four-factor experiment. The experiment may be displayed in a three-column-by-four-row *orthogonal array*. Orthogonal statistical analysis methods may then be used. While the methodology is beyond our interest here, we may want to keep in mind the viewpoint implicit in experimental design: "If you torture the data long enough, it will confess" (anon.).

The glue example typifies the world of design and material selection. There are examples like it everywhere. For instance, maybe gold is usually specified in an electronic circuit because of its high conductivity. A designer experiments with an aluminum alloy as compared with gold. The alloy tests out fine over a wide range of operating conditions. The gold, costing 100 times more, performs much better at midpoint use conditions but softens and loses contact at higher temperatures. The aluminum alloy turns out to be the better choice.

Quality Free?

Westerners have just begun to get accustomed to the idea that quality is free, that quality is inherently good, that the next quality improvement is always justified. Now along comes Taguchi and his convincing arguments about seeking the cost–performance combination that is just right. Is there a conflict here? Perhaps a slight philosophical one, but nothing to fret about.

The customer, after all, dictates the correct course of action. The right course *still* is to reduce variability, and never cease reducing it. The loss function may seem to say stop, because in the current state of the art the available options all cause the loss function to rise, not fall. That is temporary. We go on looking for new options, like new alloys or glueless bonding, that drive variability down.

The Western design community, at least in big companies, is captivated by the Taguchi methods—but not, I'm afraid, for all the right reasons. Will the methods encourage product designers to go back into hiding to play with signal-to-noise ratios, analysis of variance, and orthogonal analysis on the computer—techniques too specialized for "the manufacturing and marketing people" to understand? We hope for a different effect: that R&D people are coaxed into communion with customers in quest of loss information, and into interactions with makers in order to test materials under shop conditions.

If the message of this chapter had to be reduced to a single sentence, it would have to be one that has almost become a cliché: *Quality is everyone's business.* And while everyone can make a difference, it turns out that the designers have the most leverage. The topic continues in the next chapter.

Chapter 8

Design Leverage

The designers design it and then "heave it over the transom" to manufacturing. Manufacturing tries to build it. It's unbuildable, and that brings forth the first round of engineering changes. It still isn't makable, which requires a second round of engineering changes.

People make wry jokes about accountants, buyers, managers—anybody. R&D people are often the butt of some version of the heave-it-over-the-transom joke.

It is a bum rap. The R&D people are not to blame. The blame belongs to their companies for not making sure that (1) design has a customer focus and (2) design is closely integrated with the rest of the organization. When (1) and (2) are true, problems disappear like dirt in a laundry detergent ad. In other words, the designers have enormous power to prevent—or cause—later problems.

Research

The research community has carried Western industry through some rough years—the years of neglect of development engineering, process engineering, quality engineering, and manufacturing. Even the stock market values investment in research: Economists at the U. S. Securities and Exchange Commission found that stocks of companies that announced R&D projects rose an average of 1.8 percent in the four-week period after the announcements.[1]

The Japanese are searching for ways to improve their outlook and overcome their reluctance to spend for basic research so that their economic miracle may be more firmly grounded. Kazuhiro Fushi, research director for Japan's fifth-generation computer project, says, "Japanese managers don't have the patience for basic research."[2]

If impatience explains Japan's relative lack of success in long-term research, perhaps it also helps explain its talent for developing and producing products for here-and-now customers.

Designing for the Customer

Scientists may design for science, but design engineers must design for the customer. While everyone might agree with that, everyone *won't* agree on what designing for the customer means.

Intel made its mark in semiconductors by designing and producing memory and logic chips for the mass market. Advanced Micro Devices (ADM), on the other hand, specializes in finding new uses and unmet needs; "engineers then conceive a new design . . . aimed at solving a specific problem."[3] Potential customers have a look and make their suggestions. After that the chip design is completed and becomes a new proprietary product—with built-in customers.

People say that ADM is customer-oriented. That seems true enough, but does that make designing and selling for the mass market less so? Which do customers prefer, Burger King's have-it-your-way, or McDonald's you-know-what-you-are-buying?

Clearly both approaches attract loyal customers. Both also demand a product design that meets the customer's requirements and is easily produced with high quality. What we lose sight of is that two simple design concepts enhance design quality for both the mass market and the specialty market: (1) Minimize the part count. (2) Use modular design.

Part Count

Reducing part counts is growing into a popular sport, an integral element of the WCM drive in top companies:

- IBM: Three of IBM's best-publicized products in the 1980s have part counts that are a fraction of predecessor products (IBM's own predecessors as well as those of competitors). One is the PC (personal computer), the second is the 3178 logic unit (one of the modules that make up the 3178 terminal), and the third is the electric typewriter.

- General Electric: GE's first JIT project in major appliances was dishwashers. The design engineers were challenged to design for simplicity, and they came up with a dishwasher with 40 percent fewer parts than the previous model had. The dishwasher was a runaway bestseller.
- Chrysler: The highly successful van wagon was designed to have only three body styles (the J-car and M-car had ten) and 50 percent fewer parts than predecessors.
- Hewlett-Packard: The touch-screen II (personal computer) was designed to have 150 parts, as against 450 for the first edition of touch-screen and 20,000 part numbers for the division's previous assortment of computer models.
- Saga Corp.: The largest "manufacturer" of meals in college dining rooms in the United States cut its number of products from 6,000 to 1,200.
- Asuag-SSIH: The Swiss consortium came up with the hot-selling Swatch (for Swiss watch), which has only 51 parts, far fewer than any other analog quartz watch.

Details of the Swatch success help explain the importance of part count (1) in making product development engineering and process engineering meld together into one hard-to-distinguish function and (2) in making manufacturing simple. Other manufacturers, including the Japanese, made watches in three processes: mechanism, case, and final assembly. Since there aren't many parts, there aren't many steps in making the Swatch. In fact, it is made by robots on a single production line, with a laser to seal the crystal to the plastic case. "Manufacturing costs are spectacularly low, labor minimal."[4]

The Swatch is sold in many colors and styles. Variety is available even though the basic part count is very low. The low price allows a consumer to own several, to be mixed and matched with clothing or mood.

Low part count is even more important for quality reasons. IBM's primary initial purpose in cutting part counts seems to have been quality: Few parts mean few whose quality needs to be certified and few suppliers who need to be audited. When there are many parts and makers, certification looks like a never ending job. *None* of the parts for the IBM 3178 logic unit is inspected (except on an audit basis), because all are certified.

Modularity

IBM's 3178 logic unit is a module that may be combined by the customer with a variety of keyboards, screens, power cords, and other modules. While each of the individual modules is a "vanilla" design—no options—the ways of mixing the modules provide appeal for a variety of customers. In sum, the joint design-production-marketing strategy resulted in a high-volume, low-cost product with broad market appeal.

Modular engineering changes (ECs) also have an impact. A slew of ECs can disrupt the factory—and the distribution system, too—as much as machine breakdowns do. The disruptive effects can be dampened by snap-on, bolt-on, plug-in modular ECs.

One factory that has been praised, but not for low part counts and modularity, is the John Deere tractor works in Waterloo, Iowa. The factory is equipped with the latest process technology and was planned with JIT features as well. Some of the technology, notably a few large automatic storage and retrieval systems, are in opposition to the JIT concept. Today's tractors, however, are large and complex and are made in many models with many features, which mean large numbers of parts. Most of the parts go through several machine centers. High part count, plus many manufacturing steps, seemed, to the designers of the Deere tractor works, to rule out direct material flow. So they put in high-rise storage units.

Parts standardization and modular design can help. To get deep cuts in part counts, however, Deere would need to offer fewer options and features to the farmer. That risky strategic decision is not for the design engineer to make. Perhaps it is the purview of the marketing-design-manufacturing team.

Marketing-Design-Manufacturing Team

Few companies have had an effective marketing-design-manufacturing team. The isolation of product designers is finally being seen as a serious problem, which has spawned a mix of solutions.

Deere & Co., along with Stanadyne Diesel, for example, now have factories where product engineering and manufacturing engineering are under the same engineering manager. In one Tektronix division design engineers were told that one member of each design team would follow the product into manufacturing—but that person wasn't named in advance. For several years IBM has had an early-manufacturing-involvement (EMI) program. A manufacturing engineer is assigned to work at one of the design labs to make sure manufacturability is considered in the design; the ME usually must move to another city for the assignment, typically for two years.

Hewlett-Packard's Medical Products Division has gone even farther. It has assigned the R&D engineers to the ME department and the MEs to R&D. In the spring of 1985 the reassignment sheet looked something like Figure 8–1 (names and other data are slightly altered). The first three on the list, Art W., Jerry I., and Paul T., are R&D engineers; they have three-month assignments in manufacturing engineering to work on the 78534 transistor project. Paul M. is an R&D engineer who is taking a "permanent" assignment as chief of the ME department. Skipping down to where the MEs start, Larry L. is taking a "permanent" assignment in R&D to fill an open requirement.

The "drastic" action of rotating the engineers was taken to combat bad coordination. The rotation had good results. In 1979 it had taken seven or eight months to get a new arrhythmia monitoring device into volume production; by 1984 it was taking only one to three months.

Other goals were pursued—and generally realized—at the same time. One is "no pilot runs; get it right the first time"; that goal has largely been achieved. Another that has been achieved is for the "I-to-L (investigation-to-lab) document" to contain a complete manufacturing plan; this shortens the planning lead time a good deal. Others

Names	Present	Assigned	Time	Reason
Art W.	R&D	ME	3 mo.	78534 transistor
Jerry I.	R&D	ME	3 mo.	78534 transistor
Dick T.	R&D	ME	3 mo.	78534 transistor
Paul M.	R&D	ME	Perm.	ME manager
Janice L.	R&D	ME	10 mo.	78534 support
Jack J.	R&D	ME	Perm.	78534 support
Larry L.	ME	R&D	Perm.	Open requirement
•	•	•	•	•
•	•	•	•	•
•	•	•	•	•

Figure 8–1. R&D/ME Switch at H–P, Medical Products Division

are building prototypes in manufacturing, not in R&D; high-quality documentation so that new employees can learn quickly and production volume can be "ramped up" fast; and getting up to the planned output rate at least by the 200th unit produced.

The whole organization is responding quickly to opportunities in the market place. The old concept of response to the customer was fragmented and narrow.

Design Without Delay

We have gotten used to the flawed idea that fast response to customer orders is simply a matter of keeping warehouses full of finished goods. There is not a good parallel to this in design engineering, because designs are mostly not inventoriable. The good idea that languishes on drafting tables loses value fast. For that reason, just-in-time—or just plain fast—design has great appeal. (It does not require getting used to, as is the case with JIT production).

Fast design does not mean hurried, slipshod design. It just means taking out the delays, shortening the design lead time, and developing product specifications that are right for the customer and for the producer.

Spec Jungle

Most product specifications are like jello in a bowl: wobbly and mushy. With a single stroke the design group, if it gets its hands around the spec problem, can slash its own lead times and lead times in purchasing and production as well.

When designers are kept in isolation, there is no way they can know in advance whether their specifications inflict pleasure or pain on later stages in the industrial cycle. A related problem: Creating the design is rewarding for the engineer or scientist; getting a prototype to work is gratifying; but specifying it so the production people can make it in volume is tedium. We have to take out the tedium and inject interest and challenge.

It is not impossible. Dr. Kaoru Ishikawa, famous for developing the fishbone chart, among other things, points out that a ballpoint pen has six hundred characteristics that might be specified. Tell that to the engineer designing the pen, and it might take five years to get all the specifying done. The task can be reduced. The idea is to be careful about features important to the customer, which may be only a small fraction of the characteristics that could be specified.

Robert Johnson of Medtronic Corporation comments on our failures to bring the designer to the customer: "We found that our vendors had difficulty taking our specifications seriously when we didn't."[5] Johnson is talking about specs for purchased materials; the customer for those materials is Medtronic's own production facilities.

As Ishikawa proclaimed years ago, "the customer is the next process"—not so very far away. See what that nearby customer's requirements are to make a product easily and without error. Part of the goal is to avoid overspecifying: Don't call for gold-plated material when plastic will do; gold just elevates the cost. Don't specify a 0.001 tolerance when 0.01 is the requirement of the customer; 0.001 may freeze out potential bidders or be unmakable by the supplier selected. Johnson of Medtronic puts it this way: "Develop 'hard' versus 'soft' specifications, or loose tolerances tightly enforced rather than tight tolerances loosely enforced."[6]

The message is that the designer cannot heed *only* the customer's requirements; the maker's capabilities must be known as well. The maker may be within the designer's own company or an outside supplier. In either case there is potential for harm if the designer specifies materials or tolerances that are beyond the capability of the maker.

Design therefore is iterative: Check a design aspect with the customer, check with the maker; redesign, check, check; redesign, check, check. Manufacturing engineers, buyers, and quality engineers are partners with the designer in keeping in close touch in both directions. Design actually is a team effort. The designer is brought out of isolation and into the mainstream activities of the enterprise. Developing specifications has been time-consuming and joyless; the new approach is rewarding, because the designer excercises professional judgment in setting specs, is not accused of throwing things over the transom any more, and spends less time on spec development than before.

So far we have examined concepts that take out error and delay in design engineering. Now let us consider an actual case.

Cutting Engineering Lead Time: A Case

One company, by applying JIT/TQC, cut its lead time for detail engineering from six weeks to about nine days. The company's product, which sells for more than $75,000 apiece, contains gears and shafts and is 3 to 15 feet in length. The department is organized by size of product into three sections. Each customer order is unique and must be specially engineered. Here is the sequence of steps that led to the lead-time reduction.[7]

The engineers self-reported their activities, which were expressed as percentages, as follows:

Prepare proposals	32%
Design	18%
Detail	23%
Check	5%
Review order	5%
Reacquaint	11%
Reassignment	6%

The first item, preparing proposals, was for prospective business, not booked orders. Proposals were given high priority, and they consumed nearly one-third of the department's time.

An interdisciplinary task force, reviewing the percentages, zeroed in on the last two items: 17 percent was spent going back and getting reacquainted with an interrupted job or getting up to speed on a job that was assigned from one engineer to another.

Further study revealed causes of the interruptions:

1. Stop detail engineering to prepare a proposal
2. Imbalance of work among the detail engineering sections
3. Order-entry data missing

The last problem was easily corrected. A joint team of order-entry and engineering people worked up checklists, and order-entry people were trained to use them.

The task force also had a solution to the first two problems: Reorganize the department by product subtype. Each group would generate proposals but would also specialize on detail engineering for certain product subtypes. A high-level steering committee rejected the task force's recommendation. The committee felt that organizing by subtypes would reduce flexibility, a no-no according to JIT principles. Instead of reorganizing, the sections in the end were dissolved; that eliminated the need for three section supervisors.

The interruption problem had to be solved another way, which turned out to be a type of kanban: When an assembly was completed, a signal went back to the "route/rate group" to prepare another job packet; route/rate sent the signal back to detail engineering.

The production rate in assembly was fairly constant, say, two units per day. Unfortunately, detail-engineering job completions per day were not constant. Detail engineering was therefore allowed two to four days of "finished goods" (completed detail engineering jobs). When the queue fell below two, detail engineering worked overtime; when it rose above four, people were reassigned to task forces, tooling reviews, troubleshooting, quality problems, value analysis, and other useful work.

As it turned out, the upper queue limit was forever being exceeded. Rather than reduce the queue, the steering committee elected to reassign less technical personnel to other departments, which reduced the department payroll.

Some other ways that engineering lead time was cut included the following:

- Undimensioned drawings were found to be suitable for 80 percent of requirements.
- Cross-footing of dimensions on drawings provided some "fail-safing."
- Sketches were acceptable for forgings and for packing and shipping.
- Repetitive calculations, especially for gearing, were done on the computer.
- Most prints were refiled by size and by "phantom job order"; the old way, which seldom was useful, was to file by job number with cross-referencing by customer.
- Instead of preparing sepia or mylar drawings for everything, "same as, except" drawings were used in copying machines.

The next question was what to do about the 32 percent of department time spent on proposals. The proposal success rate was about 40 percent, and accepted proposals had to go through the department a second time in order to tighten up the engineering.

A do-it-right-the-first-time solution was adopted: The department prepared proposals more thoroughly so that, if accepted, most of the detailing was already done. That further cut lead time; it also reduced the number of change orders, since the customer had access to a more complete engineering package.

Proposals came to be treated like any other job. In the past, marketing needs dictated that proposals be given top priority, which caused many of the job interruptions in engineering. With engineering lead times cut to eight or ten days, marketing no longer required that proposals get special treatment, and the interruptions went away.

Formerly the department had three control clerks. They tracked progress, prepared ETC (estimated-time-to-completion) reports, accumulated cost data, and checked inventory against bills of material (BOM). When the lead time melted, so did the need for the tracking and reporting. The pull system simplified material management and cut out the need for checking materials against BOMs. The control clerks were reassigned or, if lacking in seniority, laid off.

While the improvements were going on in detail engineering, things were changing in the factory as well, and some of the factory changes yielded engineering benefits. For one thing, formation of cells in the factory caused bills of material to collapse; that is, there were fewer levels that had to be identified in the product structure. One of the two BOM clerks proved to be unneeded.

Without going over all of the improvements, we may examine the net head-count savings from the JIT/TQC changes:

Position	Before	After
Manager	1	1
Working supervisor	3	0
Control clerk	3	0
Detailers	7	4
Designers	10	10
Checker	1	0
BOM clerk	2	1
Total	27	16

The net reduction is 41 percent. Furthermore, a computer-aided design system, which had been justified earlier, no longer was justified after the simplifications and changes had been implemented.

CAD/CAE

The WCM concept of design has been sharply altered. At the same time the world of product design is being nudged by technology. After decades with scarcely any change in methods of developing specs and prints, industry has found good uses for computers and facsimile copiers. Computer-assisted design (CAD) and computer-assisted engineering (CAE) already rank among the more valuable uses of computers in industry.

For one thing, CAD offers capability to design frames and load-bearing members with strong, lightweight skeletal structures. Producers of machine tools and storage and handling gear need to make use of that capability, because their WCM customers need the mobility of lightweight equipment.

Facsimile copiers make it possible to send a drawing anywhere in a hurry, which cuts transit delays and increases flexibility to balance workloads among plants.

CAD and CAE speed up the design task by making rough drawings smooth and taking over drafting chores. A central CAD data base may be tapped by designers located in different plants in different cities. Designers look to the data base and use the company-standard part, when one is available, instead of inventing a new one. Among the substantial benefits is containing the growth of part numbers in the company.

Even more important, standard parts are *proven* parts. In the past, Xerox typically put 80 percent newly designed components into a new model of copier. The results: a long design cycle followed by a long debugging cycle and tardy entry into the marketplace. Xerox's new 9900 copier used only 30 to 40 percent new components, which helped cut the design-to-market time in half.[8]

Low part count was an early topic in the chapter and worth returning to near the end. The overall message of the chapter is broader than the part count issue, however. The message concerns our concept of what design engineers are supposed to do, which may be summed up as follows.

The proper role of design engineers is to maintain a factory presence so they come to understand how parts and materials are made and used. Armed with that knowledge, the designer is better able to engineer problem-free easy-to-do-right products. When engineers design modular products with low part counts that can be produced on simple equipment, the shop floor becomes the focus for most of the subsequent problem-solving. On the other hand, when products and processes are complex, there never seem to be enough staff hours to straighten out the mess.

Chapter 9

Partners in Profit: Suppliers, Carriers, Customers

Exact as much as possible at the lowest price from your suppliers and carriers of materials; provide the least possible service at the highest price to your customers.

Harsh sounding, but good business? If it ever was, it's not any more.

If you have world-class manufacturing pretensions, those you buy from and sell to may not be business adversaries. They are co-producers, co-makers, or partners in profit (Harley-Davidson's term). You want your business partners to be the best, but they will not be if:

1. You beat down the price so much that your provider or customer is unprofitable, unable to invest in improvements, and perhaps unable to stay in business.
2. Your withholding of information on capacity plans, product plans, and demand forecasts causes your supplier/carrier to design, buy, build, and ship late—or early.
3. Your failure to specify requirements clearly makes it impossible for your supplier to assure quality at the source.
4. Your failure to share your knowledge of best business practices contributes to their inability to keep up and stay attractive as your providers or customers.
5. Your energy is expended in the search for new providers and customers, which results in a continual succession of startups and no movement up the learning curve.

6. Your lack of interest and reluctance to keep in close touch leads them to treat *you* as an adversary.

The worst of the standoffish practices have been perpetrated upon suppliers, but the bad practices are reciprocal. Therefore, I address the partners-in-profit concept from the standpoint of both suppliers and customers, with the middleman, the carrier delivering the goods, fitting into the picture as well. The place to begin is with suppliers, and the way to begin is with supplier development.

Supplier Development

Supplier development means making the supplier "like family." It is not worth the effort and cost unless there is a clear intent to stay with the supplier for the long haul. The long haul is the multiyear life of a part, and perhaps more than that. It may be the life of the companies or plants, and it may take in several generations of a family of parts or class of commodities.

The rationale for supplier development is simple: The quality goes up and the price goes down. Since too many suppliers means too little attention to each of them, supplier development starts with supplier reduction.

Shrinking the Supplier Base

What could be more sure to strike fear in the heart of a supplier than stories like these?

- Twin City Disc (Control Data): Suppliers reduced from 900 to 250 (80 percent certified)
- Xerox Reprographics Division: Suppliers reduced from 5,000 to 300
- GM, Canada: 99 percent of components sole-sourced
- IBM Typewriter Division: Suppliers reduced from 640 to a target of thirty-two

Will large numbers of supplier companies bite the dust? Surely not. If supplier reduction runs its course, these should be the results:

1. A typical supplier plant sells in much larger volumes to a much smaller number of customers than before.

2. Long-term contracts replace short-term purchase orders.
3. The supplier receives training, advance planning information, and sometimes even financial assistance.
4. Some contracts provide for delivering to a regular daily rate rather than to irregular demands.
5. Buyers at the customer's plant take over the headache of making the freight arrangements.

This is not to say that the buying company ought to be motivated by benevolence. Contractual requirements should be tough so as to drive the supplier into the mode of continual and rapid improvement.

Cost Containment, Polaroid Style

Polaroid has developed a unique approach, called zero base pricing (ZBP), to set tough target prices.[1] The first step is for a Polaroid buyer to ask the supplier to fork over data on its unit costs. The data are fed into a computer, so the buyer can test the effects of cost changes on the price. The ZBP program does so by means of Lotus 1-2-3 spreadsheet routines. The buyer also does manual projections of labor and material costs.

Buyers are not to accept cost increases as justification for a price rise. Instead, at that point, Polaroid people visit the supplier's plant and offer tips on how to contain costs.

In one case Acme Nameplate & Manufacturing Inc., in North Carolina, asked for a price increase based on higher costs for aluminum, which is the raw material for making nameplates for cameras. Polaroid's buyers paid a visit and came up with a way to offset the rising cost of raw materials: eliminate one packaging step.

In another case, the supplier got Polaroid to make the key improvement: Polaroid's buyers told Industrial Filters & Equipment Corp. of Burlington, Massachusetts, to cut its costs. The chemical filter supplier answered that it could do so if Polaroid would give it a commitment for a whole year instead of the usual pattern of sporadic orders. Polaroid took the advice, and the filter company held its price steady through 1984.

Polaroid is marketing its ZBP approach and computer package. Whether ZBP sells well or not, many top Western companies are talking about or implementing the basic concepts: target pricing and cost containment help for suppliers.

Andrea Carlson, president of Duall/Wind Plastics, a Polaroid supplier, has forebodings: "What would happen if all our customers decided to participate in our business? We'd have a real mess."[2]

It would be a mess indeed if each supplier plant had trickles of business with hundreds of customers, and the customers' names were changing every year. While that has been true in the past, the future should be different. The WCM scenario of each customer having just a few good suppliers applies in the reverse: Each WCM supplier plant has just a few good customers. If *just a few* customers come for cost data and to comb your plant for latent improvements, it's not a mess.

Frequent Personal Contact

Polaroid's zero base pricing is aimed at getting off to a good start—a low price for the buyer and reduced cost for the maker. At that point the customer company's outreach program has just begun. Wayne Mehl, former vice president and general manager at Rolm Telecommunications, tells about a full-blown effort to keep in close personal touch with suppliers:

> What we have done at Rolm is to start a program where we've gone to these vendors. We went to this one particular one who makes our power supplies in the center of tornado country. . . . The first thing we did was we prepared a monthly summary of our joint inventory—what we had in work in process, what we had in the store room, and what they had—and we looked at that as a whole. We sent our statisticians and our people back there to work with them. They did not know about statistical quality control. . . .
>
> We sent some people back to work on their assembly line, to understand their problems. We had some of their people come out and work on ours, putting their product in our products. There's been terrific progress made and we have a terrific rapport. . . . We had certainly jerked them around and pushed them out and pulled them in and so forth in the past. Now we've gone back there and thrown a huge ice cream party for them and things like that. And there's a lot of connection with that particular vendor at all levels.[3]

When Mehl says "at all levels," he is talking about a degree of communication between companies that has been rare even between divisions, or plant-to-plant, within the same company. Figure 9–1 schematically shows the idea of that kind of bridge-building.

People at all levels need to visit their opposite numbers in the

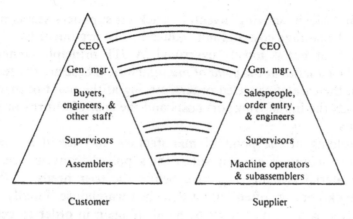

Figure 9–1. Building Bridges

other company, because there is coordination to do and there are misunderstandings to clear up. Having contact only between a buyer and an order-entry person often is tragically ineffective. The relationship is healthy when a shop floor assembler or supervisor will just pick up the phone and call someone in the supplier company to tell about a problem.

Having people at all levels taking the time to visit another plant has a cost. On the other hand, the results reduce material-related problems, which lowers needs for support staff, middle managers, supervisors, and direct labor. Then the problem can be what to do with excess staff. A partial answer is that reduced internal problems make more staff available to send on missionary trips to other plants—and thus speed up the pace of supplier development.

Pushing Material Back on Suppliers

Early reports on JIT purchasing in the automotive industry did not sound at all like Rolm-style bridge-building. They sounded like bullying: "Big automakers with clout shove inventories back on suppliers" is the way the subheading might have read in a *Wall Street Journal* story.

That has indeed been going on, and in a few other industries besides the automotive. In view of the dire straits Western automakers found themselves in, it can be argued that the inventory cost problem had to be dealt with right away. The bridge-builders could follow and help the suppliers with their costs and other obstacles.

At first blush, shoving inventory back on suppliers seems merely to move the storage cost and not reduce it. The argument has a grain of truth to it but is mostly overruled. A JIT principle comes into play: *Store material at the point of manufacture.* These are the reasons:

1. In the case of canceled orders, storing at the point of manufacture avoids the initial transport costs and the cost of returns or transshipments.

2. Holding at the point of manufacture may avoid a handling step. When materials are shipped at the supplier's convenience, some of the material is likely to arrive before the user needs it. It goes into a stockroom or, often, into a detached warehouse. Finally, when the material is needed, it must be handled again in order to get it to the production line. Hewlett-Packard and IBM have greatly expanded "dock-to-stock" deliveries. Material from "certified" suppliers goes right to the production line; that avoids the extra handling and storage that come from putting it first into a receiving stockroom, quality-hold area, or warehouse.

3. Holding at the point of manufacture avoids damage. I visited a frozen food plant that had a detached warehouse filled with corrugated case stock and cartons. Much of the material was badly damaged: corners dinged by fork trucks and by being mashed against other pallet loads, dust, humidity, steel strapping pinching down on tilted loads, and so forth. Clearly the damaged cartons and cases were not usable on the plant's automated cartoner and case-packer equipment. Damage of that kind in warehouses is the norm, not the exception. And if the goods in storage aren't damaged, they may become obsolescent or overaged.

4. The maker should store the component materials and be held responsible for their cost, because that is the best incentive for the maker to learn how to avoid making the components before the customer needs them. A manufacturer of large metal frames for Hewlett-Packard computers agreed to a daily delivery schedule but continued to build in monthly quantities. A few months later H-P found an increasing incidence of out-of-square frames. It turned out that the supplier's tooling was wearing out. The supplier rushed right over to H-P to fix the problem and found a month's worth of frames needing rework. At that point the message sunk in: The supplier improved outgoing inspections, adopted JIT production, and asked H-P for help in selling JIT/TQC to its other customers.[4]

5. The amount the supplier has to store can be very small if customers will keep the daily delivery quantity steady and not change their

minds all the time. Some customers cannot do that, however. There-fore, the challenge is for the world-class supplier to learn how to be flexible in order to make the products fast when customers change their minds.

Those arguments apply to internal suppliers—one work center making parts for another—as well as to external ones. The arguments apply as well to finished goods. We shall see far fewer distribution warehouses in the world as manufacturers learn how to collapse pro-duction lead times and make to customer orders instead of to forecasts.

Are there also risks in pushing materials backward to suppliers? The cautious among us may harbor concern about what might happen if we don't have a healthy cushion of supplier materials and an act of man (strike) or act of God (fire) destroys the supplier's capability to produce.

Risky Business

My occasional colleague David Taylor tells this true story. While he was chief of purchasing at Hewlett-Packard, Greeley, Dave's boss, Gary Flack, charged him with finding "at least two sources" for every part number. As is usual with Dave, he put his wholehearted energies to the task.

He was nearly ready to certify "mission accomplished" when Gary called a meeting. Gary said, "Uh, Dave. Remember what I told you about finding at least two sources?"

"Yes," said Dave expectantly.

"Well, I've been doing some reading," said Gary.

To make a long story short, Gary had been reading about JIT, and his about-face direction to Dave was: Find *one good supplier* for each part number.

Since the first policy was soundly based on avoiding the heavy risk of a single source, single-sourcing must carry that risk—unless there are ways of dampening it. Happily, there are.

Here is one: Have two (or more) sources by commodity but one (or very few) by part number. As an example, Company X may buy bearings from Supplier A and Supplier B; A provides part numbers 1, 3, 5, 7, . . . , and B provides 2, 4, 6, 8, ... If a tornado tears A's plant apart, B is there as a backstop.

A real example: Honda in France buys left tail lights from one supplier and right tail lights from another.[5]

What if the "Amalgamated Bearing Workers" struck both A and B? The answer: If you have only a hundred suppliers instead of several thousand, it becomes possible to get to know each of the hundred very well. If there is the smell of a strike in the air, you detect it early. You arrange an alternate source, or you opt for the old solution: Build inventory.

Anyone with purchasing experience will be able to think of pages full of ifs, ands, and buts—exceptions to the supplier development concepts that have been discussed. One example would be a worldwide shortage of the thing you want to buy. Another is when a single company holds the patent or is privy to the technology of making something, hence you are a captive market. Still another is when you seek to deal with high-quality or low-cost sources oceans away.

World-Sourcing

In the last few years many or most of our larger industrial companies have caught the world-sourcing fever. At Ingersoll-Rand, for example, buyers have access to a global data bank that tells where a part can be bought at the least cost. "We scour the world," says Fred Hatfield, an Ingersoll manager in the United Kingdom.[6]

World-sourcing flies in the face of the WCM concept just discussed: Develop a few good local sources and stick with them. The same companies that are doing most of the world-sourcing also are generally the leaders in JIT/TQC implementation. Does the left hand know what the right hand is doing?

Healthful Competition

World-sourcing *does* support a dominant concept of JIT/TQC: serve the customer. The customer is not served if costs and prices are so high or quality so poor the customer won't buy the product. Thus, if there is a large cost or quality advantage in buying a part from across an ocean, we may have to do it.

Worldwide competition is healthful for industry and for each nation's economy. It is also what has spurred our leading Western manufacturers to do something about their abysmal cost and quality performance, to search the world for techniques and concepts for slashing lead times, defect rates, and machine malfunctions.

Orderly competition, at least, is healthful. Unfortunately, the competition among parts makers in different nations has been disorderly in recent years. It has been based partly on unreal costs bent out of kilter by swings in exchange rates and not just on real costs of manufacturing.

Standardization

There is a piece of good news: Standardization—which is basic to JIT/TQC—is proceeding at a faster pace in order to make it easier to change sources on short notice. Buyers at Ingersoll-Rand who seek the lowest-cost supplier worldwide have more leverage than in the past, because many parts for its compressors and tools have been standardized. Fewer part types bought in larger quantities lead to lower costs and more bidders.

Nonstandard tooling and methods, as well as nonstandard parts, are enemies of quality and obstacles to removal of buffer stock. FMC Corp.'s giant ordnance facility in San Jose has devised standard tooling for quick setup of NC machines (tooling that is usable in a variety of other kinds of machines as well), and the company is transferring the standard tooling to its plants worldwide.

Part of the method is having four tool positioning holes drilled with the same spacing on the work table of every machine. The work piece clamps in a standard way to a base plate that has four holes drilled in it to line up with the four holes in the work table. Then the base plate fastens to the work table by inserting four "ball-lock" fasteners through the four holes. The ball-lock devices, which are patented, require only two and a half turns of a key by hand to anchor the base plate firmly (see Figure 9–2, page 164). Base plates may be designed at any plant and are easily shipped to any other plant for immediate use.

Disadvantages

When world-sourcing is done for cost/exchange-rate reasons alone, the cost advantage had better be substantial, because it has to offset some large disadvantages:

- Bad coordination on designs and quality requirements
- Large inventories in transit, heavy with the risk of high defects or a quality disaster

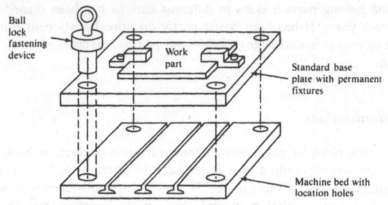

Ball lock fastening device

Work part

Standard base plate with permanent fixtures

Machine bed with location holes

Figure 9–2. Ball-Lock Fastener and Standardized Base Plates

- High obsolescence costs when orders already in transit are canceled or when engineering changes intervene
- Local bad feeling and distrust when a local source is abandoned

On the last point, most manufacturers who would be world class have been preaching about trust and long-term commitments with local suppliers. A sure way to destroy credibility is to go back to supplier musical chairs—only now at the world level. When the cost advantage of out-sourcing is too large to pass up, the local community needs to be told. In the long run, however, customer companies must reduce out-sourcing by building a strong local supplier base.

By extension, each WCM plant must develop a strong local *carrier* base. New freight concepts and progress in their implementation are discussed next.

Carriers

One of the first companies to contact me, a few years ago, about conducting a seminar on JIT was a trucking company, Rider/PIE. In my ignorance, I did not know exactly why they were interested. The dates did not work out, and I did not conduct the seminar, but Rider/PIE learned about JIT anyway. That was clear by the ads for one of Rider's subsidiaries that were appearing every month in some of the trade journals dating back to 1983:

> Combining the needs of "just in time" with the resources of a major transportation company to produce the process that results in low cost, high service, total transportation—"JUST IN TIME"

Freight

When the JIT awakening began in North America, people were predicting that the common carriers would be the losers. Manufacturers were advised to use independent truckers or get their own fleets. The advice was based on prior experience: extremely poor delivery performance by the common carriers.

Trucking deregulation in the United States in 1980 changed all that. The common carriers are eager to serve today, and they are fitting into the JIT purchasing picture nicely.

For example, Hewlett-Packard, Greeley Division, contracts with a common carrier to make a daily circuit to pick up materials from seven suppliers and bring them to Greeley docks.

The same carrier stages a trailer load of styrofoam at one of H-P's docks. Assemblers fetch foam directly from the truck, and when the quantity gets low, a phone call to the carrier brings another trailer load. The carrier has a terminal just a few miles away, and the service is swift. The trucker hauls the empty trailer to Styromolders, the Colorado Springs producer of the foam—about a two-hour trip—and brings a full load back to the terminal. Styromolders owns the styrofoam until it leaves the terminal for H-P.

The trucker's terminal in this case is the middle stop in a two-stage kanban system, and the trailers serve as the containers. Formerly the foam came in cardboard boxes. The full boxes took up large amounts of floor space at H-P, and labor was required to take it out of the box and dispose of the trash.

Xerox in Webster, New York, appears to have the best-developed JIT trucking network in North America. Xerox trucks pick up one hundred part numbers every day from twenty-five suppliers within a 50-mile radius. Also, a new pilot program calls for daily pickup of parts from one main and a few smaller suppliers in the Chicago area, 600 miles away. An independent Chicago freight consolidator makes the daily circuit.

Another example: Ten suppliers in Dallas ship daily in a truck going to their customer, McDonnell-Douglas in St. Louis.

The need for fast, reliable transport from JIT suppliers seems to favor trucks over rail freight. The railroad companies show some signs of trying to respond to the challenge. They had better respond quickly, because at some plants rail sidings are being torn out and replaced with truck docks. The "Buick City" project in Flint, Michigan, has included this step.

At GM, Canada, seventy freight studies were conducted as part of a JIT purchasing effort. Most of the studies recommended a shift from rail to truck. The net cost improvements, as of early 1985, were:

- $2.8 million inventory reduction (smaller delivery quantities).
- $216,000 less for racks
- $10,000 less freight cost—a surprise since rail freight usually has a cost advantage

The automaker also makes use of a new type of truck trailer with gull-wing doors. Sliding railside doors are already available in the plant, so some of the rail docks can be used to unload the new trailers. That permits complete loading and unloading from the side so that valuable dock space is freed fast. An advertisement for Fruehauf's new gull-wing trailer reads:

> No sooner has the trucker backed his rig into the assigned berth than the enclosed dock area virtually explodes with activity. Forklift drivers mount up and stand at the ready as internal hydraulic arms smoothly lift both sides of the gull-wing trailer, exposing two rows of diesel engines mounted on pallets. In a smooth, coordinated movement, the engines are plucked from the trailer and delivered directly to the production line—just in time.
>
> Fifteen minutes after setting the parking brake, the truck driver is off on his next revenue-producing assignment. The unloading operation would have taken hours with conventional equipment, and the rest of the driver's day would have been shot.

There are strong signs that Canada may deregulate its trucking industry. In the meantime, GM, Canada, has negotiated agreements with various U. S. and Canadian regulatory agencies to ease some of the restrictions. A truck going from the United States to Canada had required a city driver at the load point, a highway driver, and then another city driver. The new agreements provide door-to-door trucking with a single driver. A number of suppliers are now shipping this way, for savings of $4.5 million.

GM, Canada, also got agencies to agree to simplified trucking rates: a flat rate per mile regardless of what kind of product and whether the truck is full or half-empty.

Geography

While some freight carriers and regulatory agencies are showing they can adapt to JIT, there is still the problem of distance. People say that JIT purchasing works in Japan because Japan is a compact country where suppliers are located near their customers. They assert that in the vastness of North America, freight costs and delivery times are too great for JIT purchasing. The costs to the economy of having suppliers build plants "next door" seem prohibitive, except where the volume of materials from a given supplier is enormous.

IBM's typewriter plant in Lexington, Kentucky, is one of the exceptions where the volume *now* is very high per supplier. IBM spent $350 million renovating the plant and implementing JIT. Those changes were part of a "high-volume, low-cost" strategy for typewriters. Parts standardization and other changes led to the reduction in suppliers, mentioned above, from 640 to a planned goal of 32. Simple arithmetic—$640 \div 32 = 20$—reveals that the remaining suppliers will average twenty times more sales with IBM than before. For that volume the freight savings from being nearby can offset the costs of relocating to Lexington, so some of the suppliers surely will do so. Each supplier will, of course, carefully judge how serious IBM seems to be about sticking with a supplier-for-life policy.

JIT Warehouses, No—Truck Sharing, Yes.

Not only have truckers been trumpeting their JIT capabilities, but so has the warehousing industry. JIT warehousing? Sounds like a contradition—and it is. Yet there have been ads for it in auto industry trade magazines. The ads advised distant suppliers to ship their infrequent truckload quantities to the JIT warehouse in Detroit, and the warehouse would make the daily deliveries to the automakers.

The JIT warehouses should all go broke. If they hold the stock instead of someone else, nothing has been accomplished. Stocks, lead times, and scrap/rework have not been reduced, and no pressure has been exerted upon the suppliers. In fact, the addition of another middleman is sure to increase stocks, lead times, and all related costs.

In the summer of 1983 I gave a JIT/TQC seminar at an Eaton Corp. piston plant in Kearney, Nebraska. Someone told me that Eaton had been building plants in rural areas far from Detroit for years, "trying to outrun the union." In fact, in that year, 1983, Eaton was to bulldoze its last plant in Wayne County, Michigan. That was about the same time the automakers were telling their suppliers, including Eaton, "We want daily deliveries." Daily deliveries from Nebraska? Less-than-full-truck freight costs would eat them alive.

People at the Kearney plant were saying, "I guess we'll have to build a warehouse in Detroit." Once a month a semi load of pistons could be forwarded to the Detroit warehouse, a distance of 923 miles. Small panel trucks could deliver to the automakers every day. Those were just early rumors. The decision-makers knew better.

Goodyear has a V-belt and hose plant in Lincoln, Nebraska, which is 793 miles from Detroit. Same freight problem, same rumors about building a warehouse in Detroit.

Des Moines, Iowa, 604 miles from Detroit, has a few small manufacturers of automotive parts. I doubt that any of them can fill a truck more often than weekly.

Kearney, Lincoln, and Des Moines are all on the same road to Detroit. The obvious solution to their common problem is a common truck. Pick up pistons in Kearney at 5 A.M., belts in Lincoln at 8:30 A.M., other parts in Des Moines at 1 P.M., and make deliveries in Detroit before the morning shift begins the next day. Schedule the pickup and delivery times like a bus run, and repeat the schedule every day.

Figure 9–3 summarizes, schematically, the three types of shared trucking that have been discussed. The first is the one just described: a straight-line truck route. The second and third, mentioned earlier, are the local cluster and the remote cluster. There are numerous other

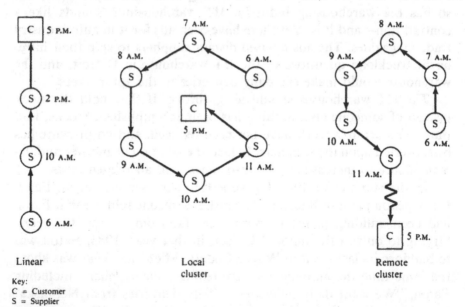

Linear

Local
cluster

Remote
cluster

Key:
C = Customer
S = Supplier

Figure 9–3. Shared Trucking

possibilities, such as a pair of neighboring companies sharing a truck that makes a daily circuit of common supplier companies.

Who makes these shared trucking arrangements? Perhaps suppliers could band together; perhaps trucking companies will try to promote shared-truck services. The most reasonable way, however, is for the purchasing department in the buying company to make the arrangements. They know who and where the suppliers are.

Shared trucking made no sense when there was annual rebidding and constant changes took place in the supplier base. With supplier stability, shared trucking should become normal. The pace of implementation is slow, but it will not stop. Industrial freight worldwide will have the new look.

WCM Marketing

Is the supplier community being carried kicking and screaming into the just-in-time era? Not exactly. I suppose nearly all suppliers dread the thought of JIT at first. A bit of knowledge of the potential benefits to the supplier changes all that. Major manufacturers have been holding "vendor days" to spread the message.

Whether or not the supplier believes the benefits will flow downward does not matter much. Doing what the big customers want may be the only way to get a big contract.

What *do* the customers want? What are they asking for in those vendor days? Everything, it seems. And they used to ask for so very little!

In supplier companies the sales department is first to be confronted with customers' tough new demands. Since sales will depend on meeting those demands, the sales department may become a center of agitation for change. To start with, advertising copy and sales presentations have to be redone.

I have consulted with sales departments, or joint sales–production groups, in a few companies on how they should get organized to meet their customers' demands. My general list of what sales should concern itself with is in Figure 9–4, "Making a Hit with Your World-Class Customers" (page 170). The figure identifies what needs to be in a sales brochure if it is to offer maximum appeal. Since the customer wants these things, sales should be prodding manufacturing for answers to questions such as those following the figure atop the next page.

Demonstrate
- Quality at the source
- Process capability
- Declining nonconformities
- Declining WIP, LT, space, flow distance
- Operators cross-trained, doing PM
- Operators making presentations on:
  —SPC   —quick setup
- Operators charting:
  —problems   —processes/methods
- Hours of operator training in TQC/JIT
- Concurrent design
- Competitive analysis
- Equipment/labor flexibility
- Dedicated capacity
- Exact counts—in customer's container
  or standard containers

Figure 9–4. Making a Hit with Your World-Class Customers

- Can we guarantee quality at the source? Do we have process capability? (Do we even know how to determine it?) Our customers want to know.
- Do we have charts and graphs all over the plant tracking declining nonconformities and rejects? Do we have more charts tracking declining WIP, lead time, space, and flow distances for key products? Our customers say these are the ways to show whether we are committed to continual and rapid improvement. If we aren't doing these things, are we at least planning to do them?
- Customers want to know about our shop floor folks. Are they cross-trained and doing their own preventive maintenance? Are any capable of making a flip-chart presentation on statistical process control? Do we have operators who have developed before-and-after charts on quick setup? (Machine operators from Goodyear's V-belt division have gone on sales trips and made SPC presentations to customers. These are rank-and-file URW members.)
- Our customers want to know if our operators chart problems as they occur during the work shift and if they are involved in process and method improvement studies. Also, how many hours of training in TQC/JIT have our operators received? Any?
- Will our product design people work with the customer's designers? They want us to design concurrently the components that we furnish so that (1) their end product design does not restrict our ability to design the best possible components and (2) the product gets out of design and into manufacturing fast. The customer also wants to see our competitive analysis lab. If they

are going to give us a long-term contract, they want to know that we aggressively keep up with products the competition comes out with.

- Is our equipment flexible? Is our labor flexible? Our customers say they won't change their mind as often as in the past, but when they do, we had better be able to respond fast.
- They also talk about wanting us to dedicate some capacity to them. At a minimum this means a certain number of machine-hours and labor-hours. Better yet, customers would like to see us set up a "factory-within-a-factory" or a cell devoted to making their products.
- Finally, our customers want never again to have to do a receiving count to see if we sent them the quantity they ordered. (They will check now and then.) Some customers want us to package in their production quantities and put it in their special sack or pigeon-hole box.

If there are any suppliers capable of making *all* the claims in Figure 9–4, I do not know about them. WCM customers do not expect to find such excellence in the supplier community. What they *do* expect is that their suppliers have these capabilities on their agendas.

There is a gratifying byproduct of this agenda: It gets sales and production talking to each other in the same language, addressing the same goals. That is true not only within the supplier company but across industry. Figure 9–4 is a list of universals for industrial marketing worldwide.

Chapter 10

Simple Models, Simple Systems

At a Westinghouse location where I presented a seminar, some young engineers confronted me at coffee break. They were on a joint project to simplify the flow of kits of material from stock to the factory floor. They asked if I thought a computer simulation would be useful. I said no.

We used up some time talking about other unpromising ideas, until one of us mentioned the twin-kit concept: For each major assembly, there are two parts containers, each fully labeled with "kanban" data; each container holds one kit of parts for assembly. While one kit is being emptied on the assembly floor, the other is rushed back to the stockroom to get quickly refilled and sent back "by return mail."

The twin-kit suggestion caused minds to race, and the engineers threw out a succession of better ideas; for example, "Why don't we do some of the kitting on the receiving dock and avoid one handling step?" and "Maybe some of the suppliers could count out the parts in our quantities so that we just toss their package into the kit."

Visual Model

The twin-kit concept did not have to be simulated. The cycle time for using a kit in assembly was known to be several hours, plenty of time to get the twin kit refilled and returned to the floor. Little planning is required: Just try out a few twin kits and *see* what happens. (The ultimate solution is to get rid of kitting entirely. In this particular case, no kitting may be the next step for the high-use parts; kitting may persist for some time for low-use parts, simply because there are tens of thousands of them at that Westinghouse site.)

The test is visual—or, as the management science people would say, a visual model is used. Mathematical models and computer simulations can be reserved for truly complicated problems.

Complex Models

It wasn't long ago that a factory was thought to be among the best candidates for the complex models, because none of us was able to view a factory in simple terms. It did not occur to us that any but the smallest factories could be modeled and managed visually. Now we know it is possible, because the factors causing the complexity— long lead times and setup times, undependable production and deliveries, and inflexibility—are removable.

A whole generation (or more) of industrial engineers and management science people have been educated to use complex models as tools to unravel the complexity in places like factories. It never worked very well and so was frustrating. Our practicing IEs and other plant management people seem happy to move on to visual models, which yield more satisfying results.

Visual Simulation

"Don't just plan there, do something!"

That exhortation reflects today's mood. After years of overplanning and underdoing, we are taken with Peters and Waterman's phrase, "a bias for action."[1]

A bias for action does not mean no planning. Planning is rational and necessary. The bad habits were in planning at arm's length— staff people doing it a building away from the action—and taking too long to do it.

A novel approach to fixing the planning problem is "the coffee cup simulator." The method was devised and used at 3M's Hutchinson, Minnesota, videocassette plant in converting to JIT production.[2]

Coffee cups stood for kanban containers, and pieces of paper inside the cups identified the material, the quantity per container, where it came from, and who used it. A large sheet of brown paper on a big table represented the factory, and squares drawn on the paper were the machines and benches. Setup times, capacities, and other machine data were written in the squares.

The simulation method was to arrange coffee cups on the sheet, then to bring in floor operators, foremen, maintenance people, and others to offer their opinions on how it would work. Their inputs about the many uncertainties—like machine down time, up-and-bad time, rework, what products to run on which lines, and late material arrivals—resulted in moving, adding, or taking away coffee cups. Everyone had to be satisfied that the pull system was sound. After two months of bringing people up to the simulation room and making changes, it was time to do it on the factory floor. The plan worked.

The coffee cup simulator killed three birds with one stone: It planned the kanban system; it got the operators involved in the planning so that they might feel ownership; and it provided JIT training for everyone—and the training was not in abstract concepts but was tied to everyone's job.

Could computer simulation have done the job? Only the first one, planning the kanban system. Computer simulation uses numbers and would mystify lay people; hence it could not provide ownership or training. What industry needs is computer graphics simulators, cartoon-like figures in motion on the screen. I'm not sure if the idea is practical, since screens are so small as compared with the large sheet of paper used at 3M for layout drawings.

If, on the WCM journey, computers are of limited usefulness for factory system planning, how about for execution? In other words, what kinds of information support should the computer provide in operating a WCM plant?

Information Systems

In 1983 one plant that manufactures rubber products was off to a great start on a just-in-time pilot project. Everyone got involved, and inventories were slashed. Then corporate directed the plant to implement its multimillion-dollar system to track orders through the factory—even though flow paths are highly predictable for the products made there. The JIT project went dormant.

JIT sucks delays out of the flow and causes manufacturing processes to become closely coupled. Closely coupled work centers can communicate visually—the kanban system. Many or all of the reasons for scheduling and tracking work flows by computer disappear. In the rubber products plant the simple way never had a chance.

Process Accounting

Information systems have other purposes besides scheduling and tracking work flows. They yield cost data, and we must know costs in order to set prices and to make go/no-go decisions about products. Most of the time our cost systems only roughly tell what the product cost is. Allocating indirect and overhead charges is one problem. Another is assigning direct labor costs among the products made.

The vendors of information systems are doing a good business selling shop floor recorders so that operators can clock in and out of each job they work on. The computer can then add up direct costs by job order. Some companies that have had those systems for years don't need them any more. Simple manufacturing leads to simple, more accurate cost collection.

Sometimes the way to simplify is to change from job-order to process accounting. The last time I visited Tennant Co. in Minneapolis (in 1984) I asked why it was still using job-order accounting on its most advanced JIT line. My hosts explained that Tennant was still using a computer package that did not allow for process accounting, but they were working on it.

The product was Tennant's 432 walk-behind floor scrubber. The factory, including the 432 area, had been equipped with shop floor data recorders. Operators entered data on labor hours and material usage for each job order or assembly order. (In final assembly, there was one assembly order for each scrubber). With the recorded data, the computer calculated labor cost, material cost, and total cost per scrubber.

That way of costing made sense when the 432 was made in batches intermixed with batches of other scrubber and sweeper models. A shift to simple process accounting became possible when, in 1982, the 432 was set up as a JIT line separate from the other products. All that is necessary now is to add up costs for the whole 432 assembly department by period and divide by units made to find unit cost— no need to accumulate costs by individual job or work station.[3]

Burden—by Lead Time

Another job of an information system is to assign factory burden—indirect and overhead charges—to products made. No one has ever been satisfied with the rough methods by which burden is sprinkled around. When factories are organized with people, machines, and product flows at odds with each other—and with the support functions at a distance—the job of fairly allocating the support charges is impossible. The accountants and the information systems do the best they can.

The WCM factory changes all that. Some of the support tasks, like quality and maintenance, are done by operators, and the operators and machines are organized by the way the product flows. Besides that, the flow time, over which burden charges accumulate, is shrunk several-fold. Allocating burden by rough averages is no longer necessary.

Bright accountants in a number of companies are working out new, simpler approaches, and the fruits of their efforts for the most part are not yet available. I am aware of some of the new ideas, one of which is using lead time in allocating burden.

The lead time notion is shown in Figure 10–1. The plant in the figure makes three products, A, B, and C. The lead time to produce a unit of A is one day, of B is four days, and of C is ten days. The sum of the lead times is 15. Product A ought to be assigned $\frac{1}{15}$ of the burden, B deserves $\frac{4}{15}$, and C gets $\frac{10}{15}$. The burden fractions

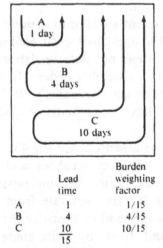

	Lead time	Burden weighting factor
A	1	1/15
B	4	4/15
C	10	10/15
	15	

Figure 10–1. Allocate Burden by Lead Time

are weighting factors; they must be multiplied in some way by dollar volume of products made in a given period.

This approach seems fair, because most of the indirect and overhead charges are for time spent dealing with delays and problems that add lead time. The approach is clever, because it induces the supervisor over product C to move mountains to cut the lead time and thereby reduce C's giant share of the burden. The supervisors over A and B will help, because cuts in lead time on any product help shrink the total burden pool.

At one plant, accountants have made some progress in implementing the concept of weighting burden by lead time: Hewlett-Packard's Greeley Division. There is talk in a number of other companies about plans to do the same thing.

Direct Costing

When operators take over support tasks—they take on quality and maintenance first—the burden costs of those functions become direct costs. With direct costing there is no allocating of burden to be done. The direct costs are true costs, which provide an accurate basis for making decisions.

IBM appears to be among the most aggressive companies in switching to direct costing. IBM's typewriter facility in Lexington, Kentucky, used to have rooms full of cost accountants. As part of a total facility overhaul, in which the plant has become a showcase for at least some WCM concepts, there are just two accountants, one for "outside" and one for "inside" inventories.

WCM offers other ways, besides operators taking over the function, to convert burden to direct cost. The factory-within-a-factory concept opens the door to putting certain support people and their tools under a product manager. Figure 10–2 lists some of the candidates: material handler, stock clerk, scheduler/dispatcher, quality technician or engineer, maintenance technician or engineer, buyer, and some general and administrative (G&A) staff. In the past people with those titles always worked in staff departments. They worked on many different products, and the accountants had to untangle the costs of their services so as to assign the costs to the products. (A 1983 doctoral dissertation reveals that, as compared with American manufacturing companies, surveyed Japanese companies place "a greater degree of importance . . . on direct costing and [a] lesser degree . . . on standard costing."[4]

Direct costing: Assign some of
these to product mgr. &
cross-train for line work:

- Material handler
- Stock clerk
- Scheduler/dispatcher
- Quality tech./engr.
- Maintenance tech./engr.
- IE tech./engr.
- Buyer
- Some G&A staff

Figure 10–2. Factory-Within-a-Factory

When the factory is arranged into flow lines, organizationally as well as physically, it makes sense to take full advantage of the situation: The material handlers, stock clerks, schedulers, and dispatchers are usually not hard to reassign. Their offices move to the flow line, their budgets go to the flow-line manager, and their costs become direct costs. They join the production team, and it is a good idea to cross-train them as machine operators and assemblers. The cross-training increases labor flexibility; gives people more skills, which offers some protection against layoffs; and breeds better understanding of the big picture.

An example may illustrate the idea for one of the support functions. Figure 10–3 shows the location of receiving/shipping stock handlers and clerks on a plant floor under three conditions.

Figure 10–3A shows the common layout: The products flow every which way around the large plant. The "stock in" and "stock out" areas cannot be associated with any product. One materials management department serves the whole plant.

Figure 10–3B shows the factory segmented into three zones, one for each of the three product flow lines. The truck-dock side of the plant is rearranged into three stock-in and stock-out areas, one for each flow line. People from materials management are now in three sets, each working for a different product line manager. Their wages are direct-costed to the product lines.

Figure 10–3C shows what the plant would look like if the building itself were flexible enough to allow receiving and shipping from three of the four walls of the building. This is the building configuration that visitors to Japan have found so unusual. Perhaps it will become usual outside of Japan as new buildings go up or as old buildings are remodeled.

Direct costing the technical and professional people—quality,

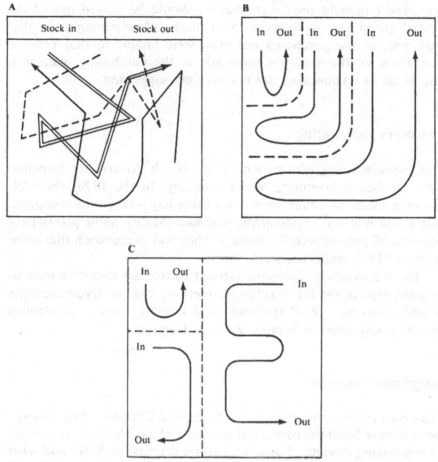

Figure 10–3. Stock Handling: From Burden to Direct Costing

maintenance, industrial engineering, purchasing, and G&A—is not so easy. Some companies have done it through paperwork: Each reporting period an engineer turns in the number of hours worked for each product manager; the data processing system takes it from there. That "pseudo-direct costing" approach may be better than just throwing the hours into the burden pool. It falls far short of true direct costing, in which the engineer actually works for the product manager and is a member of the problem-solving team. Where practical, true direct costing is best.

The purchasing function is probably the hardest to convert to true direct costing. Most purchasing departments have buyers specialized by commodity, and there are strong arguments for doing so. In one company I thought one of the buyers should be moved out of the central group and go to work for a product line manager. In that case most of the purchased materials were unique to that product line. Even so, the idea was traumatic to the purchasing managers, and as far as I know they did not take my suggestion.

Inventory Accounting

One manufacturing area in which top North American companies have excelled is inventory record accuracy. In the 1970s the *cycle counting* method—count some items every day—swept the continent, along with material requirements planning (MRP). Some plants have achieved 99 percent record accuracy. They had to approach that accuracy, or MRP would not work.

The stockkeeping discipline learned in the last decade stands us in good stead in the JIT era, but the methods change. Cycle counting is still good, but "WIP tracking" and keeping stock in controlled central stockrooms are becoming excess baggage.

Simplified Counting

Here is an average situation in an advanced WCM plant: Design engineers have reduced the part count fivefold and have halved the number of engineering changes. There is a tenfold decrease in WIP, and what there is is counted out in exact quantities in a known number of standard containers; some of the containers have "egg carton" dividers so that it is easy to be sure of the quantity in them. Where the identity of the item is not obvious, a card for each container gives precise identifying information. The standard containers always reside in exact predetermined locations.

Those conditions make stock counting quick and easy. A total physical inventory count can be taken weekly (or more often) with virtually no error.

In some JIT plants the assemblers do all the counting, perhaps once a week in an hour or less on a Friday afternoon. Where that has been tried (for example, at H-P, Greeley, and H-P, Vancouver), the assemblers find the counting to be boring; they want to get it over with quickly, which is an added incentive to come up with more ideas to cut the stock levels further, keep everything properly located and labeled, and not squirrel away extra parts in bench drawers and cabinets.

WIP Tracking

"Where is Work Order XYZ-777?"

"Just a minute. I'll call it up on my screen. Here it is. XYZ-777 left operation 30 yesterday, and today it's in deburr."

The computer has made the above scenario possible in thousands of Western companies. The key to it is daily move notices fed into the computer. The ultimate system uses bar coding: Just wand the order as it leaves a work center.

The procedure not only tells where the work orders are (tracks the WIP); it also provides value-added data so the value of the inventory can be known at all times.

All complications are allowed for. Order canceled and WIP stuck in midstream? No problem. The computer system assumes that the work goes into storage after each operation. For orders that are canceled (or reduced, slowed down, or altered by an engineering change), the computer already considers the stock to be in storage; the files are correct, and no further transactions are necessary until a later order comes along to use up the residual stock.

The computer system just described is rational when the lead time to complete an order is weeks or months. The WCM factory, however, completes orders in hours or days. As compared with the old-style plant, the WCM plant may have one-twentieth the number of orders in process and one-tenth the amount of stock to account for. It is time to turn off the WIP tracker.

Four-Wall Inventory System

When lead times have really been crunched—down to one or two days from raw material to packaged goods—the four-wall inventory system is the way to go: Enter the raw material into inventory records when it comes inside the four walls, deduct it when it leaves as finished goods. Have a "scrap ticket" system to keep track of abnormal usage. Count what's inside the walls now and then to purify the records.

The amount deducted when the material leaves the plant as finished goods is the standard material, taken from the bill of materials (BOM) file. The procedure for deducting the standard quantity is called "back-flush" or "post-deduct." (Some progressive thinkers are talking about even doing away with backflush—going to "trackless" material control.)

The inventory file and the BOM file are still in the computer and still must be highly accurate. Order entry, explosion of the customer order into component materials ("BOM explosion"), and inventory accounting are still computerized as well.

What is eliminated are computer transactions tracing the flow of the work from stockroom to work center to stockroom to work center and so on, through all operations. There are three reasons why WCM makes all the tracking unnecessary. First, the product does not spend enough time in the plant for multiple inventory transactions. Second, lack of rework minimizes abnormal flow paths and times. Third, the flow of the product is so disciplined and flow distances are so short that one can *see* where orders are—or, more properly, the status of the production flow—at any time.

Advanced JIT plants in North America generally are not yet able to adopt the four-wall approach fully. The obstacle is suppliers whose quality and delivery reliability are suspect or who ship infrequently. Prudence or necessity dictates keeping extra amounts of their materials on hand—weeks or months of it. That much stock should be charged into a stockroom after receipt. Later, deduct it from the inventory balance in the stockroom and charge it to the factory. Finally, deduct it from the factory records and charge it out of the factory as finished goods. That makes three inventory transactions instead of the two under the four-wall system.

What if there is a long-cycle operation in the factory, for example, a two-day burn-in? That might be another place for an inventory transaction: Charge work into burn-in and then out of it later. The rule is, wherever material stops for a few days, perform inventory accounting. Time adds value, and value is in want of control.

Of course, there are some industries that are never going to get their lead times down to days. They are likely always to need several inventory transaction points inside the plant.

There is also the question of class C materials (for example, fasteners and resistors) bought in large amounts perhaps semiannually. One way to deal with such materials is to charge them into the four-wall inventory records upon receipt; then, at time of use, to deduct from inventory balances—but don't charge to the product until it leaves as FGI. ("HP-JIT," one of the early JIT computer software packages, has this one-way transaction feature.)

Besides streamlining the data processing, WCM provides for collapsing the number of steps in production plans. As we shall see below, the streamlined production plans lead to still fewer computer transactions.

Eliminating Work Orders and Operations

The long lead times are in the job shops, which are high-variety, low-volume producers. If the job shop has only a few thousand part numbers to contend with, there is hope for eliminating the work orders and cutting out nearly all of the shop floor inventory transactions. Chapter 6 included explanation of how Hewlett-Packard did just that for the HP-9000 scientific computer. The customer order governs work in the final stages of production. Pull signals (kanban) ripple back through prior stages. The pull signal, not computer-generated work orders, authorizes production.

If the total of part numbers is hundreds of thousands (or millions—for example, in shipbuilding), the WCM plant will be able to reduce greatly, but not eliminate, work orders. Work order reduction comes about when scattered work centers are pulled into cells. At the same time, cells slash the number of moves across the plant.

Take the parts for a wooden chair, for example. Assume that plant organization is clustered, jumbled. There might be six work orders: (1) front legs, (2) back legs, (3) leg support pieces, (4) seat, (5) back members, and (6) top piece. Each work order has about ten operations (some of the early operations would be saw to length, saw to width, plane, rough sand, and finish sand), which means ten trips across the plant.

Change to cellular plant organization, and it might be possible to have only one work order and no trips. A single work order goes to the cell, which contains all the equipment—perhaps two saws, a planer, a sander, and one or two others—to make the chair parts.

Before the shift to cellular organization, there were sixty inventory transactions (six work orders, each with ten operations/moves). Afterward there is one transaction. In production control lingo, the cells permit collapsing the bill of materials and shortening the routing. That is, the BOM has only one level instead of ten. (We are considering

183

only the chair components, not the whole assembled, finished, and packaged chair.) There is no routing, since all the work is done in one cell.

One of the main Western beneficiaries of collapsing BOMs and routings is a shipbuilder, Bath Iron Works in Maine. Bath has been spending several million dollars a year for several years following consulting advice from Japanese shipbuilders. Bath has modularized the designs and has set up cells and flow lines (they call them "flow lanes") in buildings all over the yards (outdoor work has been reduced by 60 percent). Whole modules are built in one place from electrical and piping systems that themselves were put together in one place. The number of moves has been greatly reduced, along with inventories. Deliveries of twenty-four Navy frigates through 1985 were running nineteen weeks ahead of schedule, and man-hours were down by 30 percent on many tasks. "We have come as close as you can to a production-line concept," states William Haggett, Bath's president.[5]

Major-Event Planning

We have seen ways by which WCM reduces the computing chores in the postmanufacturing (accounting) and during-manufacturing (shop-floor execution) phases. Now let us back up to premanufacturing.

Computers in Premanufacturing

Here are premanufacturing activities where the computer may play a central role:

- *Order entry.* At GM of Canada 40 percent of suppliers receive their orders by direct computer-to-computer links with GM (as of early 1985). Furthermore, 40 of the suppliers have access to GM's inventory records for the part numbers they supply. That permits the supplier to check GM's records and be assured that the order and due date really are valid. This use of the computer helps allay the distrust between supplier and buyer companies that has plagued us in the past.
- *Design.* Computer-aided design (CAD), computer-aided engineering (CAE), and computer-aided manufacturing (CAM) provide a technological assist in slashing engineering lead times;

they also provide a common data base to far-flung designers, which helps assure use of standard parts and avoid waste of time in adding new ones. The computer is useful in configuration control—including keeping track of engineering changes—as well.

- *Master production scheduling* (MPS). By all means put the MPS into the computer. For all regularly demanded products, the MPS, or, more properly, the final assembly schedule, should simply be a production rate. Then run the bill-of-materials processor to determine the production rate for component materials.
- *Cut-over.* For regularly demanded products an MRP-like program is needed to calculate, by back-scheduling, exactly when a new production rate should go into effect for component materials. In other words, calculate a "cut-over" date and hour. After that, kanban may take over—no work order scheduling—until the next change in the production rate.
- *Purchasing.* This is the other end of order entry. Besides the computer linkages to suppliers, the computer provides clerical efficiencies in purchasing. In addition, for JIT suppliers it is efficient to wand a bar code on the kanban upon receipt. That conveys receipt information to purchasing and to accounts payable. Toyota uses this approach extensively. (But, as was indicated above, companies with very short lead times should *not* need to use bar coding on the shop floor.)

Most of these uses of the computer in manufacturing are what might be called *major-event planning.* Major events are new orders, new rates, new products, new processes, and new product designs or engineering changes (ECs). They have important effects on most of the resources of the firm, including the outside suppliers.

Clustering the Major Events

It may seem that major events, like new orders and engineering changes, occur every day, and if so, the computer would be running the major-event planning routines continually. For regularly demanded products, marketing needs at least a few days to assess whether demand has changed. Therefore, computer runs for changes in production rate are unlikely to be needed more than weekly, and usually not that often.

If manufacturing receives engineering changes every day, then it is time to change policies. The Japanese auto industry has learned to cluster its ECs. For example, ECs are allowed only once a month, generally on the same date as new rates go into effect. Problems get worked out in a few days, and then manufacturing runs smoothly the rest of the month. Since most companies and their suppliers follow the same timing in cutting over to new schedules and other major events, the whole industry benefits from predictability not available in the rest of the world.

Kawasaki in Nebraska clusters its major events, and Hewlett-Packard's Computer Systems Division has been considering it (and perhaps by now is using it). I look forward to the day when leading companies in the auto industry and the electronics industry agree to introduce clusters of major events on the same day of the month. The constant random disruptions that plague OEM and supplier companies in these industries would dissipate, and all the companies would benefit.

Manufacturing Resource Planning

North America has a large lead over the rest of the world in using the computer for major-event planning. The tool, which has been perfected and widely implemented over the past twenty years or so, is material requirements planning (MRP). We have seen that JIT obviates the need for MRP for shop floor execution and inventory accounting. MRP subroutines that calculate mid-range effects of major events, however, will continue to useful.

MRP is versatile in that a number of subroutines work from the same data base, the same set of numbers. An extension of material requirements planning, called manufacturing resource planning (MRP II), delves into use of that data base to calculate such things as cash in/cash out, equipment needs, labor needs, and when to change tools.

The world-class manufacturers in Japan have a lot to learn from North Americans about using the computer for major-event planning. While they learn those lessons, the North Americans have the task of turning off the features of MRP that are made redundant when JIT goes on stream.

What about Western plants that are just starting or are in the middle of factory information system projects? The best advice is to *slow down*. Get the plant right, and then put in the computer support.

Managerial Control

Having looked narrowly at some of the systems issues, we may sum up with an overview. The information-based control loop that governs manufacturing operations has necessarily been long in the past.

Figure 10–4 shows the loop schematically. The double-bordered geometric is the source of data: the operator and the machine. Quality assurance (QA) and production control (PC) people on the floor check the source data against their standards. Their findings go onto check sheets or directly into computer memory. Summarized results are available to QA, PC, and accounting. They sift the data and send variance reports to line management in the factory. The onus is on the first-line supervisor to take corrective action. The loop is closed when the operator and machine are adjusted.

Visual control, a prime WCM objective, greatly shortens the control loop. The ideal loop—two versions of it—is shown in Figure 10–5. In the lefthand version, the operator measures key performance factors and posts the data on charts right there on the floor. The operator adjusts the machine or manual procedures right away whenever there is a variance in quality or rate.

When the adjustment is beyond the control of the operator, the righthand version applies: Problems that persist show up day-after-day on the shop floor charts. The supervisors bring in operators from other areas, engineers, buyers, supplier reps—whoever can help—and form a project team to study and solve the problem.

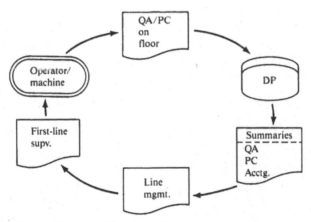

Figure 10–4. Control Loop—Conventional

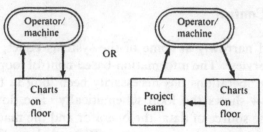

Figure 10–5. Control Loop—WCM

The idea of shortening the control loop and cutting out reporting should have general support, since everyone complains about too much reporting. In every organization there are campaigns now and then to cut out redundant reports. The populist approach is just to stop sending out certain reports and see if anyone screams. A better approach is to put the charts and graphs on the shop floor and cut off the computer summaries to the management echelons. Managers then *must* get out into the factory on a regular basis to exercise control.

Chapter 11

Managing the Transformation

The art of progress is to preserve order amid change and to preserve change amid order.

—Alfred North Whitehead

Is world-class manufacturing a pie-in-the-sky idealist's dream? Not at all. While WCM is demanding of change in all parts of the manufacturing enterprise, the changes are attainable. Briefly the reasons are:

Simplicity: No need to hire a bevy of consultants for a multiyear program of guidance

Overwhelming logic: No need to wait for studies to be done to provide proof that the concepts are right

Quick, visible results: WCM means not only continual improvement but *rapid* improvement; fast reductions in scrap and rework, not to mention racks full of materials taken out, more than pay the bills until the big benefits—growing numbers of customers opting to buy from you—show up.

Low cost: WCM is *not* investing in expensive plant and equipment.

Personal excitement, fulfillment, and rejuvenation: The wimp on the beach on whom people kick sand becomes number 1; being number 1 is not exciting, but getting there sure is.

No one is left out.

That's fine, and I can accept all this (you might say), but how do we transform ourselves from where we are now to what you describe? How do we get there? Japan's thirty-year journey does not serve as a proper model for implementation. The rest of the world should pick and choose the best approaches for their circumstances and reject what does not work well.

Until recently, there were not enough successes in Western industry to sort through. Now there are. Conclusions in this chapter draw from a fair-sized sample.

Resistance

The simpler implementation issues pertain to who does what. The hard ones concern getting commitment. Gaining commitment from the factory operatives is proving to be the smallest problem.

What about first-line supervisors? One study revealed a lot of resistance by supervisors to *employee involvement.* [1] As academic studies go, this one seems well done, except that it is the usual verb-without-object kind of study that the universities churn out. The question is, employee involvement in *what?* At the time the study was made, the widespread feeling was that EI was good in and of itself. No one seemed to know what employees should be involved in, and so that survey could not be specific on the point.

Now we know that employees should be involved in SPC, in quick setup, in getting equipment to work right, in teaching and learning, and in a hundred other things that used to be someone else's job. I have not noticed supervisor resistance to those things. The supervisor is the master teacher, which is not a bad role, especially since it begins with learning about SPC, quick setup, and the other tools.

Many people are saying that the middle managers are the resistors. In companies where middle managers have been thoroughly exposed to JIT/TQC/TPM/EI, however, the middle managers say they are eager. They say their bosses are the problem, that the people at the top do not understand, or only understand some of it.

The number of Western chief executive officers (CEOs) and chief operating officers (COOs) who care intensely about JIT can be counted on the fingers of one hand. Jack Warne, president (retired) of Omark Industries, is such a person. The number of CEOs and COOs who are on the quality bandwagon (that includes Mr. Warne) is far larger but still a small percentage.

Corporate officers are going to put energy into WCM only if they see clear connections with their heavy responsibilities. Dealing with risk ranks among the heaviest of those responsibilities. Let us look at how WCM affects the issue.

Risk Avoidance

Many of the kinds of Americans who in the past might have bought a Harley-Davidson motorcycle—a "hog"—today buy a Chevy Luv or an over-powered oversize-tired four-wheel-drive pickup truck. The market for its unique product fell out from under Harley-Davidson, and it was touch-and-go as to whether the company could survive.

Harley is much smaller today, but it is surviving. Furthermore, a growing number of the survivors in the company, union rank-and-file included, are getting cocky. They are coming to believe themselves now capable of making money producing anything from bedsprings to computer frames to curtain rods to electric cables.

The Harley assembly plant in Pennsylvania now assembles mixed models: assembly lots of one. They call it "jelly beans." Jelly beans assembly signifies flexibility. Those who have learned to do it may feel that if motorcycle sales stay poor, maybe they could run a mix of air conditioners and office furniture down the line.

The engine and transmission factory in Milwaukee also has become flexible. Machines that had taken hours to set up are now changed over in minutes.

Along with learning to be flexible, Harley-Davidson has immersed itself in statistical process control. Gaining SPC expertise has opened doors and revealed many paths that can be taken to stay solvent and successful. For example, Harley obtained a large contract to assemble electrical cables for IBM. I've been told that Harley produced 9 million cable sets with zero mechanical defects and only a small number of electrical defects.

JIT at Harley has yielded some unexpected benefits: On one contract for a nonmotorcycle product, Harley delivers and is paid before it pays for the materials that go into the product.

We think of the buyer of a Harley motorcycle as a tough-looking dude in a black leather jacket. There are quite a few people who live up to that image working inside the Harley plants as well. Yet they have learned finesse in manufacturing.

Glover Morgan, a machine operator, is one such person. A few years ago Morgan vociferously resisted things like quick setup and SPC. He is now one of the most vocal advocates. In fact, Morgan has been loaned to Tennessee Associates, Inc., which offers quality assurance training for manufacturing people. Morgan shows the industrial audiences how they do SPC where he comes from.

I have been describing Harley's use of certain WCM techniques, like SPC and mixed-model assembly, by which the company has gained a measure of security. But techniques alone are not likely to grab the attention of our industrial executives. What else does WCM offer in the way of crisis immunity or recovery capability? What does the big picture look like?

Disaster Insurance

In certain of the world's large cities, if I park my car in a slum area, I may be confronted by a youth who says, "Give me three bucks and I'll make sure nothing happens to your car." I pay the price, but I am outraged.

What protection is there—short of extortion—to make sure that nothing happens to *my company?* Clearly, the best protection is good management. If fire destroys a plant or a major product bombs in the market place, good management may be able to rescue the enterprise. Even if your company's product line were suddenly made obsolete—like a buggy whip company when automobiles replaced horse-drawn carriages—good management might be able to effect a recovery.

People Who Are Indispensable

Measured by the WCM yardstick, good manufacturing management virtually did not exist until rather recently. Management of world-class manufacturing companies today is an order of magnitude better than the best in prior history.

What puts those companies in another league is that their talents and their ability to shrug off a crisis do not depend on a few highly proficient managers, marketers, or engineers. If the very best of them left the company when a crisis hit, those remaining in the company would manage the recovery. Protection against disaster is flimsy if it consists of a handful of indispensable people.

WCM companies set themselves apart in that management is widely shared and people are versatile, adaptable, and flexible. WCM provides crisis protection by inculcating good management of quality, lead time, and design into the organization.

My earlier example, Harley-Davidson, is a company that has the right idea, is moving in the WCM direction, and is building confidence. We may consider the example of another company, one farther along on the WCM journey, to show how risks are reduced when there is organization-wide skill in managing quality, lead time, and design. The company is Nihon Chukuko, a small Japanese supplier of metal parts for Isuzu trucks. Part of the Chukuko story—use of the six-axis process check sheet—was told in Chapter 2.

Companies That Become Indispensable

On my visit to Chukuko, I saw evidence of operator involvement in data capture, diagnosis, and problem-solving everywhere. The walls, posts, and work benches were thick with charts showing results and accomplishments. The "war room" was also three-deep in charts: schedules, defects, projects, QC circle presentations, awards. The plant manager took time to explain the company's rigorous program to keep gauges calibrated and in use.

One set of charts in the war room gave the delivery location, date, and hour of the day for each delivery of each part. Most parts were to be delivered at 1 P.M.—plus or minus thirty minutes. Isuzu would have dock space open for a delivery in just that narrow time window. The part typically went into an Isuzu truck within two hours of delivery. This required that Chukuko be extraordinarily reliable in delivering the right parts to the right place on time.

Some of the charts on the factory walls were methods diagrams. The machine operator was charged with improving the method of making the part, and then diagramming and writing up the important details. (Chapter 2 describes a similar approach at Gorman Rupp Co. in Ohio.) The plant manager checked those sheets at intervals and raised questions when someone's methods diagram showed no improvement between visits.

Those measures assured a high rate of improvement so Chukuko could stay profitable. Exceptional improvement was called for, because Chukuko's three-year contract with Isuzu lowered the price 1.5 percent every six months.

A room about 12 feet by 16 feet held carefully labeled samples of competitors' products, metal parts made for other truck companies. It was the "tear-down room" (see Figure 11–1), and employees spent time there tearing down each competitor's part; they performed value analysis to find out the probable cost, checked tolerances and paint finishes, and evaluated materials and likely methods of manufacture.

Isuzu helped Chukuko set up the tear-down room and monitored its use. Isuzu wanted to be sure its sole-source supplier had top product and process designs. For its part, Chukuko didn't want Isuzu even to think about doing business with another maker of those parts.

Why aren't suppliers in Western industry so conscientious? Because most customer plants in the West have never offered that brand of helpful insistence and stuck with suppliers long enough to develop a pattern of mutual esteem and dependency.

Now let's consider the minus side. Chukuko's ancient equipment is crammed into an old, dingy building. Being very small, the company has virtually no borrowing power. It is reliant almost exclusively on one customer. Its products are simple metal pieces, and there are hundreds of other small factories around Tokyo that could take Chuku-ko's business if Isuzu decided to bless them with it.

Disaster Scenario

Those negatives suggest a disaster scenario: Isuzu redesigns a number of the metal parts to be made out of plastic. Being a tiny company, Chukuko could not possibly swing a big bank loan or go to the equity market to finance plastic molding equipment.

Toll the death knell for Chukuko? Probably not. Isuzu would be likely to provide financial assistance and training so Chukuko could get up to speed in plastics.

Isuzu would not do that for sentimental reasons, nor because of Chukuko's current equipment, which is primitive, or its production savvy, which is low-tech. Isuzu has made investments in Chukuko that are more valuable than machinery. Isuzu has invested talents of some of its best people and has succeeded in transforming Chukuko from average or below-average to a top supplier. Chukuko is valued for nothing less than its excellence in *management,* in *quality,* and in *product and process design.* Isuzu can buy plastic molding machines, but Chukuko's total company management cannot be bought; it can only be developed.

Western supplier companies sometimes have policies that limit the

Figure 11–1. Tear-Down Room

amount of business done with any one customer; 25 percent is a typical number. Chukuko is 90 percent with Isuzu, but the risk exposure seems small. Its WCM management capability insulates Chukuko from disaster better than anything else I can think of.

Champions and Ramrods

Still there is the question of how to get there from here. In industry we often can identify success in almost any program with a "champion." The champion is the believer who batters down obstacles and brooks no naysaying. In some cases the champion is more of a ramrod, like the fabled Taiichi Ohno of Toyota.

In some of our top companies the quality campaigns have progressed beyond the champion stage. For the most part JIT has not progressed that far, but I know of a few JIT champions (usually they are also strong TQC advocates) who are making big JIT waves in their companies.

Marcel Fages of American Standard's Building Specialties Group is one such person. Jerry Brown, Jack Geikler, and Vinod Kapoor of Westinghouse are others. Lew Springer, senior vice president—manufacturing at Campbell Soup, is still another.

Demanding Leadership

Fages got a JIT education effort mounted in his group. Two or three months later he had the following JIT projects organized: nineteen pull projects, twelve quick setup projects, twelve move-a-machine projects, and fourteen increase-frequency-of-delivery projects.

Kapoor managed JIT startups at a Westinghouse plant in Fayetteville, and later Ashboro, in North Carolina. JIT training and planning commenced but, says Kapoor, "though we seemed to be committed, the results were not forthcoming." Kapoor became personally involved and "stuck to my guns." Lot sizes were cut in some cases to one, and numerous JIT projects were organized and carried through.

At Westinghouse, West Mifflin, Pennsylvania, after a round of training and planning, site managers Brown and Geikler *demanded* action. Their insistence was expressed as a rule to the factory management group: You *will* meet the schedule every day—by 8 A.M. the next morning. If you have to stay late and can get your direct labor to stay too, that's a plus. But *you will stay.*

It took two painful months, but the plant people did meet Brown's and Geikler's challenge. Now it's routine to complete required work every day.

There is a short videotape floating around Campbell Soup Co. that was made by people at the Campbell plant in Fayetteville, Arkansas. The narrator tells about how the plant manager there attended a JIT seminar. On the plane home, with Lew Springer's calls for action ringing in his ears, the plant manager worked out something to do, and then did it right away: He slashed the inventory of aluminum pans, made on their own pan presses, from 1.4 million to 33,000 units. The reduction came about by bypassing the store room and converting the pan-press department from the push to the pull system. At the end of the videotape, the narrator says that JIT requires a champion, "and the champion is the plant manager."

That is good advice. There are bogged-down JIT and TQC campaigns here and there in most large industrial companies. You may say it is for good reason. We have decentralized, and this is the decentralization approach doing its worthy work.

Hogwash. It is plain old procrastination. It is indeed a good idea to let all have their say and not ruffle any feathers when the subject is *what* to do. We are not talking about "what" any more. We know what to do to make an average manufacturer world-class. The subject is *when,* and the answer is *now,* before the competition does it.

Total Immersion

Those like myself who advise others on procedure have been cautious in the past. We said do it now, but advised easing into action with one or just a few pilot projects. No such timidity was shown by Mr. Fages of American Standard: fifty-seven projects organized almost instantly.

The slow and easy approach has been more common; its advocates said, "Let's get a success story, and then repeat it." In the case of SPC the starting point could be any work center where people were trained and eager. Where JIT was the agenda item, advocates said to start at the tail end, final assembly or packing. The idea was to get the end of the process in tune with the daily sales rate. Then back up one step to subassembly; get that right. Then back up further to fabrication and beyond.

The back-to-front approach was okay when a plant had only a handful of believers. Now, with plants sending busloads of people to training sessions or to tour other advanced JIT/TQC plants, I think we are ready for a total immersion approach. Figure 11–2 illustrates. The challenge to every stage of manufacture and to those who purchase from suppliers is to move away from batches and toward the sales rate. Buffer stocks between each pair of processes shrink only as fast as the pair of processes become flexible (quick changeovers) and reliable (high availability, dependable quality). While the buffer stocks provide security, the flow distance, lot sizes, and lead times may be squeezed everywhere at once.

Everywhere at once means broad training followed by insistent management. At the end of one of my seminars on JIT/TQC, a fellow from the audience—a manager of a plant—stopped by to thank me and said, "You give us a lot of food for thought." I said, "No. Food for action."

Ringi-Dingey

Some people fault Westerners, particularly Americans, I suppose, for being *too* quick to act. Those criticisms are based mainly on reports about Japanese consensus management.

We have been told that in good Japanese companies startups tend

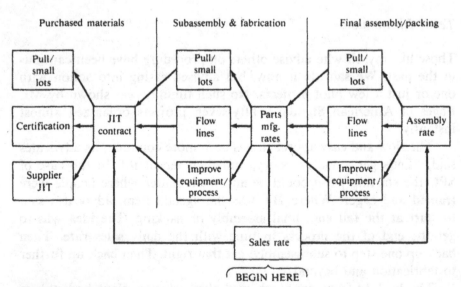

Figure 11–2. Total Immersion Approach

198

to be smooth, without a lot of mistakes. I agree with that. We are also told that errorless implementation comes from consensus management, which means taking enough time to get everyone's backing. Backing is signaled by signatures on the *Ringi* sheet. That part of it is speculation. I don't believe it.

In any large bureaucracy the system is to get everyone's signature on the document. In the U. S. Air Force it is called "staffing off": Everyone at one level in the command structure signs; then it goes up to the next level for a round of signatures. Maybe a year goes by, and nothing has happened. We don't call this consensus management. We call it red tape. Of course sometimes—on questions of *what* to do—the delay can be worthwhile.

The reasons why implementation is often smooth in Japan are these: flexible labor; flexible equipment; small supplier base; extensive standardization of parts, containers, dimensions, and other variables; simple visual controls; an absence of people in non-value-added functions; and habits of joint planning. Those grease the skids and avert startup problems.

That raises a question: Under those simplifying conditions, why does it take the Japanese so long to make decisions? Action-oriented, individualistic Western societies may have a cultural edge. Fast, accurate decisions offer an advantage over a competitor that makes slow, accurate decisions.

Competitive Pressure or the Lack of It

Competition has induced wondrous changes in the U. S. airline industry and the world auto and electronics industries. The opening of a Japanese-owned soup plant and a noodle plant in California has shaken the American food industry a bit. And so it goes.

What about companies that do not have much competition? It does not necessarily doom the company to inaction and regression. Omark Industries, for example, had the bulk of the world market for saw chain for many years, and yet Omark has always kept up with management and technical advances. Recently Stihl, a German competitor, has taken away some of Omark's customers. Some people at Omark blame it on currency exchange rates. If that is the reason, then Omark's manufacturing excellence should cause recovery of sales when the rates turn around—unless Stihl has also been transforming itself into a WCM company.

Another company that has been active in taking out inventories and compressing manufacturing lead times is Haworth Corp., a maker of office furnishings. The North American market for office furnishings has been growing at a torrid pace for several years. Producers' problems lie more in increasing capacity than in finding ways to appeal to customers. Still, Haworth's manager's scan the globe for the best manufacturing practices. They have cooperative ties to a Japanese maker in the same business, but it is a relationship with a wrinkle: Haworth people go over there to learn about equipment; the Japanese come to Haworth to learn how to use *kanban.*

In the next few years, I believe, we shall hear more such reports. There are plenty of Japanese companies that have prospered without a strong JIT campaign. Their Japanese and world competitors weren't doing it, and perhaps the general view was that "JIT is okay for the automotive people, but we're different." Now that there are strong JIT efforts in progress in the Western electronics, textile, food, medical products, pharmaceuticals, and even chemical industries, the hot breath (or maybe only the cool breath) of competition may force changes in laggard Japanese companies. Manufacturers in Korea, Taiwan, and Hong Kong have also gotten by without much JIT, and they too have much to learn and do.

One whole sector that is short on competition is government contracting. Big companies like TRW, Hughes, McDonnell-Douglas, and Sperry sometimes get mammoth multiyear contracts. Some are renewed from one product generation to another without much threat of loss to another contractor. What is more, the government makes progress payments. That is, the government pays the contractor for its piles of inventory.

These look like built-in inducements *not* to adopt WCM concepts, especially just-in-time production. Yet some of the best JIT examples I know of are in government contracts. For example, an IBM government division has one of that company's most impressive JIT projects. A factory on government contracts may be the top JIT plant within Texas Instruments. FMC's giant ordnance plant in San Jose is not yet among FMC's top JIT plants, but there are impressive JIT projects going on there.

At first I wondered why the managers and engineers in those plants were working so hard at change. Then I decided, why not? There are fewer chances to look good when working within the limits of a government contract. JIT and TQC offer ways to stand out and perhaps outdo more entrepreneurial sister divisions.

While plant-level people at the IBM, TI, and FMC facilities have themselves turned on to JIT, I don't know that the top executives in those companies are particularly interested. They may be absorbed in other issues. Sometimes it is one dominant issue; the issue of the moment could be one aspect of WCM, but not WCM as a whole.

Single-Issue Management

The homily "Don't bite off more than you can chew" translates into getting behind one major program at a time. As applied to WCM, that approach will be disappointing.

The four prime WCM pursuits are total quality control, just-in-time, total preventive maintenance, and employee involvement. As candidates for single-issue management, the last two, TPM and EI, are easily disposed of.

Employee involvement has not meant salvation to the thousands of companies that mounted EI campaigns—under a variety of names. EI is likely to pay big dividends when its object has something to do with customer needs. When left up in the air, however, EI can just as well be self-serving or even destructive. An employee group could, for example, spend its time trying to figure out how to hold down the production pace.

Unlike EI, total preventive maintenance has a clear beneficial purpose: keeping machines running right. TPM does lead to improvements the customer cares about. On the other hand, the customer has no direct interest in it, and so TPM and EI are not sound as single-issue programs.

JIT and TQC do not have the same limitations. Each directly addresses matters customers certainly do care about: Customers want short lead times, which JIT directly provides; customers want quality, and TQC directly provides that. The question is, can JIT or TQC perform well independently, perhaps implemented one at a time?

JIT Without TQC

Earlier chapters showed that shortened lead time, arising from JIT, is a powerful advantage in the market place, because it makes the producer responsive to the customer without the need for large finished-goods inventories. JIT advocates also maintain that JIT is a quality improvement approach and that inventory benefits are secondary.

JIT sounds like the engine that can drive the company to improve continually and rapidly and thereby become world-class. There are plants that have put JIT on the front burner and have delayed their TQC training.

It is no longer true, but for a time Hewlett-Packard, Greeley Division, was among the top Western plants in JIT accomplishments but had let its quality campaign lag. (As we saw in an earlier chapter, it now has a strong TQC emphasis.) The lag in TQC resulted in too many quality problems and not enough people equipped with quality improvement tools.

I don't want to create the wrong impression. JIT itself is a quality improvement tool, mainly because it cuts time delays between process stages so that that trail of causal evidence does not get cluttered and cold. (See "Quality/JIT Interlink" in Chapter 7.) The point is that JIT is only one quality aid. Other TQC tools are needed as well, or the rate of quality improvement will not be fast enough.

To oversimplify, an end result of JIT without TQC might be fast response to a dwindling number of customers.

TQC Without JIT

One of the largest American electronics manufacturers is totally immersed in quality improvement. Corporate leaders feel they should not risk disrupting the quality effort by overlaying a heavy JIT campaign. JIT training has been provided, and all JIT efforts are welcome, but a fair number of high-level people in the company feel it is best to get quality right before doing a lot with JIT.

That policy is fraught with risk to the company. I'm talking about financial risk, because companies that are not active in JIT tend to sink capital into plant and equipment by the old wrong rules: Bigger is better, get rid of the old outdated equipment, automate as fast as possible, equip for large batch production and long runs, position like machines together, make as much as possible, and run machines as many hours as there are on the clock.

Adding to the monetary costs of following those wrong rules are the quality costs. Big machines and long production runs push large lots into the system so that scrap and rework rates apply to huge qualities. Worse, the long lag times between the maker and the user put prodigious numbers of process changes into the system so that cause analysis becomes difficult or hopeless.

Quality without JIT—and vice versa—is the fork without the knife. The spoon, TPM, makes a set, and the three together resolutely draw employees into a state of high involvement.

No Tradeoffs

Cost reduction or productivity improvement has been a single-issue concern in many a company in the past. The WCM view is that cost drops and productivity rises jointly as defects and lead times fall and as equipment is made to work well.

Once everyone believed that cost and quality are a tradeoff pair, but that view has been thoroughly discredited. At least the view is discredited among manufacturing people in top companies. It may not yet be understood or believed by all the officers or by the board, and they are the ultimate decision-makers. A brief review of the no-tradeoff viewpoint seems necessary.

A 1981 article by Steven Wheelwright included a weathervane-like sketch with quality pointing north, cost pointing south, flexibility pointing east, and dependability pointing west. That, he stated, seemed to be "the American attitude."[2] The next panel of his illustration showed the Japanese approach: Quality aimed east into a box containing flexibility and dependability, which were easterly arrows only 30 degrees (instead of 180 degrees) apart; cost continued eastward out of the box.

If the article were rewritten today, the sketch would probably put lead time in place of dependability. The reason is that dependability takes care of itself when the lead time is slashed. Putting it another way, lead time reduction is brought about by pulling out the unpredictable delays; dependable delivery performance is then no trouble.

Tradeoff Myth

Belief in the tradeoff theory has been almost universal. A few generations of MBAs have taken the tradeoff baggage into the business world and presumably have made strategy accordingly.

Business college students learn about tradeoffs in a number of courses; the concept gets extra attention in the final "capstone" course, which is called business policy, administrative strategy, or some such name. The textbooks talk about finding your competitive niche or area of "distinctive competency." Perhaps your company is the cost leader in the industry. Then, the book will say, you should expect your quality to be somewhat lower, your response time a bit slower, and your flexibility less. If you get the product out the door faster than everybody else, then your quality is unlikely to be as good and your costs are higher, so charge more.

Now we know that all that is balderdash. The best manufacturers of the world are likely to be good in *all* those areas. WCM explains why.

JIT stimulates solutions to quality problems by keeping evidence fresh. It takes out the idle inventories, so there is little to scrap or rework when a bad batch is found; the effect is large cost reductions. It slashes lead times. It does not result in flexibility, but it does demand flexibility: flexible labor and flexible equipment.

TQC fans the flames: It greatly accelerates quality improvement, which lowers scrap, rework, warranty, and liability costs. TQC takes out some of the rework loops as well, and that cuts lead times a bit.

TPM and EI are in the thick of it all.

WCM for the CEO

Even if the CEO and his executive group see that WCM is a large, impressive no-tradeoff package, it still might be delegated to the operating group. WCM will receive strategic-level attention only if it has a dominant strategic flavor to it.

Philip Crosby, W. Edwards Deming, Joseph Juran, and others prominent in the quality movement have done an amazing job of showing executive-level people that quality is strategic. The purveyors of JIT have not always been so adept at presenting their case.

There has been too much talk about inventories, which can be the kiss of death. If inventories are the substance of JIT, then the tendency is to delegate JIT to the materials managers, who can do little about inventories other than keep track of them.

The real substance of JIT is lead times, and that *is* strategic. Beating your customers to a sale, undercutting their backlogs, and being able to fill orders with hardly any distribution inventories is competitive advantage. Full-blown JIT—with quick changes and flexible labor and machines—provides the added strategic weapon of quick response when customers want a different mix of products or models.

Today's manufacturing executives talk often enough about the need for being customer-oriented. They have not realized where the tools are for making the transformation from an internal to an external focus. The old internal tools are still there and are getting in the way.

Toward an External Focus

A world-class manufacturer is one that fulfills the customer's demands for high quality, low cost, short lead times, and flexibility. Those are external measures of manufacturing success, but they are measurable inside the plant. Internal measures of flexibility, for example, might be average number of jobs or machines mastered per employee and line changeover time.

We do not measure factory performance on those terms. Instead, we use secondary internal measures, and the customer doesn't care about any of them. They are cost variance, internal due dates, efficiency, and utilization. Table 11-1 stacks up the secondary internal measures against the customer-oriented WCM measures.

Table 11-1. Internal Versus Customer-Oriented Measures of Performance

Internal Measures (old way)	Customer-Oriented Measures (WCM way)
Cost variance	Cost
Meet internal due dates	Lead time
Efficiency	Quality
Utilization	Flexibility

Our internal measure of cost is not of interest to the customer, because we judge actual cost against our own internal *standard cost.* The external way is to check our cost against what the customer wants to pay or what competitors charge. Meeting internal due dates does lead to meeting external due dates, and that made yesterday's undemanding customer happy. Today's customer *expects* that it will be on time; the competitive issue is, "What's the lead time?" Efficiency and utilization clearly are of no interest to the customer, especially since some of our ways of pursuing those internal goals conflict with our ability to deliver quality and provide flexible response.

What about productivity? I don't even have it on the list, because surveys keep showing productivity low on our executives' lists of things important—well below price of stock, market share, and other items. One could argue that productivity merits higher billing, but let's hear what a Sanyo executive says about it: "I myself am not too concerned over raising productivity, because our manufacturing system [is aimed at] preventing defective products through maintenance of strict quality control that extends to machinery, jigs, and fixtures . . . so that [productivity] will automatically go up."[3]

Is the case for executive-level involvement in WCM strong enough? Where executives are convinced, a flurry of activity to get the ball rolling will follow. Consulting companies often assist with such large-scale efforts. What should the consultants' role be in WCM?

Searching for Help

On the first page of this chapter, I commented that WCM does not require much use of outside consultants. Actually, there are quite a few top-notch consultants available, and they are providing valuable help to industry.

There is a problem with the large consulting companies, however. Currently they are short on people who give WCM advice and long on people who advise and assist with the old solutions.

The consulting companies, like everybody else, need to get lean and shed some of the non-value-added functions, the ones that push incentive pay systems, automated storage systems, and computer-based shop floor control, for example. As it is now, if you go to a consulting company and declare an interest in automated storage and handling, you are not likely to be told to eliminate the inventory instead. Storage and handling system experts are still on the staff and welcome the business; besides, the complicated solution makes for a bigger consulting job.

It looks as though the consulting firms can make their greatest contribution to WCM in the training area. The colleges and universities are not very helpful right now, and there is a massive amount of training to be done. In fact, training is so important to WCM that it is impossible to complete the topic of this chapter, "Managing the Transformation," without a full treatment of training. There are enough training issues to take up a separate chapter, and so the discussion continues in Chapter 12.

Chapter 12

Training: The Catalyst

Hundreds of industrial companies now have cadres of believers in JIT/TQC, but many are frustrated over the question of how to implement their beliefs. I am asked if I can offer an implementation plan.

Implementation plans are usually boxes with words in them connected by arrows. I have such a plan for WCM. It comprises half a dozen arrow-connected boxes, and the word *training* is in each one. If you prefer a fancier word, you can put "education" in a few of them.

To be sure, many other boxes can diverge from the training boxes: appoint a task force, measure and photograph "before" conditions, revise the performance measures, regularize the schedule, launch several pilot projects, get a top-level commitment and a policy statement if you can, quickly halt or slow down all large projects that add complexity and collect waste.

Still, if there is impatience over lack of action, it strongly suggests a training gap. Waiting for training and education, however, has its own frustrating side. A large training effort is often spaced out over months, because the company's limited classroom space and limited number of trainers may accommodate only fifty people a week. While the company's WCM effort is on hold waiting for training, the stories about achievements at Omark, H-P, IBM, Tennant, Buick, and others become old news.

WCM means continual and rapid improvement. Similarly, WCM implementation means continual and rapid training. In other words, the training effort must somehow be streamlined so that it doesn't keep progress on hold.

Training for Implementation

The number of people who have attended one of my JIT/TQC seminars is in the tens of thousands (I have no idea how many more have viewed the audio- and videotapes of my seminars). I say this to show that my views on training are based on a large sample size; they are also shaped by discussions with others who provide seminars and training on the same topics.

Whom to Train

My seminars, both public and on-site at manufacturing companies, are somewhat successful in stirring people up. (Some were enthused before they came.) If a whole group is fired up, and all are staff people—from purchasing, materials management, quality, DP, personnel, engineering, accounting—nothing much gets started aside from planning. If the group includes a few line managers, things may start to pop: Task forces are formed and pilot projects are begun. While pilot projects create excitement, and usually results, a letdown may follow.

Some have taken a different approach to training and have managed to avoid the letdown. I know of no single best approach, but the successes tend to have this in common: Direct labor and first-line supervisors are in on the training early. From the start, many of the seminars I have done on-site at companies have included a sprinkling of shop floor people—for example, at Tennant Co., several Hewlett-Packard divisions, and Tektronix. In companies with unions, it is a "sin" not to include union representatives.

The usual reason for bringing in shop floor folks—at least a few—early is to stifle false rumors. There is a second reason: Show that their opinions are valued, that their understanding is important. There is a third reason: JIT/TQC is common sense; the story really can be told about the same way for corporate officers as for the rank-and-file.

There is still another reason, and this is the crucial one: Some of the assemblers and machine operators get more excited than anyone else. And why not? Who has a clearer view of the waste, excesses, mindless complexity, and—from their view—bad management than those who make the product? JIT/TQC promises enlightened management. It also aims at creating jobs that are a mixture of direct labor, indirect labor, problem-solving, and management of the resources at hand.

(Dr. Deming is reputed to insist sometimes that the top company or plant official be in attendance when he visits. Not a bad idea. I have given more serious consideration to—but so far have not implemented—a slight alteration of it for my own visits: saying I won't come unless some direct labor people are in the audience.)

A few companies, like Ray-Chem and Lorain Industries, have sent the majority of their direct labor force to my seminars. A couple of times the whole plant has shut down to attend. Recently, for example, the whole plant population from McNeil Consumer Products in Round Rock, Texas, came on buses to a seminar that I conducted at an Austin hotel. That plant makes Tylenol. I expect it to set the pill-and-capsule industry on its ear.

Speedy Training

But wait. I'm going off the deep end. There are many other ways to train people besides attending a seminar conducted by Dick Schonberger. For example, show everyone the twenty-nine-minute JIT skit developed at Hewlett-Packard, Greeley Division. Many companies have copies of the skit, and everyone loves it. Several companies have made their own skits or serious videotapes, and those are helpful. They provide a speedy, cheap way at least to get the basic idea across. They should be followed with continuing in-depth training.

Plant tours of top JIT/TQC facilities are also a good training method. Control Data sent busloads of people, including direct labor, from one of its plants in Pennsylvania to tour Harley-Davidson, and the tour was highly effective. Like quite a few other plants that are being toured a lot, Harley uses some enthusiastic hourly employees as tour guides, which is impressive in itself. Usually tours are far more effective if preceded by some general information on the concepts that are to be seen.

In-Depth Training

With the shortage of trainers, some of the more successful companies have decided to grow their own. Texas Instruments sent a large group of its most senior managers to Crosby's quality college. Those managers trained the next batch at TI, who trained the next batch. The figure that I heard in 1984 was that 15,000 TI-ers had been trained by that method.

High-level executives have always done a good deal of coaching, but actually conducting classes has been mostly unheard of. Andy Grove, president of Intel, advocated it in his book, *High Output Management*. [1] It is hard to think of a more effective way for an executive to show genuine backing of a campaign. Serving as trainer also assures that the executive thoroughly understands. It doesn't matter much whether the executive is particularly good as a trainer. Everyone understands that signaling commitment is the real purpose.

An old adage holds: When eating ham and eggs it is well to consider that while the chicken was involved, the pig was committed. [2]

In earlier chapters I stressed the notion that all factory operatives also must be trainers. A company should ensure that anyone with a head full of wisdom about how to run a machine or make a part shall not leave the job without recording that wisdom or teaching it to someone else. To make sure operating knowledge is not suddenly lost, the employer must make training and instructing a regular part of everyone's job. That means publicly posting sketches and writeups on the latest correct methods, and teaching the job to someone else whenever there is a lull.

Part of the instruction concerns operation of machines, uses of tools, and assembly sequences. Gauging dimensions, plotting on SPC charts, and posting incidences of slowdowns and stoppages are also part of the job and therefore part of what is to be taught. In other words, WCM concepts are absorbed into jobs in the factory, and factory people come to be part of the WCM training group. As trainers, they may want to know more about their subject—even to the point of reading books about it.

Book Learning

Omark Industries began its JIT journey via self-study. It bought six hundred copies of Shingo's book, *Study of Toyota Production System from Industrial Engineering Viewpoint*. [3] Study teams were each assigned a different chapter. The teams analyzed, discussed, and restated the points in the chapters. Their analyses were shared with the other teams. Since their English version of the book was poorly translated from Japanese, the analysis was very time-consuming. A bit later Omark found out about two other books: They bought five hundred copies of *Japanese Manufacturing Techniques*[4] and five hundred of *Zero Inventories,*[5] and study teams dissected those books as well.

Other companies have launched their own JIT/TQC efforts the same way: analyzed the available books chapter by chapter, compared their way against the JIT/TQC way point by point, and set forth plans of action to change.

Some companies have made readings on JIT/TQC available to direct labor employees. At General Electric's coffee maker division in Ashboro, North Carolina—now owned by Black & Decker—a supervisor had a copy of *Japanese Manufacturing Techniques.* One of his subordinates asked, "What's that book?" The subordinate ended up borrowing it. Later, plant management decided to put small libraries of such reading material in supervisors' offices. A goodly portion of the direct labor force did read some of the materials. Things have changed from a few years ago, when few managers even read books about their trade.

Formal Corporate Training

At General Electric, among the first North American companies to start up JIT projects, one step was to appoint a full-time JIT director at corporate level. Ed Spurgeon has held that job since 1983. Spurgeon's team expanded into a corporate consulting group, whose role has been training and not much actual consulting.

Borg-Warner's approach was to set up corporate-level training classes that focused on JIT/TQC as part of an effort to upgrade manufacturing engineering.

General Motors (especially Pontiac), IBM, and others have extensively tapped the wisdom of W. Edwards Deming. The Juran Institute and Juran's videotapes have played central roles in many companies' quality management training. Tennessee Associates, Inc. is flourishing today as a center for training on SPC and the Deming philosophy.

Motorola started up a Manufacturing Management Institute in late 1984. It includes "the study of world-class manufacturing management strategic planning" and "the world-class quality concept."

Early in 1984 Schonberger and some of his colleagues and acquaintenances launched an enterprise with a similar name: the Manufacturing Institute (MI). The MI conducts multiday programs for audiences from industry. The topic is world-class manufacturing with emphasis on advanced JIT/TQC/TPM/EI concepts and implementation.

The formal corporate training programs complement and are fed by information from the professional societies, most of which were formed for a training purpose.

Professional Societies

Two professional societies have been in the thick of Japan's WCM training for many years: the Japanese Union of Scientists and Engineers and the Japan Management Association. Most other countries have the problem of many fragmented societies. WCM training in the United States, for example, is split among dozens of societies. Right now the prime ones are the American Production and Inventory Control Society (APICS), American Society for Quality Control (ASQC), National Association of Purchasing Management (NAPM), Institute of Industrial Engineers (IIE), and the Society of Manufacturing Engineers (SME). Other societies that have (or could have) some impact include those specializing in maintenance, R&D, information systems, accounting, transportation, human resource development, toolmaking, and marketing.

APICS has taken the remarkable step of launching the "Zero Inventory Crusade" for the 1980s. *Production and Inventory Management,* an APICS journal, has run quite a few articles on that subject. There are more articles, however, on issues that are no longer relevant (e.g, the economic order quantity), are overly complex or narrow (e.g, computer simulations of a hypothetical factory), and are partly outdated (e.g, some of the advice on computerizing the factory floor).

Among the professional societies, one stands out for its WCM orientation: ASQC. ASQC's magazine, *Quality Progress,* has provided a steady diet of fine pieces emphasizing prevention (instead of detection) of quality and process problems.

North America has two new organizations, both still small, that emerged expressly to promote certain WCM concepts and techniques. One is the Association for Manufacturing Excellence (AME), which started out as the Repetitive Manufacturing Group of APICS. The other is the Automotive Industry Action Group (AIAG), whose membership had grown in 1985 to more than two hundred companies from the automotive industry. Among other things, the AIAG has prepared videotapes on just-in-time production. Both the AIAG and AME assemble case studies on JIT and other WCM topics for their members.

The rest of the societies provide advice that is uneven. They seem to have about as many people with a foot in the old camp—the complex and wasteful approaches—as in the new one with its opposite mission. The ambivalence is strong, for example, in the IIE, and part of the reason may be that the IIE is half academic and half practioner; the IIE's magazine, *Industrial Engineering,* is increasingly taking on the sort of statesmanlike tone that we find in *Quality Progress.*

I have intended the foregoing criticism of the societies to be mild. All in all, they provide valuable service, because the reader or conference attendee may pick and choose from the conflicting materials presented. The problem of too much specialization is not the societies' fault, because industry and academia are specialized the same way. Since academia is supposed to oversee, guide, and offer solutions, let us look at the role of higher education—and the trade and technical schools as well—in regard to WCM.

Schooling

The trade, technical, and professional schools provide industry with many of those who populate staff organizations in industry. The schools are part of the reason for the tendencies of staff to take over what line people can handle very well themselves.

Part of the problem is that most professional schools have been out of touch with industry. An exception is the accounting schools, which have kept close to their constituency—maybe more so than medical schools, engineering schools, and law schools. The inadequacies of cost accounting and cost control spring from the high state of complexity and high levels of waste in manufacturing, not from the profession itself. How can there be a simple, accurate way to account for complexity?

On the opposite side are those who have taught manufacturing management in the engineering and business schools. In recent decades they were badly and sadly out of touch. When the professional schools and industry have a falling out, it is usually because neither side thinks much of what the other side is doing. That certainly was true with regard to manufacturing in the 1960s and 1970s.

Before 1960 manufacturing education centered on things like time and motion studies, which are vocational enough to be taught in training departments in industry. The professors backed off and put their energies into queuing and sequencing models, linear programming, computer simulation, and other "scientific" tools. Modeling was in the limelight. There was little thought about the rightful place of the models—little attention to application concepts and theory—and the models received little attention in industry. (Some companies did spend money developing models, but nobody used them.)

In the 1980s relevance is back in manufacturing education. Just-in-time, statistical process control, and cellular manufacturing are hot topics in the classroom, as they are in industry. Those and the many other core topics of world-class manufacturing incorporate theory, strategy, concepts, and techniques. There is plenty for academics to sink their teeth into, and there is a vocational side that fits nicely into industry's training programs.

Vital changes in other parts of the education and training establishment have yet to occur. We might expect the most profound changes in the social-psychological side of the house. Operator-centered maintenance, operator-centered quality, and operator-centered data collection and diagnosis are not just talk; WCM *demands* their use.

From a behavioral scientist's point of view, it sounds almost too good to be true. Those concepts resemble ones that have been the focal point in organizational behavior studies for years. Industry attended the classes, nodded approvingly, and then went back to business as usual: Managers are managers, and direct labor is direct labor. The experiments labeled worker participation may be dismissed as cosmetic. Industry was not interested in genuine involvement, because there was not a compelling concept of what direct labor should be involved in and why.

Everyone a Trainer

Since training is an easy budget item to cut, training budgets have long been lean in most manufacturing companies. There are exceptions: IBM, for example, has always maintained high training budgets. Aside from the inherent benefits of training, IBM has relied on training to make its no-layoff policy possible. Training to avoid layoffs, a long-range concern, is actually retraining. It also helps make people more versatile and better able to see the big picture, but those are side benefits. WCM requires training for versatility and involvement in problem-solving, which are short-run, everyday benefits.

The message of this chapter may be summed up in three sentences:

1. Western industry must put substantially more resources into training to match the prodigious sums that WCM companies in Japan and Germany invest in it.
2. Training is the foundation of implementation.
3. Training is everybody's business.

Chapter 13

Strategy Revealed

I don't recall exactly when, as a student, I first heard a professor say "Management is a process." More specifically, the process was planning, organizing, staffing, and controlling (sometimes directing, budgeting, and others are in the list). By the professor's tone of voice and serious face, the student knew this was something to write down in the notebook.

Most students, I included, lacked the wit or the guts to say "Professor, spare me the definitions. I am here to learn how to be a *good* manager."

Good Managers

The revelation that management is a process offers no help. A manager can plan, organize, staff, and control an organization into bonanza or bankruptcy.

Later I learned from other professors and books that education is a process. So are marketing, quality, engineering, and communication. So is cooking, yet it yields overcooked peas and soggy fries as often as not. We need advice on how to manage the *processes* for high-quality results (*this* use of the word "process" refers to something concrete: the conversion of resources into goods or services).

Manufacturing managers and those who advise them have rarely taken time to reflect on what we *ought* to do. The management team at Hewlett-Packard's Personal Office Computer Division held meetings and made up a more meaningful list of what good management is. They decided it is communicating, training, promoting teamwork, clearly stating responsibilities, describing (modeling) the decision process, and setting standards for performance evaluation. It is easy to agree that this is a worthy *general* list of what any manager *should do;* if managers in a hospital, army battalion, or sales organization tried to create their own lists, they probably would come up with similar ones.

If that list tells, in general, what any good manager should do, can we get more specific about what a *manufacturing* manager should do? Furthermore, would such a list apply only to manufacturing managers, or may it not apply to everyone else involved in the manufacturing enterprise?

Good Management of Manufacturing

A manager, in the United States, is an employee who is exempt from the U. S. Wage and Hour Law. All the rest, the non-exempts, are, legally, nonmanagers.

Let's ignore the legal definition and focus on who gets involved in manufacturing management. World-class manufacturing requires that *everyone* help manage the enterprise, that all employees be involved up to their ears in the pursuit of continual and rapid improvement. Can a list be drawn up that will guide everyone's efforts along this path? I believe so. My own list, actually an *action agenda for manufacturing excellence,* follows:

1. Get to know the customer
2. Cut work-in-process
3. Cut flow times
4. Cut setup and changeover times
5. Cut flow distance and space
6. Increase make/deliver frequency for each required item
7. Cut number of suppliers down to a few good ones
8. Cut number of part numbers
9. Make it easy to manufacture the product without error
10. Arrange the work place to eliminate search time
11. Cross-train for mastery of more than one job
12. Record and retain production, quality, and problem data at the work place

217

13. Assure that line people get first crack at problem-solving—before staff experts
14. Maintain and improve existing equipment and human work before thinking about new equipment
15. Look for simple, cheap, movable equipment
16. Seek to have plural instead of singular work stations, machines, cells, and lines for each product
17. Automate incrementally, when process variability cannot otherwise be reduced

Make the items on this agenda—or your plant's version of it—the driving force for manufacturing improvement. Train everyone in why these items lead to competitive strength. Post the agenda prominently in the factory. Put up charts and graphs showing rates of improvement for all items on the agenda that can be measured. Form project teams to solve problems and to remove obstacles in the way of fast progress on all agenda items. Reward people for each idea or innovation that solves one of the problems or removes one of the obstacles. Make sure that supervisors spend most of their time guiding and helping people in their efforts to make the improvements. Bring all support people—quality and manufacturing engineers, product and process designers, sales people and clerks, material handlers and human resources staff—into the thick of the improvement effort. Otherwise the support staff will drift off into pursuits that run counter to the seventeen-point agenda.

The last sentence is not just a passing remark. Please take a hard look at each of the seventeen items. Is it not true that staff people have been devising solutions in opposition to every one of them? As just one example, is it not true that at new equipment time, the staff people responsible recommend equipment that takes longer to set up, is more complex, and often has more down time than its predecessor. Of course, it runs much faster, but that, too, is a problem.

I'll not summarize the merits of each of the agenda items. They have all been discussed in earlier chapters. What remains to be done is show how those seventeen highly specific operating guidelines for manufacturing excellence should form the foundation for manufacturing strategy.

Manufacturing Strategy

Strategy has to do with plotting to gain advantage. Financial strategies—like finding takeover targets and identifying cash cows—receive most of the press coverage, but they are of no interest here. Our concerns are manufacturing strategy, marketing strategy, purchasing strategy, design strategy, and other related strategies. If we have not seen these as closely related, it is because we carved up the enterprise to the point where marketing, manufacturing, design, purchasing, data processing, and the others were not even on the same team. That will not do for the company that has world-class aspirations. A unifying strategy is required.

A Grain of Truth

Putting together a unifying strategy sounds like serious business, something to be entrusted to people who earn six-figure salaries. Is there wisdom from the Orient that might show what a unifying strategy should look like? Here is an excerpt from a session at the national conference of the American Institute for Decision Science a few years ago. I am the speaker, and this was my roundabout way of critiquing someone else's proposed survey of executives on the subject of manufacturing strategy.

> Let me tell you about an interview in which I am talking to the CEO of a very successful Japanese company about manufacturing strategy.
>
> *I:* Mr. Amae, were you able to look over the list of interview questions that I sent you?
> *Mr. Amae:* Yes, I did.
> *I:* Okay. Tell me, then. What would you say are the main elements of manufacturing strategy in your company?
> *Mr. Amae:*
> 1. *People.* We fill over 50 percent of our professional and managerial positions with engineers. This includes positions in marketing, production foremen, material control—even personnel. And we have a vigorous management development program in which design engineers are rotated into production engineering and so forth.
> 2. *People and quality.* We train all employees in total quality control.
> 3. *People and operations.* We follow the just-in-time production method, with worker-centered problem-solving.
> 4. . . . . .
>
> *I (After Mr. Amae had gone through several more points):* Mr. Amae, tell me something about the development of this manufacturing strategy. How was it formulated, and when?
> *Mr. Amae:* I just developed the strategy today after looking at your questions.

I: What do you mean?

Mr. Amae: Well, we never have formally listed the strategic factors before. I just thought about what has made us the world leader in our industry, and those factors are what I believe are most important.

At this point I revealed to the audience that "this interview actually never took place." I went on to explain that I *have* met with Japanese CEOs and other top executives, and I believe that is what might happen if I did a focused interview on manufacturing strategy with certain Japanese CEOs (and probably some non-Japanese CEOs as well).

More often, CEOs would respond conventionally by saying they appointed a manufacturing strategy committee, which in a series of meetings came up with a formal five- or ten-year plan for manufacturing. That's what our textbooks say is the rational approach. But is it?

Basics

The late Vince Lombardi, legendary (in America) coach of the Green Bay Packers professional football team, still has a sizable fan club. His no-nonsense tenets about what makes a winner are often quoted in speeches by managers in manufacturing and in a wide range of other fields. Lombardi believed in the basics, and in football that means blocking and tackling.

The largest-selling business book of all time is Peters and Waterman's *In Search of Excellence.* The authors struck a chord with populist prescriptions like "management by walking around."

In early 1985 John Robb, vice president of manufacturing for Monsanto's Electronic Components Division, spent ten hours in one of the division's plants walking around. Robb was not walking around making random observations. He was looking for one of the most vital of the basics of manufacturing, as fundamental as blocking in football—namely, statistical process control.

Robb found SPC charts in fairly wide use in the plant. Wherever he found an SPC chart, he spent time talking with the operators and supervisors who did the plotting. He asked them to interpret the charts, to explain why a point went out of control on the high side on a certain day two months ago. He wanted to show everyone how thoroughly interested he was in those fundamental charts, and he also wanted to see if those doing the plotting really understood the charts and what the charts revealed about the process, if anything.

A manager does not discover what the fundamentals are by walking around. Rather, the manager *who knows what the basics are* may find out the organization's weaknesses and strengths by walking around. I say "may" instead of "will" deliberately. The manager surely *will* find out the weaknesses and strengths if measured data on graphs are in evidence throughout the plant. The manager will get cosmetic impressions and emotion-based opinions if the graphical data are missing.

Graphing the Basics

Among the many fine plants I have toured since the WCM movement began in Western countries, one stands out for its attention to keeping the walls covered with measured data on the basics. It is the Hewlett-Packard plant making the HP-3000 Series 500 minicomputer, which has been a steady seller for a number of years. $\bar{x}$ and R charts are everywhere in the California plant where the 3000-500 is produced. The charts have been in use for several years with excellent results. For example, wave-soldering defects have dropped to between 0.5 and 1.0 per million, a performance that surely ranks with the best in the world.

A main wall near the center of the manufacturing floor has three large charts posted on it. One shows the JIT material flow. Another chart shows the total quality control process. The third, centered between the other two, contains a wealth of data plotted on graphs and charts, mostly on performance in printed circuit assembly (PCA). One graph plots PCA throughput time: down from fifteen days in 1982 to 1.5 days in 1984. Another shows WIP inventory: down from $670,000 in 1983 to $200,000 in 1984 to $20,000 in 1985. Three more graphs show scrap, floor space, and labor hours in PCA—all cut roughly in half. Several more graphs show declining defects and non-conformities. Every day PCA people post detail sheets showing number of bent leads, missing parts, and other nonconformities, and they plot defect totals on the graphs weekly.

Other charts in the plant deal with causes of machine malfunction and down time. Color-coded kanban cards and signs are also in wide use. Most are found on kanban racks between process stages. The SPC charts have been in use in the division for several years. Those dealing with flow time, space, and inventory—and the obstacles in the way of their reduction—were added more recently.

In short, the plant is set up for visual management. A manager, a quality engineer, a supplier, a customer, or a visiting class from a college campus can make a circle tour of the compact facility in an hour or two and know what is right and what is wrong. Compared with this, managing a plant by examining periodic reports seems like looking through binoculars the wrong way.

Basics as Strategy

High-level managers who plot strategy have a need for the kind of operating data that the HP-3000-500 people keep posted on their walls, but it is rare to have such information available. The internal information that has been available has been deficient and misleading. It's been filtered several times, and it is secondary data: not process quality but after-the-fact customer complaints; not how fast manufacturing can react but how responsive the warehouses are; plenty of broad measures like cost variances and labor efficiencies but no details on causes of the variances; little if any measures on *rates* of improvement. The enterprise cannot be guided strategically on secondary information.

World-class manufacturing surely does require strategic leadership. I am convinced that the best strategy is doing things better and better in the trenches.[1] The best leadership is that which insists on visible measures of what is going on in the trenches and on action there to achieve a high rate of improvement. What, besides walking around, should the leadership of the manufacturing enterprise be doing to keep the fires hot?

High-Level Management

To answer that question, a number of our leading manufacturing companies have been moving in the right direction. The approach at Xerox, focusing at first on quality, is typical. At Xerox twenty-five of the most senior managers, including the CEO, held a series of meetings and hammered out new policies on total quality control. Those executives sat still and listened to W. Edwards Deming and Joseph Juran, and they attended Philip Crosby's Quality College. Their new quality policy starts out, "Quality is *the* basic business principle for Xerox. . . . Quality improvement is the job of every Xerox employee."[2]

Werner Schuele, a vice president in the Materials & Controls Group of Texas Instruments, tells about a strategic shift at TI: "In years past, we traditionally held quarterly financial reviews with top corporate executives. For the past three years or so these financial reviews have been discontinued. In their place we hold a review four times per year with top management that is devoted solely to quality and productivity."[3]

Some companies that began their WCM quest with a quality focus have since broadened their approaches in such a way as not to stifle local action. For example, FMC Corp., a $3.4 billion conglomerate with about fifty dominant manufacturing and mining business units, developed a good "loose–tight" approach. FMC set up a corporate steering committee headed by the vice president for manufacturing. Committee members were from the corporate staff groups—manufacturing, marketing, engineering, planning, and a few others—and also FMC plant managers. The committee's main task was to develop principles of manufacturing excellence. They did not consider their role to be to advise or oversee plant-level activities. The principles, hammered out in a few off-site meetings, cover several topics. Here are just a few, in no particular order:

"We will operate process- and/or product-focused facilities."

"We will evolve from complex manufacturing 'push' systems to simpler 'pull' systems."

"We will accurately identify our customer's needs, and will design, produce and deliver products and services accordingly. The term 'customer' refers to all users of each employee's output."

"We will operate with a minimum number of organizational levels."

Controls

The last statement, getting by with fewer levels, is what many North American companies have already done, but in the name of cost-cutting and survival, not WCM. Most companies that have cut out levels and reduced middle managers knew they had too many. Some also knew their controls were heavy-handed and not very effective. What was not known was what kinds of controls there should be.

This time we are not relying on the economists, the accountants, the engineers, and the other staff people to devise the controls. The high-level group at Xerox, the one at FMC, and similar groups at many other companies are fashioning enlightened principles of excellence in manufacturing. In the past, lack of overriding principles led to complex controls that suited parochial staff interests. Now the staff people, together with line managers, have the job of devising controls, measures, and ways of collecting data to support preordained principles.

I know of no company that has gone through this fully. The control tools developed for refineries will not be quite the same as those for light assemblers or those for metal fabricators. While each type of manufacturer will come up with somewhat different tools, all will have the same flavors. The seventeen-point agenda for action, presented early in the chapter, provides the flavors in general terms; they are, in other words, general principles.

Getting Stuck and Unstuck

Having an agenda and pursuing it are two different things. People and events can sidetrack the best ideas and intentions.

Most large manufacturing companies have a few take-charge people sprinkled around. Some have many. Does the campaign fizzle when the champions leave? When higher authority puts the champions on other projects? I know of two cases like that.

Capsized Campaign

The first involves a producer of electric products. The plant manager had a good JIT effort under way. WIP was quickly reduced from seven to five weeks, and promising projects were under way. At that time the plant manager was moved to another site. The new plant manager canceled the JIT projects and got the staff to put its energies into implementing manufacturing resource planning (MRP II). Some people are calling this particular case a JIT failure.

I'm not sure that JIT failure is the proper term. Something did fail, and the example does again seem to show the precarious nature of programs and champions. A champion can throw a few switches that lead to sharp cuts in stock, scrap, nonconformities, space, and lead time. A champion may not be able to turn a plant into a world-class performer.

Plateaued

The second example is from a large metal fabrication and assembly division of a giant corporation. The division fashioned one of the early fine JIT success stories in North America. In 1982 and 1983 WIP for one product had been halved, machine operators were involved in setup time reductions, and some of the machine maintenance had been transferred to the operators. At that point the JIT journey was interrupted. Part of the reason was a new plant manager, but the main reason was a corporate decision to develop a totally new automated plant to make one fairly low-volume product. According to one manager, "Money was no object." In fact the price tag was half a billion dollars. The automation project did not erase the JIT accomplishments but did cause the JIT campaign to "plateau."

The plateau effect is something large centralized companies are susceptible to. Figure 13–1 shows in general what can happen and in some cases is happening. After an early round of training, high-impact WCM projects are begun. The projects—SPC, lot-size cuts, conversion to the pull system—yield sharp cuts in lead time and sharp

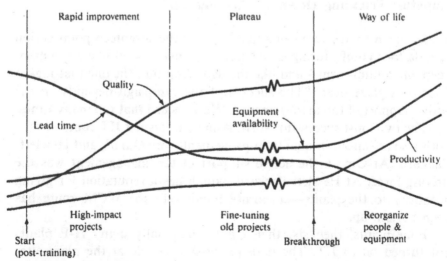

Figure 13–1. Pattern of Improvement

improvement in quality. Productivity improves just a little as fewer labor hours are wasted on delays; machine availability improves just a little, since some of the projects include fixing up equipment.

Rapid improvement in lead time and quality lasts for maybe a year or two. Then come the diversions. WCM is becalmed, and improvement is nearly flat, except for fine-tuning of old projects.

It takes momentous action—a breakthrough—to get WCM on course once again. Broad-spectrum training is needed to explain what has to be done to have a breakthrough, namely the concepts of Chapter 6: reorganizing people and equipment the way the products flow. The broad training leads to creation of cells/responsibility centers. After that, one aggravating cause of stoppage after another is corrected. The productivity rate finally turns upward at a healthy angle, and causes of the intolerable machine malfunctions are fixed so that equipment availability rises at a healthy rate as well.

How could the plateau have been avoided in the first place? By doing the reorganization back in the high-impact project phase. The reorganization projects get so many people on the problem-solving track that the rapid improvement engine is hard to slow down.

There is one problem in this formula for achieving breakthrough: Reorganizing people and machines takes boldness, which is a commodity in short supply. Some prodding may be necessary, and the best type of prod is built into the performance measurement system.

Impetus: Trickling Down or Pushing Up

I refer again to measurements that support the seventeen-point action agenda for manufacturing excellence. This may sound like a top management commitment—and like the usual cop-out, the one that makes your eyes glaze over: "The success of the campaign depends on the active support of top management." We've heard that too many times.

The two most successful North American-owned JIT companies—both also advanced in quality improvement—are Omark and Hewlett-Packard. At Omark the active support of top management was the driving force. At Hewlett-Packard, which has a reputation for giving authority to the plants—corporate hands off—the WCM route has been bottom-up.

Four plants, then six, then eight, and finally many H-P plants got turned on to JIT. The data processing people at the plant sites rewrote manufacturing software, and later some of the software ideas went to the corporate division that sells H-P software. The results was "H-P JIT," a commercial package. The accountants at the plant sites have been developing new accounting techniques, such as allocating overhead by lead time.

The plants begin to measure themselves based on their home-grown accounting measurements. Other plants find out and put in similar measurements. Soon corporate adopts them. By then JIT is institutionalized.

Whether the company is fortunate in the Omark way—strong support from the top—or the H-P bottom-up way, the WCM campaign becomes self-sustaining, a way of life.

Self-Determination

Many people work in companies in which vigorous WCM activities are going on in just a few locations. Management is applauding the efforts, and every location has people who seem eager about planning but timid about doing.

I am reminded of a JIT seminar I conducted at one of the Hewlett-Packard sites quite some time ago. At the end of the seminar Lee Rhodes, my host, posed a scenario for me. It went something like this:

"Dick, suppose I am a supervisor and I just sat through this seminar. I am all fired up and determined to get JIT going right away. So on Monday, I go first to the QA department. I ask for them to come to my shop and help train the operators in SPC. They say yes, we have that on our things-to-do list. But right now, we have a receiving dock loaded with incoming materials to inspect. More comes in every day, and I don't know when we'll have time to get going on SPC training.

"Next, I go to industrial engineering. I ask for help in setup time reduction. They point to a large stack of projects in the IE chief's in-basket and put me off.

"So I find my way to purchasing, and I ask the buyers for help in certifying suppliers so we can keep the lines running with good parts. Half the buyers are on the phone expediting orders and don't even hear me. The others are going through piles of invoices and other paper, and they tell me there is no time right now to go check out suppliers."

Lee continued in the same vein through a few more staff offices. Nobody had time to help. Then Lee posed his question:

"Dick, if you were the supervisor and that happened to you, what would you do?"

My response: "I'd do it myself."

Then I explained: We are talking about simple concepts, simple techniques. Does the supervisor (or foreman) have to have help in cutting lot sizes? in putting some of the buffer stock aside? Can't the supervisor go ahead and substitute a few small containers for large ones? Are there a few scattered workbenches and small machines that the supervisor and the assemblers could move into a cell? Can't the supervisor find a videotape or manual on SPC and get some training going?

Clearly there is no good excuse for inaction among line people who believe in the WCM principles, because, unlike most programs in the past, this is a crusade for simplicity. If you are the type of person who has never dared to take the initiative, or if your company has never encouraged it, are you putting yourself at risk by being the one to put a foot forward? Not much. JIT and TQC work, and they work fast. You and your group get your personal rewards soon. More important, the results can make people outside your group sit up and take notice. It is easy enough, for example, to cut WIP inventories in half between two work centers without ill effects. Is there risk, having achieved that result, that superiors will be angry that you took charge? It hardly seems likely. Carrying cost savings alone nearly always exceed the modest costs of JIT/TQC. They are pay-as-you-go campaigns.

Throughout this book, the overriding theme, quest, goal, or ideal is continual and rapid improvement. Pockets of continual and rapid improvement, inspired by take-charge people anywhere in the organization, form first. The pocket successes join together into product lines and then plants and finally whole companies. The individual, the groups, the plants, and the companies that learn their WCM lessons can apply them to any product, any service. Dependence on current products, machines, and customers subsides, replaced by confidence that a partial immunity to serious risk is in place.

World-class manufacturing fosters the notion of total management—in place of domination by a separate group of managers. The following two statements summarize this final message:

WCM does not employ bottom-up or top-down management. It employs blended management.

WCM management is not merely arranging resources in order to produce goods and services. It is marshaling resources for continual and rapid improvement.

Honor Roll: The 5-10-20s

Note: Some data on JIT and JIT-related achievements apply to just one product, some to a whole plant. Some of the plants listed were just a bit short of a fivefold improvement but were likely to be there by book publication time. In any case, the data are meager and cannot be used to compare one plant with another, especially since some involved high capital expenditures and others virtually none. Also, the time intervals vary. The list is representative but by no means complete.

1. Hewlett-Packard, Greeley, Colo. (flexible disc drives, tape storage units): WIP cut from twenty-two days to one day, whole plant on JIT
2. Hewlett-Packard, Vancouver, Wash. (computer printers): Space reduced about threefold, inventories manyfold, whole plant on pull system
3. Hewlett-Packard, Boise, Ida. (dot-matrix printers): Lead time cut from five days to one, WIP cut from seven days to less than one day, raw material cut from one month to ten days maximum, units per person per day doubled
4. Hewlett-Packard, Sunnyvale, Calif. (Personal Office Computer Div.): WIP cut from three weeks to three days, space reduced sixfold (no more warehouse), labor cut about fourfold, mixed-model assembly on new product
5. Hewlett-Packard, Cupertino, Calif. (H-P 3000 Series 68 mini-computer): Printed-circuit assembly lead time cut from fifteen to 1.5 days, PCA WIP cut from $670,000 to $20,000

6. Hewlett-Packard, Ft. Collins, Colo. (H-P 9000 Series 500 computer): WIP cut sixfold, WIP in printed-circuit assembly cut tenfold, asset turnover up threefold, work orders eliminated
7. Hewlett-Packard, Sunnyvale Printed Circuit Facility: Lead times cut from one month to five or six days, lot sizes cut from ninety-six to six
8. Sperry, Minneapolis (UNIVAC 1170 computer): Whole computer, from printed circuit assembly (one-piece lots, no units between stations) to computer assembly and test to pack and crate made in one small room
9. Omark, Guelph, Ontario (saw chain): Lead time cut from twenty-one days to one, flow distance cut from 2,620 to 173 feet
10. Omark, Portland, Ore. (saw chain): Lead time cut from thirty down to one to three days, WIP cut 80 percent, defects cut 50 percent, scrap & rework cut 50 percent, floor space cut 40 percent
11. Omark, Onalaska, Wis. (gun cleaning kits): Lead time cut from two weeks to one day, inventory cut 94 percent
12. Omark, Owatonna, Minn. (timber harvesting machines): Throughput time on major subassembly cut from thirty to three days, raw material and WIP cut 50 percent, flow distance cut 94 percent
13. Omark, Woodburn, Ore. (circular saw blades): Order turnaround time cut from ten to fourteen days with 75 percent fill rate to one or two days with 97 percent fill rate, WIP cut 85 percent, flow distance cut 58 percent, cost cut 35 percent
14. Omark, Mesabi, Minn. (twist drills): Large-size drill inventories cut 92 percent, lead time cut from three weeks to three days, flow distance cut from 416 to 157 feet
15. Omark, Oroville, Calif. (reloading equipment for firearms): Lead time cut from six weeks to two days, 96 percent of machines relocated into flow lines
16. Omark, Prentice, Wis. (log-loaders): On hydraulic value control handles (a pilot project), lead time cut from thirty days to a few minutes, flow distance cut from 2,000 feet to 18 inches
17. General Electric, Louisville (dishwashers): Lead time cut from six days to eighteen hours, raw and in-process stock cut by more than half, scrap and rework cut 51 percent, field service calls cut 53 percent
18. General Electric, Philadelphia (vacuum circuit breakers): Space

reduced from 2 million to 600,000 square feet, inventory cut by 82 percent (98 percent in fabrication shop)

19. General Electric, Burlington, Iowa (circuit breakers): Assembly lot sizes cut from twelve weeks to one, distance cut from 410 to 120 feet, WIP on floor cut 67 percent, rack storage cut 67 percent

20. General Electric, Cincinnati (servicing aviation turbine blades): Lead time cut from thirteen weeks to nine hours

21. General Electric, Willoughby, Ohio (supplier of ceramic parts for high-pressure sodium lamps): Shipments of finished parts cut from about monthly to daily, authorized by kanban; kanban used for internal production and for shipments to customer (dual-card kanban)

22. Black & Decker/GE, Ashboro, N. C. (coffee makers): Formerly made 10,000 units per day on three lines, three shifts, with three months between model changes; now same volume but all models made daily on two mixed-model lines, one shift, with kanban squares for line stocking; space reduced 52,000 square feet

23. Tektronix, Beaverton, Ore. (hybrid ceramic products): Lead times cut from forty-five to about four days, WIP cut 95 percent, high level of operator versatility and process ownership

24. Tektronix, Wilsonville, Ore. (graphics terminal): Lead time cut from thirty-five to five days.

25. Tektronix, Clark County, Wash. (portable oscilloscopes): Lead time cut from forty to sixty days down to two to five days, inventory cut 70 percent

26. IBM, Owego, N. Y.[1] (computer products for government customers): Flow distance cut from 31,000 to 275 feet, WIP inventories cut 70 percent, lead times cut 50 percent

27. IBM, Raleigh, N. C. (3178 logic unit): Redesigned as a "vanilla" product; automated, with JIT concepts blended in; labor cut from 130 to 10; space cut from 51,000 to 9,000 sq. ft.; raw and WIP inventory turnover improved from under fifteen to over seventy; data processing support cost per unit reduced from about $50.00 to $1.26

28. IBM, Bromont, Quebec, ("chip placement"): Process lead time cut from thirty to forty days down to seven on a ceramic substrate product (as sole-source supplier); process lead times cut from thirty to three to six days on other products, fifteen operators doing own maintenance

29. IBM, Boca Raton, La. (personal computer): New product (no before-and-after data); product designed for ease of manufacture and fast throughput

30. IBM, Lexington, Ky. (typewriters): Part numbers reduced manyfold, which slashes inventories and production lead time; number of suppliers cut from 640 to a target of 32

31. 3M, Hutchinson, Minn. (videotape cassettes): Converted to pull system with daily rate-based scheduling

32. 3M, Weatherford, Okla. (floppy discs): WIP cut from six hundred to six hours, space per unit cut sixfold, productivity tripled

33. Intel, Singapore (printed circuit board assembly and test): Lead time cut from twenty-five to six days, raw material cut three- or fourfold

34. Intel, Puerto Rico (microcomputer): WIP cut from twenty to five days; partnership with key suppliers; D-RAMs cut from thirty-five to five days; Winchester drives cut from twenty to five days; no inspection of either

35. Intel, Oregon (microcomputer): WIP cut almost as large as Puerto Rico; D-rams and Winchesters about the same results

36. Honeywell, Minneapolis (electronic air cleaners): WIP cut 80 percent in subassemblies and component parts, scrap and salvage costs cut 54 percent, space cut 15 percent, productivity up 15 percent

37. Honeywell, Phoenix (large computers): New product designed with JIT in mind, production lead time cut from about thirteen weeks to fifteen days

38. Westinghouse, Fayetteville, N. C. (motor-control centers): Inventories cut from 4.2 months to .89 months in two years, sheet-metal equipment moved and cells created to eliminate nearly all work orders and convert to kanban, 40 percent space reduction

39. Westinghouse, Asheville, N. C. (variety of motor-control products): Only one year experience with JIT; progress similar to Fayetteville but at faster rate; new plant equipped with computerized automation that was hard to set up, so $1 million in equipment sold off and replaced with simpler equipment at fraction of the cost

40. Westinghouse,[2] West Mifflin, Pa. (subway controllers, etc.): Lead time cut from twelve weeks to one, floor space cut from 125,000 to 52,000 sq. ft., material storage cut from 66 percent

to 15 percent of available space, plant capacity increased 600 percent

41. Westinghouse, Youngwood, Pa. (semiconductor division): Lead time cut 70 percent, number of job categories cut 95 percent, customer reject rate as percent of sales down 67 percent, defective material as percent of sales cut 50 percent

42. Harley-Davidson, Milwaukee (engines): Inventory turns up from 6.0 to 19.6, WIP cut four- or fivefold, units per employee up about 38 percent, flow distance for flywheel manufacturing (sixty-two machine tools) cut 62 percent

43. Harley-Davidson, York, Pa. (motorcycle assembly): Lot sizes cut from twenty to twenty-five down to one (mixed-model assembly); inventory turns up from 3.5 to 20; fork trucks cut from fifty to six; inspectors cut from seventy-five to six; defects per bike down 52 percent

44. John Deere, Dubuque, Iowa (industrial equipment): Crankshaft machining inventory cut from thirty to three days, small crawler tractor chain inventory cut from thirteen to three days, large crawler roller frames cut from fourteen days to one day on mixed-model line; reconfiguring entire plant

45. John Deere, Ottumwa, Iowa (hay and forage equipment): Began JIT only in 1983 but among the more rapidly improving JIT plants

46. John Deere, Horicon, Wis. (self-propelled lawn mowers): Build seven models every day instead of each model once a month, indirect labor cut in half in subassembly and fivefold in welding

47. Eaton, Truck Components Group, Shelbyville, Tenn., plant: Time to produce shafts cut from eight to ten days down to twenty-eight minutes, WIP cut 98 percent, floor space cut 25 percent

48. Eaton, Truck Components Gr., Kings Mountain, Tenn., plant: Time to machine transmission cases cut from one to eighteen days to two hours, WIP cut from twenty-two to twenty-three days down to four

49. Eaton, Truck Components Gr., Shenandoah, Iowa, plant: Time to produce transmission cases cut from more than a week to less than two hours, WIP cut from 438 cases to 40

50. Eaton Corp. (Hydraulics Div.), Eden Prairie, Minn.

51. Eaton Corp. (Hydraulics Div.), Spencer, Iowa

52. Eaton Corp. (Hydraulics Div.), Shawnee, Okla.: At all three

plants, machines moved into cells, standard-quantity containers, production lead time for steering units cut from seventeen to four weeks in one year, lead time for motors cut from twelve to three weeks (with one week in sight)

53. Richardson-Vicks Home Care Products, Torshalla, Sweden (cough drops): "Almost perfect" customer service level with more than fivefold reduction in WIP/FGI; overall inventory turns up from 4.4 to 13.5, line changeover time down from one shift to eighteen minutes

54. Richardson-Vicks Home Care Products, South Africa (full line of products): Line changeover time down from one shift to one hour, large WIP and FGI cuts

55. Richardson-Vicks Home Care Products, Gross-Gerau, Germany (Milton line of sterilizing agent): Factory-within-factory concept, large inventory cuts

56. Richardson-Vicks Home Care Products, Lyon, France (Petrole-Hahn hair-care product line): large inventory cuts

57. Control Data, Aberdeen, S. D. (read-write heads)

58. Control Data, Eden Prairie, Minn. (read-write heads)

59. Control Data, Minneapolis thin-film head plant (read-write heads): At all three plants, WIP cut tenfold, yields up 5 to 12 percent with no changes other than large cuts in lot sizes and conversion to pull system

60. "Buick City," Flint, Mich. (automobiles): Fender WIP cut from ten days to eight hours, flow distance in fenders cut from 8,000 to 140 feet.

61. Motorola, Seguin, Tex. (electronic controls for auto and appliance industry): Inventory cut 75 percent, lead time cut 67 percent

62. Allen Bradley, Milwaukee (contactors for motor starters): Highly automated with JIT concepts blended in; build and ship product within twenty-four hours of when customer places a computer order from any sales location worldwide (a new product; for similar products in the past, response times were in weeks)

63. Raychem, Menlo Park, Calif. (Thermofit Division): Lead time cut from three weeks to three days, WIP cut tenfold

64. Rockwell, Richardson, Tex. (telecommunications): Lead time in fabrication cut from 8.2 to 1.5 weeks, lead time for waveguide parts cut from 17.3 to 2.2 weeks, lead time in sheet metal cut from six to 1.2 weeks

65. Stanadyne Diesel Systems, Hartford, Conn.: Pull system between automatic screw machines and machining line cut inventory fivefold

66. Xerox Corp.: Company won *Purchasing* magazine's 1985 Medal of Professional Excellence. Sample reasons: suppliers cut from 5,000 to 300, raw material cut from over three months to about one month, cost reductions of 10 percent per year since 1980, cost to "spend a dollar" cut from $0.09 to $0.035

67. Tennant Co., Minneapolis (industrial sweepers and scrubbers): Four final assembly lines with components built on-line or delivered daily

68. Burlington Industries, Reidsville, N. C. (custom-length drapery fabric): Lead time cut from four to six days down to under one hour, WIP cut 97 percent (from 5,000 to under 150 units), floor space cut from 13,000 to 4,300 sq. ft.

69. Double A Products, Statesville, N. C. (hydraulic valves): Entirely kanban (from screw machine to grinding/buffing to assembly), run families of spools on screw machines, cut out nearly all work orders, cut paperwork by 70 percent, inventory turns up about fourfold

70. Texas Instruments, Sherman, Tex. (defense weapon systems): In metal fabrication, cut WIP from 18,000 to under 1,000 pieces, cut production lead time from fourteen days to about two days, cut scrap and rework four- to fivefold; in magnetics, cut WIP 30 to 60 percent, cut production lead time 50 to 70 percent, cut scrap 50 to 100 percent; overall, cut floor space 40 percent

71. Apple, Fremont, Calif. (Macintosh): New product (no before-and-after data), product designed for ease of manufacture and fast throughput, inventory turns twenty to thirty times a year

72. Lincoln Electric Co., Cleveland (welding equipment): Long history of use of many WCM techniques, such as cellular production and no stockrooms or warehouses (but inventory turns are only four to six, probably indicating a need to cut setups and lot sizes)

73. Owatonna Tool, Owatonna, Minn. (electronic products): Lead times cut from forty-four to 2.74 days

74. Abbott Laboratories, Las Colinas, Tex. (diagnostic drug analyzer): Flow distance cut from 1,100 to 180 feet; $800,000 inventory takeout

75. FMC Corp., Aiken, S. C. (cargo hatches): WIP cut 86 percent, setup times in machine shop cut 60 to 95 percent

76. Nashua Corp., Nashua, N. H. (disc packs and discs): After nine months of JIT, in disc pack assembly, WIP cut from 330 to about five packs, space cut 75 percent, rework cut from about 10 percent to nil, productivity (including yield) up 35 percent; similar or better productivity improvements in disc production

77. Applicon, Billerica, Mass. (CAD/CAM equipment): Lead time cut from seventeen weeks to one week, inventory cut from $5.5 million to $400,000

78. Digital Equipment Corp., Colorado Springs, Colo. (computer disk drives and controllers): In Winchester disk drive final assembly, lead time cut from 2.0 to 0.25 days, WIP cut from $5 million to $900,000; in diversified disk product subassembly, WIP cut from $119,000 to $18,000, rework cut from 300 to zero units, productivity up 63 percent

79. Kawasaki, Lincoln, Neb. (motorcycles): Assembly lot size cut from 200 (or multiples thereof) to one, total inventories cut fourfold, WIP reductions more than fivefold

80. Toyota, Long Beach, Calif. (truck beds): Kanban throughout, assembly frequency for a given model cut from monthly to daily, throughput time cut from six down to one to 1.5 days, fork trucks cut from eighteen to twelve, labor per unit down from 8.3 to three hours

81. Nissan, Smyrna, Tenn. (trucks and automobiles)

82. NOK, Inc., LaGrange, Ga. (oil seals and mechanical seals)

83. Honda, Marysville, Ohio (motorcycles and automobiles)

84. Sony, San Diego, Calif. (TVs)

Notes

Chapter 1:   Faster, Higher, Stronger (pp. 1–16)

1. Richard J. Schonberger, *Japanese Manufacturing Techniques: Nine Hidden Lessons in Simplicity* (New York: Free Press, 1982).
2. Philip B. Crosby, *Quality Is Free: The Art of Making Quality Certain* (New York: McGraw-Hill, 1979).
3. See Charles E. Sorensen, *My Forty Years With Ford* (New York: W. W. Norton, 1956), p. 174; and Harvard Business School, "Henry Ford and the Ford Motor Company," Case no. 9–307–092 (Soldiers Field, Boston: Intercollegiate Case Clearing House), p. 18.

Chapter 2:   Line Operators and Operating Data (pp. 17–38)

1. Rensis Likert, *New Patterns of Management* (New York: McGraw-Hill, 1961).
2. Robert B. Reich, *The New American Frontier* (New York: Times Books, 1983), p. 75.
3. "Gorman Rupp Avoids Layoffs for Half a Century," *The Productivity Letter,* American Productivity Center, Houston, July 1985, pp. 1–2.
4. A. J. Geare, "Productivity from Scanlon-Type Plans," *Academy of Management Review,* July 1976, pp. 99–107.
5. Harry Thompson and Michael Paris, "The Changing Face of Manufacturing Technology," *The Journal of Business Strategy,* 3, no. 1 (Summer 1982): 45–52.

6. "Employee Involvement Gains Support," *The Wall Street Journal,* December 12, 1984.

Chapter 3: Staff as Supporting Actors (pp. 39–55)

1. Hideki Yoshihara, "Japanese Plants Abroad: Little Basics Mean a Lot," unpublished paper, Pan-Pacific Business Conference, Honolulu, March 26–28, 1984.
2. Shigeo Shingo, *A Revolution in Manufacturing: The SMED System* (Stamford, Conn.: Productivity Press, 1985).
3. Wayne Robinson, lecture at just-in-time seminar, Toronto, March 22–23, 1984.
4. Taiichi Ohno and Tomonori Kumagai, "Toyota Production System," *Proceedings of International Conference on Industrial Systems Engineering and Management in Developing Countries,* Bangkok, November 1980.
5. Mitsubishi Electric Co. is reputed to be the originator of carry-on-ban.
6. Andrew Friedman and Joan Greenbaum, "Japanese DP," *Datamation,* February 1, 1985, pp. 112–18.

Chapter 4: Overstated Role of Capital (Automation in Slow Motion) (pp. 56–76)

1. John McElroy, "Quality Goes In Before the Part Comes Out," *Automotive Industries,* November 1984, pp. 51–52.
2. Much of the information about the IBM 3178 is drawn from Ernie Huge, ed., *The Just-in-Time Newsletter,* no. 6 (Association for Manufacturing Excellence, Inc., December 31, 1984), pp. 2–10.
3. Robert H. Hayes and Steven C. Wheelwright, *Restoring Our Competitive Edge: Competing Through Manufacturing* (New York: John Wiley & Sons, 1984), p. 133.
4. *Ibid.,* p. 357.
5. Jeremy Main, "How to Battle Your Own Bureaucracy," *Fortune,* June 29, 1981, pp. 54–58. Besides the *Fortune* article, information comes from a discussion with Joe Nevin, formerly White's righthand man at Citibank.

Chapter 5: Economy of Multiples (pp. 77–100)

1. Robert H. Hayes and Steven C. Wheelwright, *Restoring Our Competitive Edge: Competing Through Manufacturing* (New York: John Wiley & Sons, 1984), p. 19.

2. Cited by Mehran Sepehri, "A Machine Builds Machines at Apple Computer's Highly Automated Macintosh Manufacturing Facility," *Industrial Engineering,* April 1985, p. 60.

3. Robert E. Harvey and James B. Pond, eds., Special Issue on FMS, *Iron Age,* August 16, 1985.

4. *Ibid.,* p. 31.

5. E. F. Schumacher, *Small Is Beautiful* (New York: Perennial Library, 1973).

Chapter 6: Responsibility Centers (pp. 101–122)

1. "Jumbled"—just the right word to describe job shop organization—was used similarly in Robert H. Hayes and Steven C. Wheelwright, *Restoring Our Competitive Edge: Competing Through Manufacturing* (New York: John Wiley & Sons, 1984), p. 209.

2. "Black Ships Are Coming," *Forbes,* January 31, 1983, pp. 67–75.

Chapter 7: Quality: Zeroing In (pp. 123–143)

1. David A. Garvin, "What Does 'Product Quality' Really Mean?" *Sloan Management Review,* Fall, 1984, pp. 25–43.

2. Kaoru Ishikawa, *Guide to Quality Control* (Tokyo: Asian Productivity Organization, 1972).

3. Neil MacKinnon, "Launching a Drive for Quality Excellence," *Quality Progress,* May 1985, pp. 46–50.

4. Shainin presented the precontrol method at the 1954 conference of the American Society for Quality Control. He "revisited" the technique at the 1984 ASQC Annual Quality Congress. Dorian Shainin, "Better Than Good Old $\bar{x}$ & R Charts Asked by Vendees," *1984 ASQC Quality Congress Transactions,* pp. 302–7. I thank Ray Wachniak of Firestone for some of the history on precontrol.

5. H. J. Bates, "Vendor Quality Rating and Statistical Process Control," speech to 126th meeting of the Rubber Division of the American Chemical Society, Denver, October 25, 1984.

6. Hy Pitt, "A Modern Strategy for Process Improvement," *Quality Progress,* May 1985, pp. 22–28.

7. Richard J. Schonberger, "Just-in-Time Production: The Quality Dividend," *Quality Progress,* October 1984, pp. 22–24.

8. *Statistical Quality Control Handbook,* 2d ed. (Indianapolis: AT&T Technologies, 1956), p. 217.

9. "Japan Does Away With Quality Control," *BusinessIndia*, February 13–26, 1984.

10. Genichi Taguchi and Yu-In Wu, *Introduction to Off-Line Quality Control* (Nagoya, Japan: Central Japan Quality Control Association, 1979), p. 3; the book is an extension of a 1966 Japanese-language publication by Taguchi.

11. *Ibid.*, p. 2.

12. Example is adapted from *ibid.*, pp. 7–9.

Chapter 8: Design Leverage (pp. 144–154)

1. "Have Takeovers Gone Too Far?" *Fortune*, May 27, 1985, pp. 20–24.

2. "Japan Focuses on Basic Research to Close the Creativity Gap," *Business Week*, February 25, 1985, pp. 94–96.

3. "Jerry Sanders's Act Is Cleaning Up," *Fortune*, October 15, 1984, pp. 210–16.

4. "The Swiss Put Glitz in Cheap Quartz Watches," *Fortune*, August 20, 1984, p. 102.

5. Robert W. Johnson, "Vendor Self-Inspection Sets the Stage for Just-in-Time Deliveries," *Quality Progress*, November 1984, pp. 46–47.

6. *Ibid.*

7. Thanks go to William A. Wheeler III (formerly with Rath & Strong, now with Coopers & Lybrand) for the case study from which this true example was extracted: "Case Study: Premanufacturing Steps in a Job Shop," unpublished, 1985.

8. *The New York Times*, Wednesday, November 6, 1985, pp. D1 and D6.

Chapter 9: Partners in Profit: Suppliers, Carriers, Customers (pp. 155–171)

1. "Polaroid Corp. Is Selling Its Technique for Limiting Supplier Price Increases," *The Wall Street Journal*, February 13, 1985.

2. *Ibid.*

3. Wayne Mehl, "Strategic Management of Operations: A Top Management Perspective," *Operations Management Review*, Fall 1983, pp. 29–36.

4. Rick Walleigh, "What's Your Excuse for Not Using JIT?" unpublished paper, Hewlett-Packard Computer Systems Division, March 15, 1985.

5. Cited in the French edition of *Japanese Manufacturing Techniques: Nine Hidden Lessons in Simplicity* (*Comment appliquer les techniques de gestion Japonaises*) (Strasbourg, France: les Dossiers du Savoir-Faire, 1983), pp.

7–17. Christian Moisy, translator and contributing author, provides the information.

6. "Moving Abroad: Strong Dollar Has Led U. S. Firms to Transfer Production Overseas," *The Wall Street Journal,* April 9, 1985, pp. 1 ff.

Chapter 10: Simple Models, Simple Systems (pp. 172–188)

1. Thomas J. Peters and Robert H. Waterman, Jr., *In Search of Excellence* (New York: Harper & Row, 1982).

2. G. P. Behrens, "3M," *The Just-in-Time Technical Development Newsletter,* no. 5 (Association for Manufacturing Excellence, Inc., September 30, 1984), pp. 2–3.

3. Some discussion of these concepts appears in Ragnor Seglund and Santiago Ibarreche, "Just-in-Time: the Accounting Implications," *Management Accounting,* August 1984, pp. 43–45.

4. Charles E. Hawkins, "A Comparative Study of the Management Accounting Practices of Industrial Companies in the United States and Japan," doctoral dissertation, University of Nebraska, 1983, p. 5.

5. "Bath: A Tight Ship That Could Spring a Leak," *Business Week,* May 20, 1985, pp. 88–90. The "leak" has to do with the labor contract.

Chapter 11: Managing the Transformation (pp. 189–206)

1. Janice A. Klein, "Why Supervisors Resist Employee Involvement," *Harvard Business Review,* September–October 1984, pp. 87–95.

2. Steven C. Wheelwright, "Japan—Where Operations Really Are Strategic," *Harvard Business Review,* July–August, 1981, pp. 67–74. Wheelwright credits David E. Kinney, General Electric Co., with the sketch showing the Japanese approach.

3. Hideki Yoshihara, "Japanese Plants Abroad: Little Basics Mean a Lot," paper presented at Pan-Pacific Business Conference, Honolulu, March 26–28, 1984.

Chapter 12: Training: The Catalyst (pp. 207–215)

1. Andrew S. Grove, *High Output Management* (New York: Random House, 1983), p. 41.

2. I found the old adage in a paper (unpublished, no date) by William L. Howard of Coopers & Lybrand, "Implementing Change: The Crisis in Middle Management."

3. Shigeo Shingo, *Study of Toyota Production System from Industrial Engineering Viewpoint* (Tokyo: Japan Management Association, 1981; U. S. distributor, Productivity, Inc., Stamford, Connecticut).

4. Richard J. Schonberger, *Japanese Manufacturing Techniques: Nine Hidden Lessons in Simplicity* (New York: Free Press, 1982).

5. Robert W. Hall, *Zero Inventories* (New York: Dow Jones–Irwin, 1983).

Chapter 13: Strategy Revealed (pp. 216–228)

1. Some academics offer theoretical reasoning in this vein. For example, Schutzenberger says, "What we have done so far is to show that the 'strategy' is simply one of tactics" and "that any tactic may be viewed as some sort of strategy." M. P. Schutzenberger, "A Tentative Classification of Goal-Seeking Behaviours," *Journal of Mental Science,* 100 (1954): 97–102.

2. Frank J. Pipp, "Management Commitment to Quality: Xerox Corp.," *Quality Progress,* August 1983, pp. 12–17.

3. Personal correspondence with Werner Schuele, August 11, 1985.

Appendix: Honor Roll: The 5–10–20s (pp. 229–236)

1. Cited in *Owego Focus,* newsletter from IBM Federal Systems Division, February 1, 1985, p. 7.

2. Cited in "Assembling a World-Class Shop," *Pittsburgh Engineer,* Summer 1985, pp. 16–17+.

Index